A PHOTO-LOCATION AND VISITOR GUIDEBOOK

PHOTOGRAPHING
SOUTH WALES

PEMBROKESHIRE • BRECON BEACONS • CARMARTHENSHIRE
GOWER • CEREDIGION • SOUTH EAST WALES • POWYS

DREW BUCKLEY

PHOTOGRAPHING **SOUTH WALES**
BY DREW BUCKLEY

First published in the United Kingdom in 2018 by fotoVUE.
www.fotovue.com

Edited and project managed by Mick Ryan – fotoVUE Ltd.
Additional editing by Susie Ryder – *www.ryderdesign.studio/editing*
Ⓡ Design and layout by Ryder Design – *www.ryderdesign.studio*

All maps within this publication were produced by Don Williams of Bute Cartographics.
Map location overlay and graphics by Mick Ryan. Maps contain Ordnance Survey
data © Crown copyright and database right 2017.

A CIP catalogue record for this book is available from the British Library.

ISBN 978-0-9929051-8-7
10 9 8 7 6 5 4 3 2 1

Front cover: *Heather and gorse at sunset – Rhossili Down, Gower (p.328). Canon 5D III, 24-70mm f/2.8 at 26mm, ISO 100, 5s at f/13. Tripod. Polariser, 3ND & ND Grad. Aug.*

Rear cover left: *A snowy Pen y Fan at dawn, five image stitch (p.256). Canon 5D III, 24-70mm f/2.8 at 24mm, ISO 100, 1/50s at f/13. Tripod. ND Grad. Jan.*

Rear cover right: *Sgwd Gwladus in autumn, Waterfall Country (p.232). Canon 5D III, 16-35mm f/4 at 16mm, ISO 50, 10s at f/22. Tripod. Polariser & 3ND. Oct.*

Opposite: *Looking up into autumn trees. Symonds Yat Rock (p.416). Canon 5D IV, 24-70mm f/2.8 at 24mm, ISO 200, 1/13s at f/7.1. Tripod. Polariser. Nov.*

Printed and bound in Europe by Latitude Press Ltd.

To the attentive eye, each moment of the year has its own beauty, and in the same fields, it beholds, every hour, a picture which was never seen before, and which shall never be seen again.

Ralph Waldo Emerson

CONTENTS

PEMBROKESHIRE COAST NATIONAL PARK – NORTH

PEMBROKESHIRE COAST NATIONAL PARK – SOUTH

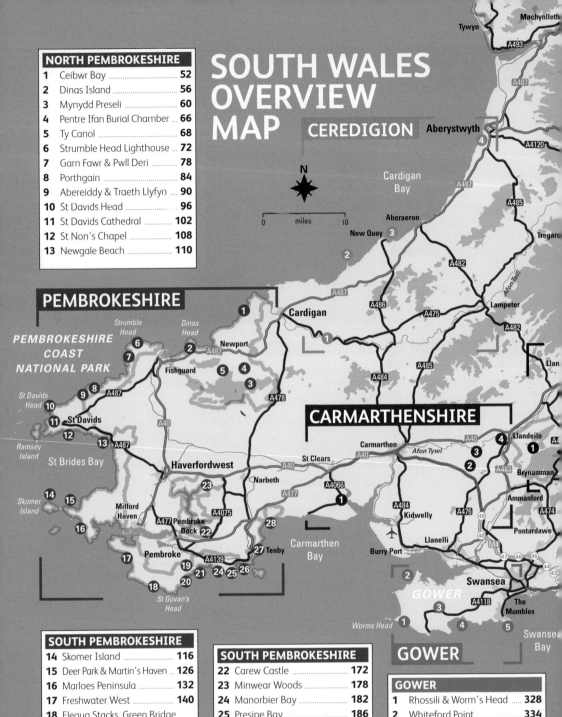

SOUTH WALES OVERVIEW MAP

CEREDIGION

N

Cardigan Bay

0 miles 10

PEMBROKESHIRE

PEMBROKESHIRE COAST NATIONAL PARK

CARMARTHENSHIRE

GOWER

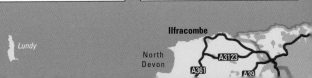

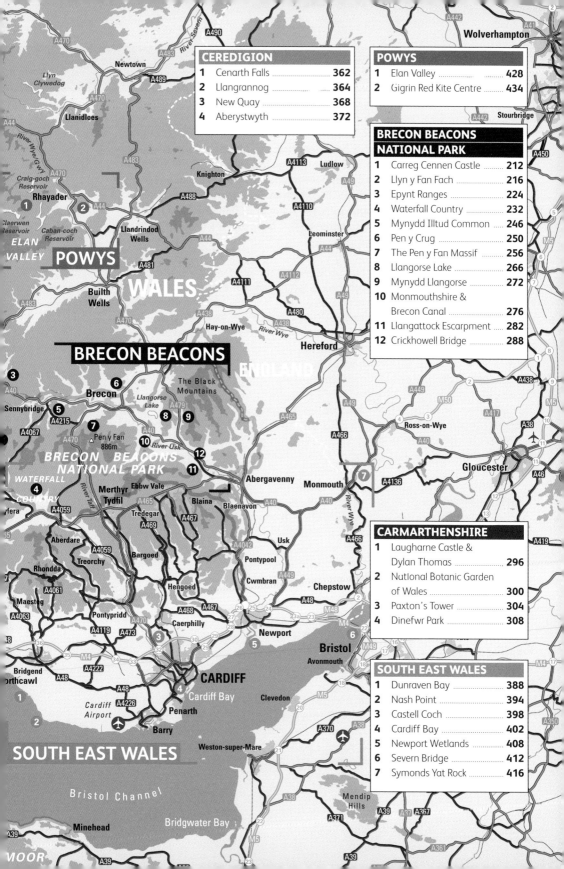

ACKNOWLEDGEMENTS

What a fantastic journey this book has been. First and foremost, an overwhelming thanks must go out to Mick and Stuart for inviting me onto the fotoVUE author team. Without them, this title may not have happened and it's a real privilege to have my name as part of the fotoVUE collection. It all started way back in 2014, after many emails and phone calls, the three of us finally met up for a brew on a rainy day in Grasmere, to agree on this book and it's been an utter joy to complete.

Any project of this magnitude can't be rushed and it takes an enormous amount of time and effort spent for all parties involved. Thanks for the words of encouragement along the way chaps and also big thanks to Mick for pouring over the tens of thousands of words, editing and honing my ramblings into the well-structured text it is today. Thank you to Don Williams for the superb maps, and to Nathan Ryder for all his hard work on the layout, and Susie Ryder for her additional editing of my text. It's been truly great to work at my own pace throughout, as it's grown and evolved over time, all made possible by that editorial freedom, much appreciated.

Many thanks to Kate Humble for writing my foreword, whom I spent a fabulous day out with last summer on a photo shoot for *BBC Countryfile* magazine. We walked and talked for many miles along the river Wye. Kate is a lovely lady who appreciates the beauty of Wales as much as I do – the perfect ambassador for this book.

Thank you to my countless friends and clients who were always asking "How's the book going?" or "When's the book out?" – this was always spurring me on to keep powering through writing up all of the chapters (most of which were written at silly o'clock in the morning!). Also to everyone who helped out with local knowledge for some viewpoints or access advice, you know who you are. Most of the images in this book were taken in the last few years as I wanted to produce my very best work for this title. Some images, however, do stretch back a decade ago to my early days when I started to become more serious about my photography.

Many years prior to that, it was some brotherly influence that first got me hooked on the world of photography. I spent countless hours as a kid gazing at the wonderment of the 35mm SLRs that my brothers had. They both need thanking for sowing the seed and helping to start my lifelong passion for photography.

Sincerest gratitude to my lovely mum and dad. They not only raised me right but they also upped sticks and moved all three of us away from the big smoke for a better upbringing in the fresh air and coastal views of Pembrokeshire. Without that move, life would have been very different I'm sure. I would not have had the opportunity of appreciating the beauty of the natural world, and quite possibly wouldn't have followed the path of doing what I love. Thank you. x

No Annie's were harmed in the making of this photograph.

Thank you from the bottom of my heart to my fantastic partner Andrea, who's supported me all of these years. She's spent plenty of time waiting around with our dog Sidney (who you may spot in the book) while I stood by the tripod waiting for the light to change, faffing around packing camera bags or even losing me for days at a time while I travelled around the country taking photos. Love you loads and thank you. x

Finally, at the end of January this year we welcomed our darling daughter, Annie, into the world. I hope she grows up appreciating the outdoors as much as we do and embracing everything there is in the great outdoors. This one's for you …

Drew Buckley
June 2018

Atlantic Puffin at the Wick, Skomer Island (p.116).
Canon 5D IV, 24-70mm f/2.8 at 35mm, ISO 400, 1/400s at f/9, Polariser & ND Grad, June.

Foreword by Kate Humble

South Wales has been my home for the last decade and yet still I wake up every morning and wonder at how I had the luck to find myself living in such a special place.

One of the many things I find so bewitching about the area is the sheer variety of landscape, from coast to mountain, forests and meadows, steep-sided river valleys and gentle rolling hills.

Buzzards and raven soar overhead, woodpeckers drum in the woods, kingfishers dart along the rivers, skylarks fill the air with their extraordinary song. And I'm by no means the first to have been seduced by this part of the country. William Gilpin was an 18th century cleric, writer and artist. He visited the Wye Valley in South Wales and was so bowled over by its beauty he coined a new word for it: picturesque. And the effect of this landscape wasn't unique to Gilpin.

For centuries it has been inspiring poets, artists, writers and photographers, Drew Buckley amongst them. Drew and I met when he was commissioned to take photographs for an article I was writing about the Wye Valley Walk. I thought he'd take a few snaps and then be off, but he walked with me, for several hours, and the resulting photographs had an immersive quality that is only achieved when a photographer takes the time to understand, appreciate and respect the subject they are trying to capture.

And you will see this quality in the collection of his photographs that follow. Drew has captured not just the beauty of South Wales, but its essence, the thing that makes it truly picturesque.

Kate Humble
Wye Valley, South Wales
June 2018

Kate Humble is a television presenter and writer specialising in wildlife and science. Humble served as President of the RSPB from 2009 until 2013 and runs her own 117-acre working farm, Humble By Nature, with her husband Ludo Graham in Monmouthshire.

More at: **www.katehumble.com**

Opposite: Kate Humble and Teg the dog, Wye Valley. July.

INTRODUCTION

South Wales is a land of big skies, lush green countryside, idyllic wooded river valleys, towering waterfalls and high snow-capped mountains, all fringed by a fabulous coastline, golden beaches and turquoise waters.

There are two national parks here; the rolling hills, serene lakes and wild mountains of the Brecon Beacons, whilst in the county of Pembrokeshire in south west Wales is the only coastal national park in the UK, with 186-miles of rugged rocky coastline home to quaint fishing harbours, secret coves and award-winning beaches.

It is a landscape shaped by thousands of years of history, myths and legends. Everywhere there are links to our past: the remains of iron age forts, bronze age burial chambers and prehistoric stones with many medieval castles standing amongst the picturesque landscape.

I decided to focus firstly on the coastline and mountains of the Pembrokeshire Coast and Brecon Beacons National Parks and then explore the variety of areas beyond them that have a rich array of photography subjects and locations on offer. Whilst the Pembrokeshire coast and Brecon Beacons feature heavily in this book, beyond them there are many woodlands, waterfalls, castles, lighthouses and lakes to explore too.

Some of the locations I have included are well-known photographic haunts, others are less well-known, discovered during many years of living and exploring in South Wales. All of the places described have a theme; they are personal favourites that have inspired and motivated me over the years. If I've not included one of your favourite viewpoints or locations then I apologise, however I can guarantee that each and every one has been thought out and meticulously planned to be shown off at its best; be it the timing of lighting or seasonal conditions.

Use the knowledge and images in this book as a head start and then let your personal creativity take over, putting your own unique stamp on each location. Travelling the breadth of South Wales, this book has been a joy to create over the last four years. I've visited some new locations along with many familiar ones. I think it's always important to set yourself targets and doing this book has really pushed me to head out with the camera covering new ground and ticking off locations, with some requiring a re-visit – or four! – to get the shots I wanted.

This journey has made me fall even more in love my local area and I hope this book will help and inspire you on your photographic journey through South Wales, and that you enjoy spending time in this fabulous part of the world.

Drew Buckley
Pembrokeshire
June 2018

Opposite: The Anvil, Deer Park (p.126).
Canon 5D IV, 24-70mm f/2.8 at 27mm, ISO 50, 1/2s at f/18, Polariser, 0.6 Soft Grad. Tripod. Sep.

A man and his dog silhouetted on Aberystwyth harbour. (p.372).
Canon 5D IV, 24-70mm f/2.8 at 70mm, ISO 250, 1/3200s at f/10. Jan.

Thanks to a great network of major roads, motorways and plenty of rail links from neighbouring England, South Wales is closer than you think.

Getting to South Wales

As Wales borders England on its eastern side, there's a variety of routes that cross the border into South Wales. Depending on how far up or low down in the UK your journey begins, this will dictate the road you travel in on. For most scenarios travelling from the east or southern England, you will cross over the Severn river on either the original bridge, or the new one (Second Severn Crossing) along the M4 motorway. Both of these are toll bridges and you only pay one way, which is westbound. If travelling from slightly further north, I would opt to exit the M5 motorway southbound at junction 8, then head down the M50 motorway bringing you to a roundabout near Raglan, then either choosing to travel towards Swansea via the A465 or Newport via the A449. When travelling from higher up in England or Scotland to South Wales, exit the M6 motorway southbound at junction 20, then travel via the M56/M53 motorways before joining onto the A483 dropping down through the countryside towards Newtown, then either going west to Aberystwyth on the A470/A44 or south to Builth Wells on the A483.

Distances and driving times

Birmingham > Aberystwyth	122m	2hrs 41mins
Canterbury > Cardiff	220m	3hrs 52mins
Exeter > Swansea	150m	2hrs 35mins
London > Cardiff	150m	3hrs 00mins
London > Tenby	238m	4hrs 32mins
Nottingham > Swansea	196m	3hrs 37mins
Peterborough > Aberystwyth	207m	4hrs 11mins
Reading > Carmarthen	172m	3hrs 02mins
Manchester > St. Davids	204m	5hrs 05mins
Newcastle > St. Davids	347m	7hrs 21mins
Edinburgh > Swansea	429m	7hrs 38mins

(Mileage and times supplied by *www.theaa.com*)

Main roads with South Wales

The M4

South Wales has a great network of main roads and they are generally pretty direct. The main artery of South Wales is the M4 motorway. This travels for over 70 miles from the Severn river and country border crossing in the south east, by Cardiff and Swansea towards Pont Abraham in Carmarthenshire. From here the road is then named the A48 dual carriageway west towards Carmarthen and on to St. Clears. At St. Clears the main road splits for north and south Pembrokeshire.

The A40

Before the M4 motorway existed, the A40 was the original 'London' road, which still travels from Fishguard in Pembrokeshire, right across South Wales, through Carmarthen, Llandovery, the Brecon Beacons into the Forest of Dean and England, on towards London. It's mainly a single carriageway but does have some dual sections, usually on hills to pass slower lorries and towing vehicles.

The A465 Heads of the Valleys road and the A470 Brecon Beacons road

The A465, nicknamed the 'Heads of the Valleys' road, goes from Swansea to Hereford, helping travellers who are going northwards to cut the bottom corner of Wales off. There's also a good array of major roads that cover the whole of the valleys, Brecon Beacons and south east Wales. The A470 is exceptionally scenic as it climbs over the Brecon Beacons passing the Storey Arms outdoor centre, one of the main starting points for the walk up Pen y Fan mountain. The main roads generally avoid going through towns and villages, but there are slower sections with the speed limit limited to 20mph in built-up areas.

Opposite: Long exposure and light trails of passing traffic on the A477 at sunrise. Canon 5D III, 24-70mm f/2.8 at 47mm, ISO 50, 30s at f/16. 6ND & ND Grad. Tripod. Oct.

Looking across the Usk valley to the Sugar Loaf (p.282). Canon 5D IV, 24-70mm f/2.8 at 27mm, ISO 100, 1/50s at f/16. Polariser & ND Grad. Tripod. Oct.

Minor roads

There are numerous back roads, B roads and country lanes that criss-cross most areas; it's how most locals get around and they are all well maintained. These narrow roads are used by cyclists, horse riders, walkers, agricultural vehicles and for driving stock. Drive with caution and be prepared to stop.

There's usually enough room to pass if you meet oncoming traffic down a country lane, although passing places are abundant on the narrower sections; however don't be surprised if you need to reverse sometimes. Some of the higher altitude lanes around Powys and the Brecon Beacons can be treacherous in winter, with ice not uncommon and sometimes a covering of snow. In winter only the main roads tend to be treated with salt so take care on wooded back roads, up and down hills and over shady bridges.

Peak times and places

Places to avoid on bank holidays and sunny weekends include Tenby and Barafundle Bay in Pembrokeshire, Pen y Fan in the Brecon Beacons, Rhossili and Three Cliffs in the Gower and Cardiff Bay and Symonds Yat Rock in south east Wales. These areas and the roads to and from them will be congested at peak holiday times, but are usually quiet first thing in the morning and late in the evening. Most areas can be by-passed by consulting a map and using minor roads. Around the rush hour times, many of the main roads will congested, especially around the South Wales motorway junctions and roundabouts in Carmarthen, so it is best to wait until after 7pm to leave or start your journey.

Parking

There is a mix of National Trust and National Park car parks near many locations with most being pay and display. Official car parks are marked on the maps by a blue parking symbol **P**. There are many informal parking areas but park at these places at your own risk. Also, avoid driving up onto the grassy verges and do not block any farm access gates or bridleways.

Travelling around South Wales

By bus

A network of local and cross-country buses knit into the rail network to cover most towns, villages and rural areas of South Wales. For occasional journeys, just pay as you board. In Cardiff, day, weekly and monthly tickets are available. In the national parks, there's specific bus services for walkers and cyclists. Pembrokeshire have their own coastal buses, the 'Puffin Shuttle' and 'Coastal Cruiser' among others. These make joining up coastal walks a breeze, as they stop at nearly all of the best places. While the buses in the Brecon Beacons make up part of the TrawsCymru network.

By train

The principal railway line in South and West Wales runs more or less parallel to the south coast, connecting Chepstow, Newport, Cardiff, Swansea, Carmarthen and Pembrokeshire. Branch lines from Newport, Cardiff and Bridgend serve The Valleys, the Wye Valley and the Vale of Usk. From Carmarthen and west, the train decreases in size to just two carriages and the line splits at Whitland; going south to Pembroke Dock or north to Fishguard. There are several scenic railway lines in Mid Wales too. The 'Heart of Wales' line connects Swansea and Llanelli to Shrewsbury, cutting diagonally across the rolling hills and countryside of Mid Wales, visiting Llandeilo and other towns en route to England.

Travelling to South Wales

By bus

The National Express coach network links major towns and cities in the UK. Direct routes to Wales include:

- London Victoria Coach Station > Cardiff, Swansea, Pembrokeshire
- London Victoria Coach Station, Birmingham > Aberystwyth
- London Gatwick Airport, London Heathrow Airport, Bristol > Cardiff, Swansea
- Manchester, Hull, Nottingham, Leicester, Birmingham > Cardiff, Swansea, Pembrokeshire
- Edinburgh/Glasgow > Manchester > Cardiff, Swansea, Pembrokeshire

Megabus provide low cost intercity travel in the UK, with a coach service running from London and Bristol to Newport, Cardiff, Swansea, Carmarthen and Pembroke Dock.

The 'Heart of Wales' train line at Llandeilo station. Canon 5D IV, 70-200mm f/2.8 at 185mm, ISO 400, 1/2000s at f/5. June.

Ferry departing Pembroke Dock, Wales for Rosslare, Ireland. Canon 5D IV, 24-70mm f/2.8 at 50mm, ISO 250, 1/80s at f/13. Polariser. June.

By train

The main direct rail route to Wales is the fast and frequent service from London Paddington, Reading, Bath and Bristol to Newport and Cardiff, with easy connections to Swansea, Carmarthenshire and Pembrokeshire. The train journey from London to Cardiff takes only two hours.

From London Heathrow Airport, there's a fast, direct rail service to Paddington, where you can change onto a direct train to Wales. From London Gatwick Airport, you can travel direct to London Victoria, then hop on the tube to Paddington or Euston to continue your journey.

From the North, Virgin, CrossCountry and Arriva Trains Wales run regular services from Scotland and the north of England to Cardiff taking between four and eight hours.

By air

There are direct flights to Cardiff Airport from Aberdeen, Birmingham, Newcastle, Belfast, Edinburgh, Glasgow, Norwich and Jersey. Though for anything other than these locations, it's best off hopping over the border and using Bristol Airport which has a greater destination choice.

By ferry – from Ireland

Pembrokeshire is lucky enough to have two ferry ports as its disposal, transporting vehicles and passengers to Ireland. The ferries travel twice daily and take approximately four hours travel time to Rosslare in Wexford. Pembroke Dock is run by Irish Ferries and Fishguard is run by Stena Line. Both ports link into major roads that in turn join onto the A48 and east onwards towards the M4 motorway, providing a fast connection between the United Kingdom and Ireland.

Where to stay in South Wales

South Wales has a variety of accommodation on offer and a great selection of places to eat and drink. The main draws are the two national parks of the Pembrokeshire Coast and the Brecon Beacons, and choosing a location centrally in either of these areas will work well as a base – especially when planning to venture out early for sunrise so that you will have minimal driving time to a location. Both areas have good amenities and you're never too far from good shops and restaurants. Here are some recommendations to get you started.

www.tripadvisor.co.uk .... **www.visitwales.com**

As regards to camping, there are over 400 campsites and caravanning parks. Search South Wales listings at: **www.pitchup.com**

Accommodation

• The Paddock, Haverfordwest	SA62 5QL
• The Cambrian Inn, Solva	SA62 6UU
• Canaston Oaks, Narberth	SA67 8DE
• Monk Haven Manor, St Ishmaels	SA62 3TH
• Shoals Hook Farm, Haverfordwest	SA61 2XN
• St Govan's Country Inn, Bosherston	SA71 5DN
• Giltar Hotel, Tenby	SA70 7DU
• Bluestone Resorts, Narberth	SA67 8DE
• The Brown's, Laugharne	SA33 4RY
• Llwyn Helyg Country House, Llanarthney	SA32 8HJ
• The Cawdor, Llandeilo	SA19 6EN
• The Cliff Hotel & Spa, Cardigan	SA43 1PP
• Black Lion Hotel, New Quay	SA45 9PT
• Carno House, Aberaeron	SA46 0JP
• Aberystwyth Park Lodge, Aberystwyth	SY23 3TL
• Ty Morgan's, Rhayader	LD6 5BH
• The Mirador Boutique, Swansea	SA2 0QX
• King's Head Inn, Llangennith	SA3 1HX
• The Lodge, Llanfrynach	LD3 7AJ
• The Grange Guest House, Brecon	LD3 7ED
• The Exchange Hotel, Cardiff	CF10 5FQ
• Jolyon's, Pontcanna	CF11 9LJ

Campsites

• Tretio Caravan Park, Tretio, St Davids	SA62 6DE
• Trellyn Woodland Camping, Abercastle	SA62 5HJ
• Stackpole Under the Stars, Stackpole	SA71 5BX
• Carreglwyd, Swansea	SA3 1NN
• Three Cliffs Bay Holiday Park, Swansea	SA3 2HB
• The Three Golden Cups, Southerndown	CF32 0RW
• Faerie-thyme, Kidwelly	SA17 5DR
• Blossom Touring Park & Camp Site, Abergavenny	NP7 8BG
• Pencelli Castle Caravan & Camping Park, Brecon	LD3 7LX
• Woodlands Caravan Park, Devils Bridge	SY23 3JW
• Fforest Fields, Llandrindod Wells	LD1 5RT

Breakfast, lunch & dinner

Cafes for breakfast

• Food at Williams, Pembroke	SA71 4NP
• Nash Farm Shop and Cafe, Cosheston	SA72 4SS
• Caddies Cafe, Haverfordwest	SA62 4NN
• Casa, Brecon	LD3 7AA
• Uplands Diner, Swansea	SA2 0EY
• Cariad Cafe, Swansea	SA4 3YE
• Starvin Jacks, Swansea	SA1 3DH
• The Deck, Cardiff	CF10 5GA
• The Secret Garden Cafe, Newport	NP20 1JT
• Firstclass Cafe, Chepstow	NP16 5PF
• The Gatehouse, Kidwelly	SA17 5AX
• Old Mill Cafe, Llanddowror	SA33 4HR
• The Red Kite Cafe, Aberystwyth	SY23 3AB
• Food For Thought, Cardigan	SA43 1JL

Restaurants / lunch & dinner

• The Cambrian Inn, Solva	SA62 6UU
• The Salt Cellar, Tenby	SA70 7DU
• Cwtch, St. Davids	SA62 6SD
• The Mooring, Tenby	SA70 7HD
• Coast, Saundersfoot	SA69 9AJ
• The White Swan Inn, Llanfrynach	LD3 7BZ
• The Three Horseshoes Inn, Brecon	LD3 7SN
• The Bear Hotel, Crickhowell	NP8 1BW
• The Angel, Abergavenny	NP7 5EN
• The Red Kite Inn, Ammanford	SA18 2JD

Top: *The Bear Hotel – Crickhowell.*
Above: *Seafood in Tenby – Salt Cellar.*

Top: *Camping pods – Stackpole Under the Stars.*
Above: *Steak night in Solva – The Cambrian Inn.*

• Slice, Swansea	SA2 9DE
• Beach House Restaurant, Oxwich	SA3 1LS
• New York Deli, Cardiff	CF10 1BB
• Cafe Citta, Cardiff,	CF10 1BG
• The Grazing Shed, Cardiff	CF10 2FR
• Franco at Frolics, Bridgend	CF32 0RP
• Plough & Harrow, Monknash	CF71 7QQ
• Mojo The FoodBar, Newport	NP19 7AA
• Diablo's on the Quay, Carmarthen	SA31 1TN
• Whitfords Cafe Bar, Burry Port	SA17 0BH
• Arthur's, Laugharne	SA33 4SS
• Pizza Tipi, Cardigan	SA43 1EZ
• Ty Morgan's Bistro, Rhayader	LD6 5DS
• Pysgoty, Aberystwyth	SY23 1JY
• Sugar and Spice, Llandrindod Wells	LD1 6AB

Indian restaurants

• Yasmins, Newcastle Emlyn	SA38 9AJ
• Red Indigo, Crickhowell	NP8 1DL
• Mehfils, Pembroke	SA71 4JS
• Panshee, Swansea	SA1 3QN

• Spice Grill, Mumbles	SA3 4DL
• Duchess of Delhi, Cardiff Bay	CF10 5AN
• Mowgli's, Cardiff	CF24 4NH

Fish & chips

• Rowlies, Pembroke	SA71 4NP
• The Shed, Porthgain	SA62 5BN
• D. Fecci & Sons, Tenby	SA70 7HS
• Lime Crab, New Quay	SA45 9NP
• Chip Box, Aberystwyth	SY23 2AR
• Morgan's Traditional Chippy, Carmarthen	SA31 1PZ
• Westend Fish Bar, Brecon	LD3 8AN
• Migels Fish Bar, Llanelli	SA14 8RE
• Youngers Fish Bar, Cardiff	CF14 4AE
• Copperfish Bar & Takeaway, Mumbles	SA3 4EN

Wild Daffodils near Bridgend. Canon 5D III, 300mm f/2.8 at 300mm, ISO 1000, 1/500s at f/5. Tripod. Mar.

South Wales through the seasons

SPRING – March, April, May

Although South Wales is mild all year-round thanks to its mainly maritime climate, colourful spring flowers and fresh woodland leaves don't make themselves shown until late April into early May. Especially the higher, upland regions of Powys and the Brecon Beacons where snow and frost are still possible up until May. For much of March and April, the countryside and coastline still has a wintry look and feel to it, with most of the foliage remaining a dullish brown and the seas turbulent. The first colourful flourish that signifies spring is always Wales' national flower, the daffodil. The timing of this changes every year depending on what sort of winter the region has, but in most cases, these vivid yellow flowers peak in early March, usually coinciding with Wales' national day, St. David's Day on March 1st.

In late March, the lush green leaves of wild garlic burst through, covering up the dull browns of the decaying woodland floor, followed by their white flower heads a few weeks after. During this time seabirds arrive back to their coastline breeding grounds in their thousands; the first of the swallows, house and sand martins and swifts are spotted in early April. On high pressure days, you can experience cold, clear and still nights creating misty mornings. These conditions are best viewed from the nearest high point and are more likely to occur at inland locations as opposed to the generally warmer and windier coast; keep an eye out for high humidity, little or no wind and low temperature forecasts. Looking down on a valley with trees and hills poking out of the 'sea' of clouds, is remedy enough for that early start. Once the wild garlic flowers fade in early May, the bluebells take over, carpeting the ancient woodland floors in rich purple and blue hues, complimenting the vivid greens of new leaf growth. The trees seem to take an age to fill in, but around the end of May everything explodes into life and the woodland floor is rendered into shade once more.

Golden hour near Mynydd Llangorse (p.272). Canon 5D III, 24-70mm f/2.8 at 70mm, ISO 100, 1/10s at f/14. Tripod. June.

SUMMER – June, July, August

Summer is a busy time in South Wales. Thousands of visitors flock to the inland and coastal hotspots over this sunny season, especially once the schools break up in late July. Before this time, you'll generally find even the busiest of locations relatively quiet on a weekday, but some main places are best avoided, especially beaches where many footprints can ruin the pristine sand and any potential images. Thankfully with the knowledge found in this book, there's always some secret places away from the crowds. Anywhere that requires a walk to get to, usually results in little or no-one else around and places along the coast path or in the upland hills, will be far less populated than say Tenby or Rhossili for instance. The hot midday sun in summer is probably the worst conditions to photograph under as you'll fight with harsh shadows and contrasted exposures. On days like these, I tend to favour shaded areas such as woodland and waterfalls as the now leafy tree canopy will diffuse any light into much more balanced images; plus backlit leaves can be quite effective if included too.

June is a time when birds and mammals are at their peak activity raising their young. Seabird colonies are a hive of activity with busy parents feeding the chicks, while nocturnal mammals such as badgers and foxes, are more likely to be seen in the daylight due to the shorter nights. Sunrise is painfully early and sunset exceptionally late, making it a tough time for a landscape photographer. Late July kicks off show season in Builth Wells with the 'Royal Welsh', the biggest agricultural show in Great Britain and also the Pembrokeshire Agricultural Show in mid August, the largest county show in Wales.

Late July into August, is when a lot of the seabird chicks fledge and the adults leave their nesting sites, but there's still photographic interest around as it's heather season in South Wales, colouring up the coastal cliffs and upland hills with rich purples and pinks. Gorse flowers at this time too, so some of the bleaker locations across the countryside suddenly become interesting, as they're painted in a multitude of yellows and purples. Much needed rain falls through August, helping to fill up the barren lakes and rivers, making this a great time to hit the waterfalls before the green tones of summer start to turn a less vibrant shade towards the end of August.

Autumn in Forest of Dean (p.416). Canon 5D IV, 24-70mm f/2.8 at 70mm, ISO 50, 1/2s at f/3.5. Polariser. Tripod. Nov.

AUTUMN – September, October, November

As the school summer holidays end in early September, you can almost hear the countryside breathe a sigh of relief as even the busiest of locations suddenly become relatively empty once more. The sunshine is still warm, but there's a distinct bite to the air and in my opinion, the light gets better too. The hazy skies and harsh light of summer has been replaced with clearer air, dramatic clouds and longer shadows. There's a golden quality to the light around dawn and dusk, that isn't replicated at any other time of year; even in late afternoon, the conditions can be truly stunning. Every day the sunrise is getting later and sunset earlier too, music to the ears of any landscape photographer who's endured the sunrise times of summer.

The characteristic colours of autumn seem to sneak up on us throughout September and by the end of the month, every leaf and piece of foliage has a subtle russet shade to it. The wetter, humid conditions and return of colder nights, result in the opportunity of misty mornings once more. As we head into mid October, autumn goes into warp speed with rich oranges and yellows everywhere you look. Any locations that have a good amount of deciduous woodland with trees like, oak, beech and birch are the ones to aim for as these will really put on a seasonal show. Dinefwr Park in Llandeilo, Waterfall Country near Neath and Ty Canol in Pembrokeshire are perfect for this. Once again, with plenty of rainfall, the waterfalls will be spectacular and coupled with a colourful backdrop of orange leaves, it doesn't get much better. Keep an eye on the weather though as windy weather can strip trees of leaves leaving some images looking a little lacklustre, even before the autumn show has begun.

For macro shooters, fungi are now abundant on dead wood and the forest floor, while wildlife such as male deer are now battling together in the annual rut for breeding rights over their harem of females. Birds are active once more, feeding frantically before the glut of now ripe seeds, nuts and berries are gone for another year. Migratory birds leave our shores for warmer climes, while we welcome others, such as wintering ducks and wading birds. November is always tricky to predict, some years it can be cool and crisp with frosty mornings, and other years it can be mild, wet and very windy, so adapt to the conditions and plan accordingly for the weather forecasts.

Waves crash into Church Rock (p.162). Canon 5D III, 70-200mm f/2.8 at 200mm, ISO 640, 1/1250s at f/13. Dec.

WINTER – December, January, February

Like November, December can still be mild and wet, and now with the exceptionally short days combined with spells of poor weather, it can make photography a frustrating and rare past time. However, small glimpses of magic light can boost the spirits over this unproductive time on the run up to Christmas break. Along the coast in December usually brings rough seas whipped up by strong winds from the Atlantic. Spectacular wave images are possible in this time and fortune favours the brave, but take care, especially on exposed cliffs. High pressure days can provide frosts, misty mornings and sometimes with extended periods of cold and northern winds mixing with rain from the sea, snow can fall on the higher tops. While the rest of the country gets rain, the lofty summits of the Brecon Beacons will catch snow first, along with some of the higher peaks in Carmarthenshire and Powys.

It's only as we head into the new year that things start to settle down into much more classic winter weather and by the end of January it's not uncommon for most of the 'Beacons' to have a covering of snow. Lower down towards the coast, the smaller hills such as the Preseli mountains in Pembrokeshire always have snow for a few days every year. Late February 2018 saw exceptionally rare conditions with sub-zero conditions for a fortnight with lakes and waterfalls frozen over, huge snow drifts blocking roads and even the coast getting a dusting of snow. Magical to see but quite a rarity compared to previous years. For true mountain conditions in the winter you can't beat Pen y Fan and its sister peaks in the Brecon Beacons, where crampons and plenty of winter clothing and equipment are a necessity to climb these summits. Over this time it is exceptionally important to keep an eye on mountain weather forecasts and look for clear windows in the weather as the winds on the summit can sometimes be gale force, with drifting snow, ice under foot and a very cold wind chill factor.

As winter eases its grip on the landscape towards mid February, the signs of a new year are on show with the pearly white flowers of snowdrops bursting through, some early daffodils will be flowering, and also the sure sign that spring is on the way, there will be bouncing lambs across many fields and hills. Snowfall and frost is possible right up until March and April, but the worst of the prolonged cold is usually over by March once more for another year.

SOUTH WALES CLIMATE

Mist filled Usk valley (p.282). Canon 5D IV, 70-200mm f/2.8 at 200mm, ISO 100, 1/3s at f/13. Tripod. Oct.

South Wales has a maritime climate, and is often cloudy, wet and windy but mild. The mean annual temperature at low altitudes in South Wales varies from about 9.5 °C to 11 °C, with the higher values occurring around or near to the coasts. On the coast temperatures average 20 °C in the summer – but have reached 30 °C – it is usually a couple of degrees less in the Brecon Beacons. In the winter the coast and low-lying inland areas rarely have days below freezing whereas in the mountains frosty days can start in late October running through to May with snow often arriving in December. Winter conditions can be quite alpine some years with significant snow drifts, but in some years there will be no lying snow anywhere in South Wales. Autumn and spring are the best times for temperature

inversions with low-lying fog and mist. It is slightly sunnier on the coast than inland, with onshore winds clearing any clouds. South Wales can be wet, with rainfall annually at 1400mm in Swansea, the wettest city in the British Isles. Inland around the Waterfall Country in the southern Brecons it rises to 2500mm and more on the hills due to heavy orographic rainfall over the mountains. Shower activity peaks in autumn and winter due to frequent onshore winds from the Atlantic. Winter storms roll in from the Atlantic at the beginning of the year, a great time to photograph crashing waves against the cliffs. In spring the coast often has short lived showers interspersed with sunny skies, a great time for rainbows.

Walkers in snow, Pen y Fan (p.256). Canon 5D III, 24-70mm f/2.8 at 35mm, ISO 100, 1/160s at f/11. Jan.

Morning light across the Sugar Loaf, from Llangattock Escarpment (p.282). Canon 5D IV, 70-200mm f/2.8 at 180mm, ISO 250, 1/30s at f/11. Tripod. Polariser & ND Grad. Oct.

Met office weather station averages – coastal

Milford Haven, Pembrokeshire
Location: 51.708, -5.055
Altitude: 44m above mean sea level

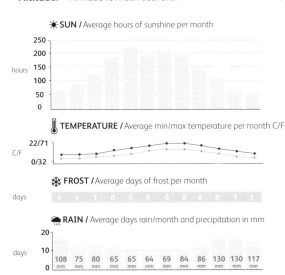

☀ **SUN /** Average hours of sunshine per month

hours — 250 / 200 / 150 / 100 / 50 / 0

🌡 **TEMPERATURE /** Average min/max temperature per month C/F

C/F — 22/71 / 0/32

❄ **FROST /** Average days of frost per month

days — 4 4 4 1 0 0 0 0 0 0 0 1 3

☔ **RAIN /** Average days rain/month and precipitation in mm

days — 20 / 10 / 0

Jan	Feb	Mar	Apr	May	Jun	Jul	Aug	Sep	Oct	Nov	Dec
108 mm	75 mm	80 mm	65 mm	65 mm	64 mm	69 mm	84 mm	86 mm	130 mm	130 mm	117 mm

Jan Feb Mar Apr May Jun Jul Aug Sep Oct Nov Dec

Met office weather station averages – inland low hills

Sennybridge
Location: 52.063, -3.614
Altitude: 307m above mean sea level

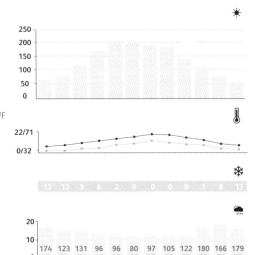

☀

250 / 200 / 150 / 100 / 50 / 0

🌡

22/71 / 0/32

❄

13 13 9 6 2 0 0 0 0 3 8 13

☔

20 / 10 / 0

Jan	Feb	Mar	Apr	May	Jun	Jul	Aug	Sep	Oct	Nov	Dec
174 mm	123 mm	131 mm	96 mm	96 mm	80 mm	97 mm	105 mm	122 mm	180 mm	166 mm	179 mm

Jan Feb Mar Apr May Jun Jul Aug Sep Oct Nov Dec

Springtime blooms at St David's Cathedral (p.102). Canon 5D III, 16-35mm f/4 at 25mm, ISO 100, 1/160s at f/11. Tripod. Polariser. Mar.

In Wales over half a million people speak Welsh, around 24% of the population. Welsh is a Celtic language that evolved from the ancient Britons and probably became a distinct language in the first century AD. The proportion of South Walians that can speak Welsh is as high as 70% in some areas with the highest numbers in Carmarthenshire (Sir Gâr), north Pembrokeshire (Sir Benfro), Ceredigion, parts of Glamorgan and Powys.

You will see the Welsh language on signs and maps everywhere, and you will hear Welsh spoken, it is a beautiful language.

Many places are only known by their Welsh name and where possible we have used Welsh place names next to English in this guidebook. Here is a quick guide to pronunciation and what some Welsh words mean in English.

A short pronunciation guide

Aw ..... as in the English cow
C .... is always a hard C as in cat
Ch ...... as in the Scottish loch
Dd ..... as in th as in there
Ff ...... as in the English f.
F .... sounds like V
Ll .... is aspirated. Form your lips and tongue to pronounce L, but then you blow air
Ng ..... as in ing
Th ...... is like the English th
U .... as ee as in leek
Ywy ... is pronounced as in English Howie.
Y .... as a vowel sound like uh or as in happy

Easy Welsh phrases

Bore da (Pronounced: Boh-reh dah): Good morning
Prynhawn da (Prin-houn dah): Good afternoon
Nos da (nohs dah): Good night
Croeso i Gymru (Croesoh ee Gum-reeh): Welcome to Wales
Iechyd da! (Yeh-chid dah): Cheers!
Tafarn (Tav-arn): Pub
Diolch (Dee-olch): Thanks
Da iawn (Dah ee-aw-n): Very good

Some translations

A

Abaty = Abbey
Aber = River Mouth or Estuary
Afon = River
Allt = Height
Ardal = District

B

Bach = Small, Little
Bedd = Grave
Bera = Pyramid
Betws = Chapel
Blaenau = Upland
Bod = Dwelling
Braich = Arm or Branch
Bryn = Hill
Bwlch = Pass, Col, Gap or Saddle
Bychan = Small

C

Caban = Cabin
Cae = Field
Caer = Fort or Encampment
Canol = Centre
Cantref = District
Capel = Chapel
Carnedd = Cairn, Pile of Rocks
Carreg = Stone
Castell = Castle
Cefn = Ridge
Celli = Grove
Ci = Dog
Clas = Church
Coch = Red
Coed = Wood
Craig = Crag
Croes = Cross
Crug = Barrow
Cwm = Valley
Cymru = Wales

D

Din = Hillfort
Dinas = Large Town or City
Drum = Ridge
Drwg = Bad/Evil
Drws = Door
Du = Black
Dwr = Water
Dyffryn = Valley

E

Eglwys = Church
Eira = Snow
Elegug = Guillemot
Emyn = Hymn
Emynau = Hymns

F

Fach = Small
Fawr = Large
Ffin = Boundary
Ffordd = Road
Ffridd = Pasture
Ffynnon = Spring or Well

G

Gallt = Wooded Slope
Garn = Cairn
Garth = Hill
Glan = Riverbank or Shore
Glân = Clean
Glas = Green, Blue, Grey or Silver
Glyn = Valley
Gribin = Jagged Ridge
Gwaun = Bog
Gwlad = Country
Gwrach = Witch
Gwyn = White
Gwynt = Wind

H

Hafod = Summer House
Hebog = Hawk

Hen = Old
Hendref = Winter House
Heol = Road
Hewl = Road
Hir = Long

I

Is = Below
Isaf = Lower

L

Llan = Church
Llanerch = Meadow
Llech = Large Rock
Llithrig = Slippery
Lloer = Moon
Llwyd = Brown or Grey
Llyn = Lake
Llys = Palace

M

Maen = Stone
Maes = Town Square
March = Horse
Mawr = Big
Melin = Mill
Mochyn = Pig
Moel = Bare Hill or Mountain
Morfa = Seaside, Marsh
Myn = Mine (Pit)
Mynachlog = Monastery
Mynydd = Mountain

N

Nant = Valley
Neuadd = Hall
Newydd = New
Nos = Night

O

Ogof = Cave

P

Pant = Valley
Pen = Top/Head/End
Penrhyn = Headland
Pentref = Hamlet
Perfedd = Middle
Pistyll = Waterfall
Plas = Large House
Plwyf = Parish
Pont = Bridge
Porth = Port or Harbour
Pwll = Pool

R

Rhaeadr = Waterfall
Rhiw = Hill
Rhos = Moor
Rhyd = Ford

S

Sarn = Causeway
Sgwd = Waterfall
Sir = Shire
Stryd = Street

T

Tal = Tall or high
Tir = Territory
Traeth = Shore or Beach
Traws = District
Tref = Town
Twll = Hole
Ty = House

U

Uchaf = Upper

W

Wen = White

Y

Ynys = Island
Ysbyty = Hospital
Ysgol = School
Ystad = Estate

Great photographs require being in the right place at the right time regardless of whether you are using a digital, film or mobile phone camera. This is what fotoVUE photo-location guidebooks are about – giving you the information and the inspiration to get to great locations in the best photographic conditions.

In the right place

Each location chapter in this guidebook describes a place where you can take great photographs. Comprehensive directions are given including co-ordinates to the nearest car park or lay-by, nearest postal codes for sat navs and smart phones, and an OS map co-ordinate.

Before you set off study a map so that you know where you are going and give yourself plenty of time to get your destination. Also read the accessibility notes to check the distances and terrain to a location's viewpoints.

Maps

Whilst there are detailed maps in this guidebook which along with the directions will get you to a location and its viewpoints, for finer navigation we recommend a printed map to go in your rucksack or camera bag.

For the best detail, recommended maps for the South Wales are the *OS Explorer Maps (scale 1:25 000)*, especially for the mountainous region of the Brecon Beacons (*Explorer OL12 & OL13 Brecon Beacons National Park/Parc*). Also recommended is the Brecon Beacons map published by the British Mountaineering Council, a 1:40 000 scale single map to the whole park, printed on tough polyethylene it includes detailed walking routes for Pen y Fan, Fan Fawr and Fan y Big

However the *OS Landranger* series (scale 1:50 000) will suffice for the rest of South Wales, they have less detail but cover larger areas.

There are several apps that allow you to download the OS maps for South Wales, all require either a subscription or purchase of the maps. Remember that it is unsafe to rely solely on a mobile phone or tablet to navigate in the mountains: always take a paper copy of the map with you.

- **Viewranger** – an excellent app, allowing you to purchase and download the maps as required. *www.viewranger.com*
- **Ordnance Survey** – another excellent app, with the option for a month or a year subscription. *www.ordnancesurvey.co.uk*

Ordnance Survey maps are available to view online free through Bing maps too. While the need for a good internet connection makes this an impractical option once on the road, it is a good option for planning before you leave: *www.bing.com/maps*

Our map symbols

Our maps are detailed but with few symbols. The symbols that are important are:

A location chapter

A location chapter is marked by a numbered circle or pin and its name.

A viewpoint

A viewpoint is marked by a small circle sometimes with the name of the viewpoint by it.

Footpaths ----------------

Not all footpaths are marked on our maps, only footpaths that are useful to get to a location and its viewpoints.

Walking man symbol

Paths with a walking man represent longer walks of a few miles, often involving steep uphill walking, and that may require navigation and use of map and compass.

Drew, above Llyn y Fan Fach (p.216). Canon 5D IV, 16-35mm f/4 at 16mm, ISO 1000, 1/640s at f/8. Tripod. Polariser & ND Grad. Sep.

Skomer Island bluebells (p.116). Canon 5D IV, 24-70mm f/2.8 at 27mm, ISO 320, 1/400s at f/10. Polariser. May.

Pub and restaurant symbols

Pubs are marked with a pint symbol and the pub name. They are included as they are good way marks and provide excellent refreshment before or in between photographic excursions. Many good restaurants near to locations are also marked on the maps with a symbol and name.

At the right time

Great photographs usually depend on light, texture and colour. In each location chapter are detailed notes on the best time of year and day to visit a location to get the best photographic results. Good light can occur any time however and often the best times to visit any location is when conditions are rapidly changing like after a storm.

The topography, sun position and the weather determine how the light falls on the land. Use the sun position compass on the front flap of this guidebook for sunrise and sunset times, to find out where the sun rises and sets on the compass (it changes throughout the year) and sun elevation (how high the sun rises in the sky).

Useful websites for this include suncalc.org and the Photographer's Ephemeris *www.photoephemeris.com*, a new 3D version renders the landscape in three dimensions, painting the light on the artificial landscape as it would appear on a clear day at any given time. **Photopills**, another app, lacks the 3D feature of TPE, but has the advantage of many other photography tools including depth of field and exposure calculators. *www.photopills.com*

Weather forecast

Check the weather forecast a few days before and the day before your photography outing. It is best to have several weather apps on your phone, or by checking on a website. Recommended are:

- Yr is weather app from the Norwegian Meteorological Institute and NRK, the Norwegian public broadcasting company. Many photographers swear by its reliability. *www.yr.no*
- Met Office Weather app: *www.metoffice.gov.uk*

Tide times

For coastal locations in this guidebook **My Tides Time** is a great free app that gives you tide tables for predicting when that sandy beach will be footprint free or when the waves will be crashing against the cliffs. You can also view sunrise and sunset times for all locations, and moonrise, moonset and moon phase information. Also useful is: *www.metoffice.gov.uk/public/weather/tide-times*

Exploration

The photographic interpretation of viewpoints is entirely down to prevailing conditions as well as your personal style and skill as a photographer.

This guidebook will help you get to some of the best photographic locations and subjects in the South Wales. The list is by no means exhaustive, use it as a springboard to discover your own photo locations. There are many other great places in the area both known or still waiting to be discovered and photographed. Study a map and look for locations or just follow your nose to discover your own.

Early morning mists and clouds envelop the Brecon Beacons, from Pen y Fan summit (p.258).
Canon 5D IV, 70-200mm f/2.8 at 200mm, ISO 100, 1/60s at f/10. 6ND & Polariser. Tripod. Sep.

Equipment

Most of the photographs in this book were taken during the last five years. All were taken with a Canon 5D full frame camera with the exception of a few earlier shots which were taken either with a Canon 7D, 50D or 30D. I've been a long time user of LEE Filters, so religiously use filtration in camera when need be; especially on the coast where I wouldn't be without my trusty polarising filter. Having built my kit up over ten years or so, I'm pretty much covered with a variety of focal lengths. The 24-70mm probably being my general workhorse along with the 70-200mm and some cases, the 16-35mm. For wildlife, I'll always tend to favour the 300mm prime, with extenders if need be, as it gives me more flexibility with focal length options when shooting on the move. Though if I have one shot or a certain species in mind, or if I'm shooting from a fixed position and need the reach then the bigger 500mm prime comes into play, as it produces stunning image quality and bokeh. I've always opted for a heavy duty carbon fibre tripod which I find vital for the long lens shooting and also is great at combating any wind or camera movement for landscape photography. Ball heads are my favoured tripod head and my must have is an L bracket for my camera. I've always had one of these bolted on my cameras for years now and they offer quick composition changes between portrait and landscape, and also help to keep the centre of gravity over the tripod – I absolutely detest flopping the camera over to one side for portrait images.

Planning

All of my images are meticulously planned down to the minute. The direction of light, pre-visualisation of a composition and also as I live on the coast, checking the tide state is very important. Then for my astro images, the planning is increased, as with certain astronomical objects only appearing for a few minutes, you may only have one shot at a certain image per year! I love scouring maps for possible locations, studying the weather forecast and looking for gaps. Living on the coast, the weather can be as dynamic as the ocean, so fast changing weather does excite me as it usually brings some superb light in between cloud breaks.

Keeping it natural

I like to keep scenes looking natural and also like to include any kind of motion in my images; be it cloud, foliage or water movement – so always tend to slow the shutter down with my landscape images, giving them a more natural and wild appearance. I'm a big believer in getting it right in camera and love playing with filters, getting the shot looking how I want it at the moment of capture, rather than playing around on the computer. However I definitely appreciate the benefits of blending exposures and HDR (done properly), so I do implement these processes if conditions call for it. All of my RAW images are processed in Adobe Lightroom and Photoshop and again, I seek to keep images true to life, keeping shadows dark and highlights bright.

Equipment list

Camera Bodies

Canon EOS 5D Mark IV
Canon EOS 1DX

Lenses

Canon EF 16-35mm f/4L IS USM
Canon EF 24-70mm f/2.8L II USM
Canon EF 70-200mm f/2.8L IS II USM
Canon EF 100mm f/2.8L Macro IS USM
Canon EF 300mm f/2.8L IS USM
Canon EF 500mm f/4L IS USM
Canon EF 1.4x III Extender
Canon EF 2x III Extender
Samyang 14mm f/2.8 IF ED UMC

Filters

LEE Filters – Graduated, Neutral Density and Circular Polariser.

Supports

Feisol CT-3471 Carbon Fibre tripod
Benro G2 Ballhead
Benro GH2 Gimbal Head
Kirk L Bracket

Drew photographing Puffins at sea.

Captions

The photo captions in fotoVUE guidebooks are in two parts:

1 Descriptive caption

First is a descriptive caption that describes where the photograph was taken, mentioning any references to viewpoints (e.g., VP1) in the accompanying text and any other useful descriptive text.

2 Photographic information

The second part of the caption lists the camera, lens, exposure, filter used, if any and the month the photograph was taken. This information is from the Exchangeable Image File Format (Exif data) that is recorded on each image file when you take a photograph.

Make and model of camera

The focal length of the lens at which the photograph was taken the photograph was taken (for non prime lenses).

Tripod or Handheld If a tripod is used, it will say Tripod. If the word Tripod is not there you will know that the photograph was taken by handholding the camera.

Filter used, if any

Canon 5D IV, 24-70mm f/2.8 at 20mm, ISO 100, 1/20s at f/11, Polariser. Tripod. July.

Lens focal length

Light–Exposure information The ISO setting, shutter speed and aperture that the photograph was taken at.

The month taken When looking at the photograph, by providing the month in the caption you will know the possible type of weather and the state of the vegetation in a particular month at the location.

CLASSIC SOUTH WALES LOCATIONS

If you want to visit and photograph South Wales' most beautiful and classic photography locations, here's my top ten.

1 MARLOES PENINSULA   P.132

2 STRUMBLE HEAD LIGHTHOUSE   P.72

3 NEWGALE BEACH   P.110

4 TENBY   P.194

5 CARDIFF BAY   P.402

6 RHOSILLI & WORM'S HEAD   P.328

7 NASH POINT   P.394

8 WATERFALL COUNTRY   P.232

9 PEN Y FAN MASSIF   P.256

10 DYLAN THOMAS   P.296

In South Wales there are many impressive landscape photography locations that are roadside, which are very useful if you have limited mobility, are rushed for time or just want an easier day. The same principles of light and weather that are described throughout this book apply to these locations and they are usually best at dawn and close to dusk, or during the day when there is changeable weather.

In book order, these are some of the most accessible viewpoints in the South Wales, either roadside (marked with the wheelchair symbol), or a short walk of less than 250m from the road (no symbol).

See each location's page for specific access details and location descriptions.

Opposite: *Full moon rises at Church Rock (p.162). Canon 5D IV, 300mm f/2.8 + 1.4x Extender at 420mm, ISO 1250, 1.3s at f/10. Tripod. Apr.*

Being outdoors is living life to the full and can be enjoyed by all, but we have to share it with others and stay safe. Here is some information and guidelines on accessing the outdoors and looking after yourself.

Public rights of way on maps

Public rights of way are linear routes which fall into four categories. They are the legal responsibility of and maintained by Highway Authorities. Details of the routes are held on the Highway Authorities' Definitive Maps.

Please stay on public rights of way and don't be tempted to wander in to fields. The following symbols are used on OS 1:25,000 Explorer maps:

Footpaths - - - - - - - - -

For use on foot only.

Bridleways — — — — —

For use on foot, on a horse or on a pedal cycle.

Restricted byways + + + + +

For use on foot, on a horse or pedal cycle, or by horse drawn vehicle.

Byways + + + + +

Open to all traffic, on foot, on a horse, on a pedal cycle or motorcycle, or in a motor or horse-drawn vehicle. However, they are mainly for use as footpaths or bridleways and are usually unsealed.

Then there are **Green Lanes** – unsurfaced rural roads – which have or may have the potential to carry motorised vehicle rights. Green Lanes are ancient routes that have existed for millennia, such as hollow ways, drover's roads, ridgeways and ancient trackways.

Permissive paths are where a landowner gives agreement for public access. There is no statutory legal right to use these routes and permission may be withdrawn. They are shown on OS 1:25,000 Explorer maps as footpaths or bridleways and the agreement may be posted at the start of the path.

Be a respectful photographer

The obvious is always worth stating: do not climb over walls or fences, shut all gates, drop no litter, pick up litter others have dropped, keep dogs at home or on lead, drive slowly in rural and urban areas, give way to cyclists, agricultural vehicles and horse riders, park considerably, don't scare livestock and keep quiet (don't play music or fly drones near others) but always say hello to fellow outdoor enthusiasts. In short follow the **Countryside Code**.

Busy viewpoints

As photography becomes more popular some accessible locations and viewpoints can become busy at times of good light. In some circumstances this can cause conflict between photographers as they look for the best spot to compose their shot. If you arrive at a location, and someone is already set up, give them space and don't get in their way. Talking and negotiating helps. They may be OK with you setting up next to them, or with you using their spot after they have done. There are usually alternative viewpoints, but just make sure you aren't in their line of fire. If there is a crowd at a particular spot, it is often best just to find another viewpoint.

Can't walk far and wheelchair users ♿

If you can't walk far or up steep slopes or if you use a wheelchair or have an injury and need to know whether a location is suitable for you, each location chapter has a brief Access notes section describing the terrain and distance from the road to a viewpoint. Most locations in this guidebook, apart from the mountain and waterfall viewpoints, are usually not far from the road, some are roadside.

If a location or viewpoint has the wheelchair symbol, part or all of it will be accessible by wheelchairs. Bear in mind that access may not be exactly as described in the text for wheelchair users, and you should use your own judgement as to how far you should proceed at any given location.

Saying all that, just driving around the countryside will present many superb photographic opportunities. Just be careful where you stop – avoid stopping in passing places for more than a quick shot – and be aware of traffic.

Winter storms and waves crash into the south Pembrokeshire coastline. Canon 5D III, 70-200mm f/2.8 at 155mm, ISO 640, 1/500s at f/13. Dec.

MOD firing ranges

If you accessing locations near Castlemartin firing range don't pick up any metal objects as they may be live shells. Check the Ministry of Defence 'Castlemartin Firing Times' website or call **01646 662 367** for firing times to find out when access and the roads are open. See page 146 for more details.

Coastal locations

If you or others are in trouble call 999 and ask for the Coastguard.
If you don't have a mobile phone, shout for help.

Many locations in this guidebook are close to cliff edges, sometimes over 100ft (30m) above the sea, and many are by the sea on beaches and down in coves. If you don't take precautions and plan your visits there is the potential to be blown of cliff edges, swept away by waves or be trapped by incoming tides.

Before you go

- If you are visiting a coastal location, wear good clothing and footwear.
- Let someone know where you are going and at what time you plan to return.
- Take a fully charged mobile phone with you.
- Check the tide timetables so that you know when high and low tides are.

Cliff tops and edges

- Stay away from cliff edges, especially if it is windy or if the ground is wet.

- Cliff edges and rock formations such as sea arches are often composed of unstable rock that can easily collapse if walked on.
- Obey warning signs and don't climb over fences to get to the cliff edge.
- Don't be tempted to explore blow holes, caves or zawns, or scramble down slopes that are often loose and end in steep drops.
- Always take a head torch with you for night photography
- If taking a selfie, be safe.

Down by the sea

People get swept in to the sea by rogue waves on calm days.

- Always stand well back from the sea whether at a harbour or on a beach.
- To avoid getting stranded always know the state of the tides, especially if venturing down into a cove or bay, and always have a plan for escape or retreat.
- Don't attempt to climb or scramble out of a cove up a cliff or steep slope.
- If you get stuck in mud or quicksand, spread your weight, avoid moving and call for help.
- Take extra care on rocky beaches that are often slippery and sharp.

Winter walking

The mountains can look their best in the winter, however the arrival of snow and ice make the mountains more dangerous to explore. Ice axe and crampons are required, along with the skills to use them. An awareness of avalanche safety is essential. A winter skills course is highly recommended for those wanting to enjoy the mountains in winter. Any hill days described in this guide should be avoided in winter by anyone that does not have the relevant training and experience.

Tenby harbour taken from a plane (p194).
Canon 5D IV, 24-70mm f/2.8 at 59mm, ISO 1000, 1/640s at f/9. May.

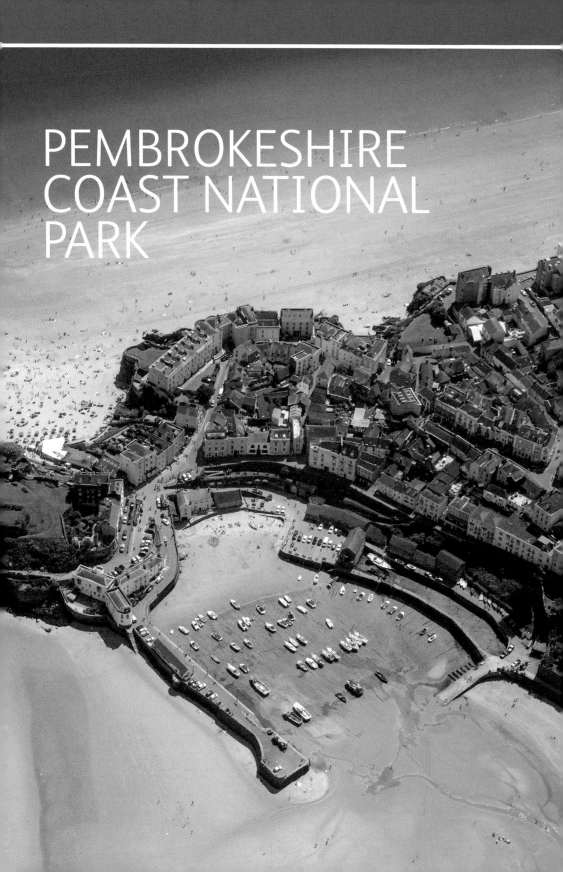

PEMBROKESHIRE COAST NATIONAL PARK

Pembrokeshire is my home and where I've spent all my life. Known for its stunning beaches, seaside villages, and rugged coastline, it also has a rich history with many castles, burial chambers, and churches. Pembrokeshire is Britain's only coastal national park with fantastic walking thanks to its unique coastal path. The Pembrokeshire Coast Path; now celebrating its sixty-sixth year, winds its way through 186 miles of the most breathtaking and stunning coastal scenery in Britain. Starting at the pebble-backed beach of Amroth in the south east of the county and finishing at St Dogmaels in the north east, the path encompasses almost every kind of coastal landscape from towering sea stacks, rocky bays and sea cliffs to vast golden beaches and grassy dune systems stretching as far as the eye can see. If you walked it all, it's comparable to climbing Everest with its ascents and descents equating to thirty-five thousand feet of elevation changes. However, thanks to the way it links up most towns and villages, it's much better to complete it in stages, taking your time and soaking up the magical views along the way.

Pembrokeshire has, and always will be, a haven for visitors and its variety of coastal destinations for a week or weekend away are second to none. The seas that surround the coast appear as a beautiful turquoise blue in the summer months and gazing into the water whilst out on a cliff top walk, you could be fooled into thinking you're in the Mediterranean. Well-known tourist spots such as Tenby Harbour, St Davids Cathedral and Barafundle Bay sell a rather typical view of what visitors to the county can expect, but go off the beaten track and the photographer will be rewarded with some fantastic locations with many unique views and compositions. The park also displays a wide array of coastal flora and fauna throughout the seasons, with an abundance of noisy seabird colonies taking up residence in the spring and summer months.

The county is split into two halves: the north with its rugged and wild coast, the Preseli mountain range, wooded valleys and remote cliff-top villages. Whilst in the south, you'll find golden beaches, and a much calmer and tranquil appearance to the seas. Having said that though, when Atlantic storms rage towards Wales, the first point they hit is Pembrokeshire and the sea can be transformed into a raging surf in a short space of time. Pembrokeshire has an essentially maritime climate, so as you can imagine, it tends to get a fair share of rain. The weather can change quickly, it's often cloudy, wet, windy and wild, sometimes all at once!

Heather and Gorse, St. David's Head (p.96). Canon 5D III, 24-70mm f/2.8 at 35mm, ISO 50, 10s at f/16. Tripod. Polariser & ND Grad. Aug.

Although misty drizzle and grey skies aren't the best conditions to show off the landscape, usually prior or after these weather patterns you may experience some rare, but fantastic light. Pembrokeshire has some great potential for majestic coastal and inland views for photography, and hopefully, you'll discover its many charms.

Map

- OS Explorer Map OL35 – North Pembrokeshire

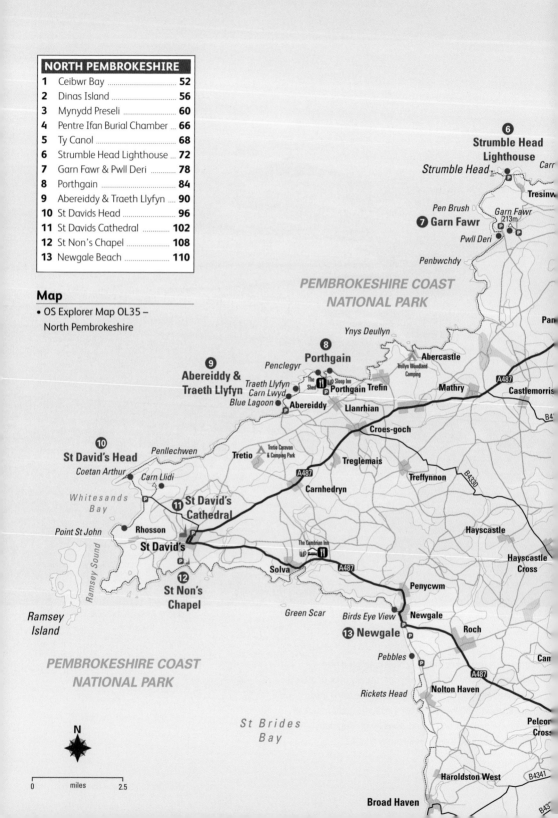

Rocky folds and strata on the coast north of Ceibwr Bay.
Canon 5D III, 24-70mm f/2.8 at 70mm, ISO 50, 1s at f/16. Polariser & 3ND. Tripod. May.

Prepared to be wowed by some of the finest and most spectacular geology and rock formations in Wales. Ceibwr (pronounced kye-bwrr) is best known for its amazing folded rock strata in the cliffs lining the north side of this small coastal inlet. The cliff tops are carpeted in swathes of pink thrift over the spring months and just a short walk to the west, is the aptly named Witches Cauldron. The Witches Cauldron is a large collapsed cave where in rough weather the sea surges creating a boiling mass of water and spray. Choughs whirl across the sky, while seals and porpoise dance in the surf, making Ceibwr a fabulous location for all aspects of photography.

What to shoot and viewpoints

Viewpoint 1 – Bay Views ♿

From one of the two parking areas you can head down into the bay and explore around the shoreline. The views are great from the parking bays if you can't walk far.

Here you will find many rock pools home to a wealth of sea life and it's here that you will feel the power of the sea as waves crash just a few metres away. I find the best views of the folded rock strata, synonymous with Ceibwr, are to be found up on the grassy headland just to the west of the bay. Thrift or 'sea pink' flowers are in abundance here and all along the coast, peaking around the end of May. This slightly elevated viewpoint will give you a much better view of the twists and curves of the folded cliffs along the north east of the bay. Following the coast path as it snakes around westwards, the path climbs up to reach an area with large rocks standing out of the water and a cave structure below. This is a great place to look for porpoise, dolphin, seal and also nesting seabirds such as fulmar and chough. This stretch of the bay provides the best photographic opportunities with a real mixture of subjects; from wildlife, flowers to coastal views. Long exposures work great here at high tides.

Opposite: Thrift 'Sea Pinks' and the rocky coastline. Canon 5D III, 16-35mm f/2.8 at 22mm, ISO 100, 1s at f/16. Polariser. Tripod. May.

Looking down into Pwll-y-Wrach (VP2). Canon 5D III, 16-35mm f/2.8 at 16mm, ISO 100, 1s at f/16. Polariser. Tripod. May.

Viewpoint 2 – Pwll-y-Wrach

Pwll-y-Wrach translates to the 'Witches Pit' and is also called the Witches Cauldron, and on stormy days it is easy to see why. Peering down into the cavernous abyss, a small inlet allows sea water into a large pool that bubbles and froths with surf. From viewpoint 1 this location is found to the west, roughly a mile along the coast path by mostly flat walking . On your left side along the way are gorse covered rocky hills, and to your right, the land drops away abruptly into the sea. Eventually the path starts to climb again, then descends the rim of the cauldron. Take care here as the path is very loose with shale and gravel under foot and it is a long way down on either side of the path. A small path takes you off the main route around to the south of the pool, but you can also view the collapsed cave from afar across the valley. The next stage is a bit of a lung buster but worth it for the views. Cross the little bridge that spans the small stream and head up the zig-zagging path as far as the top of the hill and look back, a real sight for the eyes. Bluebells grow on these grassy flanks in mid-May.

Coast path at Ceibwr Bay. Canon 5D III, 16-35mm f/2.8 at 24mm, ISO 100, 0.4s at f/16. Polariser & ND Grad. May.

Thrift 'Sea Pinks' along fence at Ceibwr Bay. Canon 5D III, 24-70mm f/2.8 at 44mm, ISO 200, 1/10s at f/16. May.

How to get here

The closest main town is Cardigan on the Pembrokeshire/
Ceredigion county border. From here there are a variety of ways to
get to the bay via the country lanes. Most routes head through the
village of Moylegrove. From Cardigan head out west on the A487
signed to Fishguard, and turn off after 3 miles signed B4582.
Follow this lane for 1.5 miles before turning right and continuing
for a further 2.5 miles, the last part of this road is exceptionally
steep with hairpins so take care. Turn left at the junction entering
Moylegrove, then a quick right at the chapel. Head down this lane
until you reach the bay. Parking is at the road side in the lay-bys,
the first one provides best access to the beach while the second
will drop you straight onto the coast path.

Parking Lat/Long: 52.077475, -4.7620194
Parking Postcode: SA43 3BX
OS Map Grid Ref: SN108457

Accessibility ♿

There is minimal walking to Ceibwr from the parking bays, although
all areas other than the road and a small part of the path is uneven.
It is especially slippery and rocky if venturing down to the shoreline
parts of the bay. Those less mobile will still enjoy the great coastal
views from the road as it is right on the edge of the cliffs.

Best time of year/day

This location is best in late spring and the summer, not only for
the vast amounts of wild flowers on show but the light angles will
suit the bay's north west aspect. Late evening light should make
the coastline rocks glow orange, while a morning visit would suit
the view across the Witches Cauldron better. Windy, cloudy, even
stormy days can provide spectacular conditions with large
waves crashing into the coastline.

*Opposite: Pwll-y-Wrach (VP2). Canon 5D III, 16-35mm
f/2.8 at 20mm, ISO 100, 1/80s at f/16. Tripod.
Polariser & ND Grad. July.*

Dinas Island is a wild and windswept promontory situated on the north Pembrokeshire coast between Fishguard and Newport. This rugged peninsula is surrounded on three sides by the turbulent Irish Sea and on its landward side is a swampy marsh cut by melt water from the last ice age, partially detaching the peninsula from the mainland, hence Dinas Island. Pen y Fan is the peninsula's highest point, standing at 142m (466ft) it boasts some of the finest views anywhere on the Pembrokeshire coast. Wildlife is abundant here and in the spring the cliffs are alive with the sound of seabirds while bluebells flourish on its eastern flanks. In the autumn seal pups are born in the rocky bays and on the south east of the peninsula is the picturesque chapel ruins of Cwm yr Eglwys. There's a lot to see on this short but challenging circular route that I describe, with many great places to stop off en-route by the coast.

What to shoot and viewpoints

Viewpoint 1 – Cwm yr Eglwys ♿

Ample parking is found in the small bay at Pwllgwaelod and from here you can start the circular walk in either direction – it is described anti-clockwise. Pwllgwaelod is a great beach for rock pools and sand formations, with views west across Fishguard Bay. Behind the beach is *The Old Sailor* serving seafood and real ale, something to look forward to at the end of the walk. Head towards the beach, then turn back eastwards (right). The first section of this path is a wide and flat suitable for wheelchairs, bikes and pushchairs and after half a mile you'll end up in the small seaside village of Cwm yr Eglwys.

Cwm yr Eglwys beach is mostly sandy with plenty of rock pools to explore and rocks to clamber over. The main point of interest will be your first glimpse of the chapel ruins. Today, just the wall of this little chapel remains, the rest was washed away in the enormous 'Royal Charter Storm' of 1859 that created all of Pembrokeshire's pebble banks. It is quite impressive to stand here and think that once it was under a torrent of water. It can still get rough here in stormy weather, but it is generally sheltered as the bay

faces away from the prevailing weather. In the summer months and if you're up early enough, it's possible to catch the sun rising through the doorway aperture or alternatively opt for an evening visit to experience some side lighting that enhances the stonework textures on the chapel wall and gravestones. When the tide is out, there's plenty to explore on the beach, with a secret beach revealed at very low tides.

Viewpoint 2 – Pen y Fan

From the graveyard you'll want to skirt around the stone wall north west and up the narrow street passing the house, before taking a right across the wooden footbridge and into the woods. This walk rises rapidly up a series of twists and turns, over uneven ground and up a series of steps – so take care, especially in wet weather as there are bare

How to get here

From Haverfordwest head out north on the A40 towards Fishguard. Follow this road for 13 miles and at the roundabout take the second exit for the A487. Drive through Fishguard town before climbing out and heading along the coast. On reaching Dinas Cross after 5 miles, turn left signed for Pwllgwaelod. Follow this lane for around a mile as it descends through woodland and the National Trust car park will be on your right at the back of the beach.

Parking Lat/Long: 52.021260 -4.9078752
Parking Postcode: SA42 0SE
OS Map Grid Ref: SN005398

Accessibility ♿

Pwllgwaelod beach is right by the car park and is extremely accessible for all via a wide slipway. The pathway that connects Pwllgwaelod to Cwm yr Eglwys is flat and well maintained too, so perfect for those with limited mobility. There is also paid parking at Cwm yr Eglwys but it can get busy in the summer and the lanes are very narrow. The rest of the walk is very undulating and like most of the coast path, can be uneven under foot.

Best time of year/day

As with most elevated coastal views, high tides work best to remove any distracting rocks near the shoreline and provide clean divisions with the land. Wild flowers like bluebells cover the eastern coastal areas in early May. The guillemots breeding season is around the same time and seals should be visible all year round, though more abundant in autumn when they inhabit the rocky coves rearing their pups. In summer, sunrise angles allow photography in the Cwm yr Eglwys bay due to its north eastern aspect. Sunsets shine straight into Pwllgwaelod beach. Heather and gorse bloom in late July, while autumn brings berries on the hawthorn trees and rich browns to the coastal bracken.

Above: Beach goers at Cwm yr Eglwys (VP1). Canon 5D III, 24-70mm f/2.8 at 24mm, ISO 100, 1/25s at f/14. Polariser. July.

Below: Coast path views (VP2). Canon 5D III, 24-70mm f/2.8 at 35mm, ISO 100, 1/30s at f/14. Polariser. July.

Coast path views heading towards VP1. Canon 5D III, 24-70mm f/2.8 at 35mm, ISO 100, 1/30s at f/14. Polariser. July.

tree roots exposed to step over. After a short while you'll finally exit out of the trees. Here you'll gaze across Cwm yr Eglwys bay and along the coast, north east towards Newport. You can take the lower but tougher route as it skirts around the coast which is very up and down and includes a steep series of steps, but personally I'd opt for the new route through the kissing gate on your left at the 'Pen Dinas' sign and across the field which cuts the corner off. Where these two paths meet is a hot spot of bluebells in springtime. They cover most of this north eastern corner of Dinas Island before the bracken starts to take over and smother the coastline. Gaze down onto Needle Rock, crammed full of guillemots and other seabirds busy raising their young before departing in early July. The last uphill slog winds up to the trig point summit of Pen y Fan where you can take a well earned breather. The views from here are simply sublime with panoramic views all around you.

To your west is the summit of Garn Fawr and past Fishguard is Carreg Wasted, the scene of the last French invasion of Britain in 1797. To the north east are the cliffs at Pen-yr-Afr (near Ceibwr Bay) while the majority of the view back inland are the summits which make up the Preseli mountains. Look out for the rugged summit of Carningli above Newport too. It's all mostly downhill now back to the car, by an easy going path, but enjoy the views out west and down into some of the rocky coves where you may see seals, especially in the autumn when Atlantic grey seals have their pups. After around a mile there's a series of forty of so steps and some impressive rock formations on the opposite coastline. These would illuminate nicely in evening light and coupled with a raging sea could provide some great images. You are on the home stretch now as the path widens and winds its way back to the car park and the pub for some well earned refreshments.

Opposite: The church ruins at Cwm yr Eglwys (VP1). Canon 5D III, 24-70mm f/2.8 at 31mm, ISO 100, 1/50s at f/14. Polariser. July.

The Preseli Mountains, or Preseli Hills, rise out of the landscape up to 536m in the northern half of Pembrokeshire. They are a complete contrast to Pembrokeshire's sandy beaches and relative lowlands of the south. Mainly grazed by sheep, this is a harsh windswept environment made up of wild moorland, heath and grassland, and is home to a wide range of plants and invertebrates, some of them quite rare. There's one pathway across the range called The Golden Road, which is a great way to access the area's many cairns and quarries. This evocatively named walking route runs along the spine of the Preseli Mountains. Gently undulating and taking in most of the main summits on its trail, it offers easy going walking along with panoramic views across the Pembrokeshire countryside.

On clear days you'll spot the hills of Ireland to the west, South Wales and to the north, along Cardigan Bay towards Snowdonia. It is easy to understand how this prominent area has ancient links with its neighbours for trade. The Golden Road is believed to date back over 5,000 years to Neolithic times, used as a main route for travellers to and from Ireland,

and for transporting gold which was mined in the Wicklow mountains. It was also one of hundreds of ancient ridgeways, high trails which people and animals used to avoid the dense forests and difficult and dangerous terrain at low levels. The Preselis are also one of the places where the Stonehenge bluestones, the inner stone circle of Stonehenge, are thought to have originated.

What to shoot and viewpoints

Viewpoint 1 – Foel Eryr
Distance 0.5 miles/0.9km, elevation gain 171ft/52m
The seven mile west-east route begins at the parking area called Bwlch Gwynt, this is the closest parking access point to reach the 468m summit of Foel Eryr. It's a main road here and vehicles can approach fast over the crest, so take care when crossing to begin your walk. It's an easy going walk to start off, with only a few boggy sections lower down, even in summer. Once passed this area, the path gets a little steeper but is well defined and it's plain sailing up to the top. The summit itself is made up of a large Bronze Age burial cairn, with rocks of mixed sizes that you'll need to clamber over to reach the trig point marker. Foel Eryr is a dramatic start and a great introduction to the

Wild ponies in the snow near parking for VP1. Canon 5D III, 24-70mm f/2.8 at 25mm, ISO 400, 1/640s at f/13. Dec.

Rocky outcrop at Foel Drygarn (VP2). Canon 5D IV, 24-70mm f/2.8 at 35mm, ISO 100, 1/200s at f/13. Tripod. ND Grad. Mar.

Preseli mountains. It translates to English as the "Place of the Eagle" so it should give you an idea of the almost timeless feeling this landscape holds. The majestic eagles are no longer seen around here but buzzard and now, red kites, are regular sights gliding overhead while wild ponies roam the raw grassland below. From the summit are 360 degree views and gazing back east over towards the car park you'll see the Pantmaenog forest nestled beneath the highest point in the Preseli mountains and Pembrokeshire, Foel Cwmcerwyn; standing tall at 536 metres. There's an ancient collection of Welsh stories called Mabinogion. One particular story tells of King Arthur and his knights fighting a battle with a mighty boar called Twrch Trwyth in the grassy cwm below Foel Cwmcerwyn. A line of rocky outcrops at Cerrigmarchogion are supposedly the graves of some of Arthur's knights, killed in battle. If you'd like to explore this area, it can be reached from the same parking area and heading east through the forest.

Viewpoint 2 – Foel Drygarn
Distance 0.5 miles/0.9km, elevation gain 295ft/90m
This Iron Age fortress dates back to around 350 BC with its double ramparts and ditches. At 363m itself, it's no easy

climb with the last part requiring a few switch backs to reach the reasonably level top. On the summit itself, there's lots of rocks at first glance, but if you look closer you will recognise it is in fact three Bronze Age burial cairns in a row, one of which features a large flat stone known as, Bwrdd y Brenin (King's Table). Legend says there is a pot of gold hidden under it.

This summit is best reached from a small parking area just outside of the town of Crymych. Heading out on the Mynachlog-ddu road for around a mile, there's a lay-by at the side of the road and the footpath is on the opposite side. Heading up the path, you'll go through a small stream then a gate before embarking uphill and across the flank of the hill. There's a series of gullies, streams and boggy patches that you'll need to hop over. After around half way up, the hill bites back and gets steeper progressively all the way to the top. Average walking time, is around ten to fifteen minutes from the car, so not a long walk but you'll know you've done it. Approaching from the northern side it's easy to forget about the weather, but once on the summit you'll definitely begin to feel the wind, which can be biting in winter. There's some great views to be had though,

Looking towards Mynydd Preseli from afar. Canon 5D III, 70-200mm f/2.8 at 110mm, ISO 800, 1/400s at f/10. Sep.

looking down the Golden Road west towards Carn Sian, Carn Goedog, Foel Cwmcerwyn and Carningli off to the right; then the views down to the coast toward Newport and on clear days, Ireland and Snowdonia. My favoured views are just over the summit on the western edge where there are photogenic jagged rocks that jut out of the land, perfectly placed foreground elements to add scale and depth to the wider views. The landscape below is mainly heather, which blooms purple in late summer. Red kite are regulars in this area, soaring on the thermals while the evocative croak of raven fits perfectly with the ancient setting.

Viewpoint 3 – Carn Goedog
Distance 3 miles/4.5km, elevation gain581ft/177m
Heading west along the Golden Road path from Foel Drygarn, you'll begin to venture towards a very important geological site. Spotted Dolerite, otherwise known as Bluestone is found in the Preseli mountains and it's at Carn Goedog where the stones were once quarried and transported to Wiltshire, used to build the inner circle at Stonehenge. A recent archaeological study confirmed this location as the site where the stones came from. Also nearby Craig Rhos-y-felin was stated as the source of one of the 'rhyolite' bluestones. Ideas of how they transported the rocks have come to light recently too. This special formation of rock, which forms natural pillars at these outcrops on the landscape, allowed the prehistoric quarry-workers to detach each megalith with a minimum of effort. Just by inserting wooden wedges into the

cracks between the pillars, then letting the Welsh rain swell the wood to ease each pillar off the rock face. The quarry-workers then lowered the thin pillars onto platforms of earth and stone, a sort of loading bay from where the huge stones could be dragged away along tracks leading out of each quarry. It is thought these were then transported overland by teams of people and oxen, each of the 80 megaliths used at Stonehenge weighed less than two tons. Quite an amazing feat of engineering in the years around 3000 BC.

Tread in the footsteps of your ancient ancestors by heading west from Foel Drygarn along the Golden Road. There's a few boggy sections, but it's a mainly flat and wide path with a few ups and downs. En route to Carn Goedog there are plenty of carns and boulder fields to stop and enjoy the views. You'll be in the middle of nowhere here; the silence and total removal from modern life is very refreshing, a great experience on a pleasant day. After climbing up and passing Carn Bica, take the pathway to your right and descend down to the rocky outcrop. You may be quite underwhelmed by a load of large stones poking up out of the ground, but it's a fabulous place to just 'be'. I'm not a very spiritual person, but there's definitely something about this place that should connect with everyone on a deeper level.

How to get here

Bwlch Gwynt parking for Foel Eryr

The parking area is immediately on the main road from Haverfordwest to Eglwyswrw. Taking the B4329 north east out of Haverfordwest, follow this road for around 12 miles. You'll reach Rosebush cross roads, and then go over a cattle grid. At the top of this hill you'll want to slow down giving plenty of warning to any vehicles behind you, before double checking for oncoming traffic before turning right into the parking area. The path up Foel Eryr starts over the road, or to head to Foel Cwmcerwyn follow the pathway out of the car park towards the forest.

VP 1 Parking Lat/Long:	51.954797, -4.8027165
VP 1 Parking Postcode:	SA66 7RB
VP 1 OS Map Grid Ref:	SN075321

Foel Drygarn and Carn Goedog

From Haverfordwest head out east on the A40 for around 10 miles, before taking the first exit north signed for Cardigan/A478. Stay on this road for 12 miles and take the first turning left as you enter the town of Crymych, sign posted for Mynachlog-ddu. Head down here for one mile and just after the road turns to the left, the lay-by will be on your left. Park here then walk down the track opposite to start the walk.

VP 2 & 3 Parking Lat/Long:	51.965779, -4.6719669
VP 2 & 3 Parking Postcode:	SA66 7SA
VP 2 & 3 OS Map Grid Ref:	SN165330

Accessibility

The Preseli mountains are definitely walking boot territory and after rainfall, even wellies are sometimes needed. It's a very wet climate with saturated ground and as such, most pathways are uneven and slippery most of the time, so it's not good terrain for those less mobile. In general the summits also involve some rock hopping over a jumble of mixed-sized stones. Always be prepared for the weather changing quickly and pack food, waterproofs and extra layers as if walking to Carn Goedog for example, expect to be out for a good three to four hours.

Best time of year/day

The Preseli mountains are the county's indicator in winter – due to their height they are the first place that sees snowfall. However because of Pembrokeshire's maritime climate and the sea on nearly all four sides, it's only during colder snaps that the hills will receive a blanket of the white stuff. When it does happen expect to witness the whole population of Pembrokeshire flocking to the hills for the day or two it will hang around. While it can be very picturesque in winter, I tend to prefer visiting in the spring and autumn due to the glorious quality of light. Thanks to the undulating terrain, the Preselis make their own weather system and coupled with passing clouds, it can really create an immense atmosphere. That said, on a summer's day, it's a lovely place to walk and you won't see many other people along this ancient route.

Drew on summit of Foel Eryr (VP1) at sunset. Canon 5D III, 24-70mm f/2.8 at 50mm, ISO 1250, 1/50s at f/11. Tripod. Feb.

Trig point on summit of Foel Drygarn (VP2). Canon 5D III, 24-70mm f/2.8 at 55mm, ISO 100, 1/400s at f/14. Tripod. Polariser. Aug.

Huge rocks at Carnmenyn. Canon 5D IV, 24-70mm f/2.8 at 47mm, ISO 100, 1/50s at f/9. Tripod. Polariser. Mar.

Wild Shetland ponies in the snow near Foel Eryr summit at sunset.
Canon 5D III, 24-70mm f/2.8 at 24mm, ISO 400, 1/80s at f/13, ND Grad. Feb.

Set in the heart of the Preseli mountains in mid Pembrokeshire, this area is known as Bluestone country. Bluestone, or Spotted Dolerite, is the famous igneous rock that was used to build parts of Stonehenge. This rock is only found in Pembrokeshire and while the journey wasn't quite as far as Wiltshire, the burial chamber that stands tall here today, is built from the same magnificently coloured rock. Pentre Ifan is a Bronze Age megalithic site dating from at least 4000 B.C.

It's one of the finest hilltop megaliths in Wales, with a gigantic 15 tonne capstone. It is said to have been originally constructed as a chambered tomb dating to the Neolithic period, but has now been denuded of earth over several thousand years. Fascinating history, an archaeological wonder coupled with amazing coastal and countryside views, it is a must-see landmark and photographic location.

What to shoot and viewpoints

In the correct use of the word, Pentre Ifan truly is an **awesome** cromlech. Its scale will definitely take the first time viewer by surprise as you gaze up at the enormous capstone, delicately poised on the points of three tapering upright stones. Originally covered in earth, the entrance to the chamber was at the southern end of the portal framed by a pair of stones, forming a semi-circular forecourt. The massive scale of the fixed portal stone, suggests that the chamber was sealed after a single burial, which would indicate that it was the tomb of a very important person, or possibly a site of several simultaneous burials. Whatever its history, it really does pronounce its dominance over the surrounding countryside .

Photographically, emphasising the size of this megalith can prove tricky but I always tend to keep the camera low and point the lens upwards. This will make the burial chamber dominate the scene and really put a scale factor into your photos. You're free to walk all around it and chose different angles, but I find the 'best' angles are to

photograph the chamber on a three-quarter angle as it were. Either from the front right (shooting in a south west direction) or round to the rear left. In all cases, try to exclude any distracting background elements such as the fence line or small trees. If shooting from the east there's an interesting composition to be had by isolating the nearby Carningli mountain summit in the aperture of the burial chamber, creating good depth and scale. If you're a neutral density graduated filter fan like me, this location can cause problems as when shooting from a low position and placing the stones against the sky, exposing correctly for the sky and the chamber is nigh on impossible on a sunny day. When conditions are like this I'd recommend bracketing your exposures and blending them into a subtle HDR (High Dynamic Range) image. Also, this location works well for black and white images, with the rocky textures and timeless stones providing an instant mood. High density neutral density filters would work great together with a long exposure creating streaky clouds in the sky. Thanks to its exposed position, the golden hours

How to get here

From Haverfordwest town, take the main A40 road out east towards Scotchwell roundabout, then the first exit north. After three quarters of a mile, take the third exit at the roundabout signed B4329. Follow this road for 15 miles, it will take you up and over the Preseli mountains. After descending down the other side you'll pass over another cattle grid before a right bend. Keep going down the main road before taking the next left junction. After two thirds of a mile turn left, then turn right after 200 yards. Half a mile down this hill you'll see the lay-by on your left. Park here and access to the burial chamber is through the kissing gate.

Parking Lat/Long: 51.999134, -4.7677338
Parking Postcode: SA41 3TZ
OS Map Grid Ref: SN100370

Accessibility ♿

A very easy location to visit with great access for all mobility levels. The parking area for this location is in a large lay-by on the side of the lane. From here, go though the kissing gate and walk down the flat path for 200m to the burial chamber. There's another gate to enter the small fenced field where the burial chamber is sited.

Best time of year/day

Morning and evening can provide dramatic side-lighting and colourful skies. Overcast days work well for moody images and close up rock textures. On clear nights, it's perfect for astro photography. Either use the moon to illuminate the stones or your torch, or silhouette the chamber against starry and Milky Way filled skies.

Above: *Pentre Ifan Burial Chamber with Milky Way. Canon 5D III, 14mm f/2.8 at 14mm, ISO 3200, 30s at f/2.8. Tripod. Aug.*

Below: *Pentre Ifan Burial Chamber. Canon 5D III, 24-70mm f/2.8 at 38mm, ISO 100, 1/50s at f/14. Tripod. Polariser. July.*

can create dramatic and colourful conditions, either benefiting from amber side lighting or silhouetting the stones against an orange filled backdrop. Mid Pembrokeshire also benefits from dark skies making it a superb place to photograph the night sky, so Pentre Ifan is a popular location for astro photography and star trails – don't forget your torch.

[5] TY CANOL

A stone's throw from the Pentre Ifan Neolithic burial chamber, Ty Canol is a beautiful ancient woodland in the heart of Pembrokeshire. The 170 acre site is one of the few remaining ancient woodlands in Wales and is rich with flora and fauna. The trees here are estimated to be over 800 years old, many of them are gnarly oaks, with the shapely boughs dripping with moss. It's also home to over 400 species of lichens which thrive in the moist and clean air conditions.

There are large rocky areas and boulders strewn across the woodland floor, all carpeted in spongy moss creating a vivid green landscape, below and above. Ponies roam through the clearings and bluebells flourish in springtime. A walk through Ty Canol is a walk back in time, a primeval scene that's not changed for millennia and it is very easy to lose track of time.

What to shoot and viewpoints

The main parking area is at the entrance to Canolfan Pentre Ifan, an education centre just off the small lane west of the burial chamber. There's room for around six or seven cars and then you'll walk down the track southwards. After following the road down the hill and around the centre, you'll enter Pentre Ifan woods. The track snakes its way through and after a short distance you'll reach a T-junction. Go left here then through a kissing gate to enter the reserve. »

Bluebells on woodland floor in golden hour sunlight. Canon 5D III, 300mm f/2.8 at 300mm, ISO 400, 1/500s at f/2.8. May.

How to get here

From Haverfordwest town, take the main A40 road out east
towards the roundabout, then the first exit north. After three
quarters-of-a-mile, take the third exit at the roundabout signed
B4329. Follow this road for 15 miles, it will take you up and over the
Preseli mountains. After descending down the other side you'll pass
over another cattle grid before a right bend. Take a left turn here
and follow the lane for just over 2 miles before turning right at the
large farm. Follow this road for half-a-mile and the entrance to the
Canolfan Pentre Ifan will be on your right, with the parking bays
displayed. Ty Canol woods is just under a mile walk from the car
down the track.

Parking Lat/Long: 52.010438, -4.7804555
Parking Postcode: SA41 3XE
OS Map Grid Ref: SN092383

Above: *The twisted, gnarly trees of Ty Canol in spring.*
Canon 5D III, 24-70mm f/2.8 at 35mm, ISO 100,
1/13s at f/16. Polariser & ND Grad. Tripod. June.

Accessibility

Most of the tracks and pathways are uneven and sometimes
muddy with one small stream crossing near the woodland. It's
generally an easy going walk with the steepest part being the hill
down/up from the parking area. There's one main pathway that
goes through the wood but make sure to explore off the track for
different views and compositions, from tree roots to boulders.

Best time of year/day

Late spring is the best time of year for those vivid green leaves
and colourful mosses. This works well on foggy days too, creating a
mysticism to the woods. It's also the time of year when wildflowers
such as wood anemone and bluebells flourish on the woodland
floor. Autumn brings its reddy orange colour palette as the leaves
begin to fall on the emerging fungi below. Overcast days work
anytime of day, otherwise choose a time of day when the sun is
low so it penetrates through the canopy with soft side lighting.

Wood Anemone on the woodland floor. Canon 5D III, 300mm f/2.8 at 300mm, ISO 1000, 1/1250s at f/4. Tripod. Mar.

Moss covered rocks and shapely trees. Canon 5D III, 24-70mm f/2.8 at 28mm, ISO 100, 1/6s at f/16. Polariser & ND Grad. Tripod. June.

There's an information board here with a map of the area to aid navigation. The wood opens up as you cross heathland and fields where there are sometimes cattle, sheep or ponies grazing. The pathway in the grass is well defined and you'll soon be stepping into the ancient woodland.

Once you walk into this tangled web of trees you are transported into a mystical world of moss-carpeted boulders, lichens and twisted gnarly oaks, all engulfed with the wonderful smell of earth and age. The tree species at Ty Canol consist mainly of oak, ash and downy birch with an understory of hazel, holly, honeysuckle and bilberry. From early spring there are many wildflowers on show. Golden saxifrage cascade down the wet banks close to the streams in February. Onwards from April, primroses, dog violets and wood anemone appear followed by the colourful May bluebells that blanket the woodland floor. This is a wild place, far away from civilisation that time forgot. It's also one of the most important sites in the UK for lichens, over four hundred species have been identified here, including many that are exceptionally rare. The woodland undoubtedly looks its best in late spring with everything being a rich green, especially after rainfall.

It's a fantastic place to see birds and mammals. As well as our native woodland species, you may also see migrant birds such as chiffchaff, redstart and wood warblers.

All these species appear in springtime to breed, filling the canopy with their birdsong. Badgers, foxes, polecats and the native dormouse all call Ty Canol home. With the dormouse succeeding in these parts thanks to a good supply of hazelnuts and honeysuckle bark, which it uses to build its nest. As it's a deciduous woodland all of the trees go that distinctive russet colour in autumn with rich reds and oranges, especially the oaks and downy birch. This is a time when it's good to look on the canopy floor for fungi, before the woodland leaves fall and cover the fungi up following autumnal windy weather. Wide to medium focal lengths work best for capturing the woodland throughout the year but it's important to keep an eye out if there's sky included in your images. Overcast days work best for photography here, providing a nice even light but try not to get too much sky in the shots, as these areas tend to contrast against the canopy leaves. I'd always opt to put on a circular polariser as this will help to cut down any surface glare and reflections from the foliage surfaces, boosting natural colours.

Opposite: A backlit bluebell flower on the woodland floor near sunset. Canon 5D III, 300mm f/2.8 at 300mm, ISO 400, 1/640s at f/2.8. May.

We are very blessed with lighthouses in Wales, especially in Pembrokeshire, and they don't get much more photogenic than Strumble Head. Jutting out along the rugged north coast of the county on a rocky promontory, this location is also one of Britain's best places to spot migratory birds and passing cetaceans (whales, dolphins, and porpoises). Grey seals breed here in the autumn, with wild flowers growing in abundance on the headland in the spring and summer.

Strumble also benefits from a great aspect looking north west, perfect for colourful sunset skies all throughout the year. Combine this with the coastal backdrop and it's a surefire recipe for greatness.

What to shoot and viewpoints

Strumble Head is a perfect place to spend a day photographing the coastline or just pulling up a chair in the observatory and scanning the seas for wildlife. Orca, porpoise, sunfish and even basking shark have all been seen around this small rocky headland. Arctic skuas, Manx shearwaters, puffins and gannets are a regular sight here

too, as is the large passenger ferry that goes to Ireland twice daily from nearby Fishguard harbour. For coastal scenes though there's a lot on offer including shapely curved bays, craggy rocks and spectacular carpets of wild flowers if you time your visit right. This stretch of the coast path is known as Pencaer peninsula and it encompasses around a mile of Pembrokeshire's rugged north coast with Strumble Head lighthouse in the middle. There's interest all along the coast here and it is possible to photograph the lighthouse from various angles using the coast path that snakes its way around the curving bays and coves.

The lighthouse is sited on its own island, Ynys Meicel (Michael's Island), built in 1908, when Fishguard became a port of call for transatlantic liners, linking passengers with the London to Fishguard railway. The lighthouse is attached to the mainland by a small metal suspension bridge. Today it is only needed for service access as the lighthouse is now operated remotely. Public access is allowed down the flight of steps as far as the metal footbridge – but not onto the island. The bottom step offers great views down into a turbulent stretch of water and is one of the best places to see the grey seals frolicking in the surf and you may spot their fluffy white pups hauled up on the rocks in autumn. >>

An Atlantic grey seal pup on the rocks. Canon 5D III, 300mm f/2.8 at 300mm, ISO 640, 1/2000s at f/5.6. Sep.

__Opposite__: Long exposure of the cliffs. Canon 5D III, 24-70mm f/2.8 at 47mm, ISO 50, 30s at f/22. Polariser & 6ND. Tripod. May.

Strumble Head lighthouse at sunset. Canon 5D II, 24-70mm f/2.8 at 25mm, ISO 100, 3.2s at f/18. Tripod. Polariser, 3ND & ND Grad. Sep.

Back up the hill between the two car parks there's a small summit near a bench that is awash with heather in late July, flowering through till September. Gorse grows along here; the mixture of contrasting colours adds a lovely colour splash to any of your foregrounds.

From up here you'll see the stark concrete walls of the sea observation building. Once a wartime lookout post, it has now been converted as a nature observatory and was opened by Bill Oddie, the comedian and keen birder. For wildlife spotting it's simple, pull up a chair and scan with your binoculars. For landscapes, the sea side of this building provides the best angles of the lighthouse. Here pink sea thrift blooms in spring along with squill and scabious flowers, as the land falls away in a series of craggy layered coves topped by grasses. A superb place to use your filters, especially a neutral density for long exposures that will soften the crashing waves into a foamy white border snaking off towards the lighthouse. Pair this with a circular polariser to really make those Pembrokeshire turquoise seas pop.

It is easy to focus on the lighthouse but looking back east along the coast can provide interesting compositions, also where the lane enters the car park area the grassy banks on the field side are always a carpet of pink thrift and vivid yellow kidney vetch in early May, quite spectacular. Heading west the coast path slowly descends and snakes around the curvy Carreg Onnen Bay where you can marvel at the islands that jut out from the mainland and the suspension bridge across to the lighthouse becomes more apparent. In summer looking in this direction is where the sun will sink into the sea, so this viewpoint is a very effective angle for silhouettes, back light or a pastel sky backdrop. Before sunset a good option is to shoot along the cliffs facing north as this will result in great side lighting, illuminating the textures of the rocky coastline.

How to get here

Parking Lat/Long: 52.029037, -5.0705793
Parking Postcode: SA64 0JL
OS Map Grid Ref: SM 894411

Accessibility

Within a short walk you can see all of what Strumble Head has to offer although everywhere isn't the flattest to walk on; some tracks that criss-cross the headland are loose under foot. The steps down to the bridge require some level of fitness. The first car park is flat tarmac and the walk to the observatory is easy enough across grassland.

Best time of year/day

Spring through to summer is most favourable with a vast amount of wild flowers on display, also this time coincides with the majority of any wildlife in the area including any rare migrating cetaceans. The best sunsets occur around this time with the setting sun angles either behind or to the side of the lighthouse providing effective lighting. Autumn adds the bonus of grey seals and their pups, more migrating birds and also the beginning of any winter storms where the waves on high tide can be very spectacular.

Above: Carreg Onnen Bay. Canon 5D III, 24-70mm f/2.8 at 39mm, ISO 100, 30s at f/14. Tripod. Polariser, 6ND & ND Grad. June.

Below: Atlantic Grey seal pup and mum. Canon 5D III, 300mm f/2.8 at 300mm, ISO 800, 1/400s at f/7.1. Sep.

Strumble Head lighthouse at sunset with heather on the headland.
Canon 5D II, 24-70mm f/2.8 at 34mm, ISO 200, 1/5s at f/16. Tripod. 3ND & ND Grad. Aug.

Located in the north of the county and often missed, Garn Fawr is volcanic rocky ridge magnificently overlooking Strumble Head and in the distance St David's Head. Its trig point stands at 213m above sea level and offers superb views of the north Pembrokeshire coastline. As with many summits in South Wales, it has a wealth of history. Garn Fawr was once a very important Iron Age hill fort, with its rocky outcrops and ramparts still visible today. The hill was also used as a World War One lookout post, with the remains of a small building still standing. The bay below to the west is known as Pwll Deri and its turquoise waters look exceptionally tropical on a sunny day. The coves and bays here are home to grey seals, while blankets of purple heather carpet the headland in summer.

What to shoot and viewpoints

Viewpoint 1 – Garn Fawr

The leisurely route up Garn Fawr is from the described car park on the eastern flank which should see you on the summit in a matter of minutes. To the right of the car park entrance is the start of the path, follow this as it skirts around the fields. After a short while, you'll notice a stone wall on your right and there is a small gap in the wall. Go through this gap and follow the worn path through the grassland towards the now visible trig point. It is a bit of a scramble up the rocks to reach the summit. Take a few more paces across the rocks and as you reach the trig point the coastline before you comes into view, and what a view it is.

Far out to the west you'll see the summits of Carn Lldi and Penberry mountains situated near St Davids, while beneath are the cliffs of the Penbwchdy headland. To the north you'll gaze across a vast tapestry of fields onto Strumble Head lighthouse and on clear days, the North Wales mountains in the distance. Out to the east is the rugged coastline snaking away from Fishguard harbour, time your visit right to see the ferry passing by on its way to and from Ireland. Finally to the east and round southwards, are the Preseli mountains and an almost infinite view of farm fields, with the Milford Haven refineries popping up on the far horizon. It really does offer spectacular panoramic views and considering it's very short ascent, it's one place I'd wholeheartedly recommend visiting. »

Looking across heather, rocks and fields to Strumble Head. Canon 5D IV, 24-70mm f/2.8 at 34mm, ISO 200, 0.4s at f/16. Tripod. ND Grad. Aug.

Heather covered boulders looking along the north Pembrokeshire coast.
Canon 5D IV, 16-35mm f/4 at 16mm, ISO 50, 30s at f/16. Tripod. Polariser, 6ND & ND Grad. Aug.

Heather and gorse flowers in evening light above Pwll Deri.
Canon 5D III, 24-70mm f/2.8 at 24mm, ISO 100, 1/25s at f/14. Tripod. Polariser & ND Grad. Aug.

While it's easy to see such a wide view and want to include it all in your images, context and scale elements are key to landscape photography, so always try to include something in the foreground for depth. Also, put on the lesser used telephoto lens and zone in on distant compositions. You'll be surprised how well this works up here, especially looking west with the layered hills along the coastline or views to the north with the lighthouse.

If you're feeling up for it, ascend to the summit via the western side of the hill from the Viewpoint 2 parking area. It's real mountain goat territory coming at it from the west and I would only recommend it after dry weather, as the paths can be slippery even on the best of days.

Viewpoint 2 – Pwll Deri

From the small parking area above the bay, you'll need to walk back down the road for a short distance before turning right through the hedge to join the coast path. Just before this there's a small grassy area with a bench which offers a fabulous view. Back on the path, you'll descend down slightly, before turning south through the gate following the edge of the headland. Continue along the path as it winds its way up and over the terrain. After a short while, it levels off and you'll walk parallel to the coast. The land drops away from you to the right for the first glimpse down into the turquoise waters of this small bay.

In late summer and into the autumn months, the eerie calls of Atlantic grey seals and their pups will be heard down below you. They mainly frequent the rocky coves and caves to the east of Dinas Mawr. It's a great time of year to witness these marine mammals going about their business; the elevated viewpoint offering good views of them bobbing about in the sea. Another seasonal highlight is in late July when much of the north Pembrokeshire coastline is carpeted with the purple and yellow hues of heather and gorse. My favourite locations to photograph these floral delights are just passed Carn Ogof, around half way along the path towards Penbwchdy Head. There's also a bench here if you'd like to take a breather and admire the views. The path up to Carn Ogof is very undulating and takes in a few curves and drops through large boulders. Jumping off the path here and doing some boulder hopping, will reward you with superb views back down into the bay, with the looming summit of Garn Fawr for a backdrop. Throw in textured boulders and colourful flowers in the foreground, and it's a recipe for some great shots. A wide angle lens would be my chosen weapon of choice, sometimes shooting in portrait orientation too, to include the foreground right in front of the lens through the frame to the far distance. I tend to shoot a lot of landscape images in portrait. I find I can show much more depth in some scenes than opting for landscape orientation. Venturing further west along the path, there's the

Pwll Deri and the rocky headland. Canon 5D III, 24-70mm f/2.8 at 57mm, ISO 400, 1/160s at f/11. Polariser. May.

Looking along the coast towards St David's Head. Canon 5D III, 24-70mm f/2.8 at 61mm, ISO 200, 30s at f/9. 6ND & ND Grad. Tripod. Aug.

occasional old stone wall which provide good photographic interest, and reaching the far west of the headland, reveals rich coastal scenes as the land snakes away towards Carn Llidi in the distance. There is so much to explore and photograph all year round, in this relatively small area.

NOTE: You can do a circular walk taking in all the viewpoints and also following the coastal paths south visiting the high cliffs at Penbwchdy Head.

How to get here

Garn Fawr

From Fishguard, follow the A40 road down towards the ferry port and at the roundabout after the filling station, go straight over. Take a left onto Quay Road and you'll climb up out of the town, follow this road for around 3 miles, before turning right signed for Strumble Head. This road is quite narrow, but the car park will be on your left after around half a mile.

VP 1 Parking Lat/Long:	52.008111, -5.0626360
VP 1 Parking Postcode:	SA64 0JJ
VP 1 OS Map Grid Ref:	SM899388

Pwll Deri

From Fishguard, take the A487 road out west for around four miles before turning right signposted for St Nicholas. Follow this lane north for 2.5 miles before bearing left onto Trefasser Cross. Head down here and as you approach a staggered crossroads by the post and phone box, take a left signed for Pwll Deri. Just before your reach the YHA, the small parking area will be on your right.

VP 2 Parking Lat/Long:	52.006138, -5.0707617
VP 2 Parking Postcode:	SA64 0LR
VP 2 OS Map Grid Ref:	SM893386

Accessibility

Neither viewpoints are suitable for those less mobile due to the undulating and uneven terrain, with the surface ranging from grass to rocks. Viewpoint 1 however does have a small viewing area with a bench close to the parking area, which is accessible from the road for wheelchairs, allowing at least one place to admire the great views down into Pwll Deri. There will be some rock hopping required to reach the summit of Garn Fawr, although good views can be had just below.

Best time of year/day

These are lovely locations at any time of day and year, with the changing seasons brings something new. Whether it's flowers blooming in spring and summer, wildlife encounters or just different sun angles changing the way the coast looks, I'd opt for a visit whatever the weather. Shooting from an elevated position always works well when the sun is low, especially during sunset; resulting in sublime golden colours and long shadows across the fields and coast below.

A popular place on the north Pembrokeshire coast is the fishing village of Porthgain. In its heyday the village was a bustling commercial harbour, exporting bricks, stone and slate around the world from the nearby quarry. Today Porthgain is a peaceful and serene harbour, mainly used for fishing and recreation. On the western side of the harbour are a series of tall, red brick hoppers that once held crushed granite. The stone was quarried from a site just around the coast towards Abereiddy and was transported from there by tramline which ran to the tops of the hoppers across the headland. Many of the harbour's other buildings hold historical links with brickwork engine houses and old kilns.

With every road junction on the approach to Porthgain, the road becomes narrower and quieter until you descend down towards the harbour. Parking is generous and free, although can get exceptionally busy in the summer months. Porthgain village boasts picturesque cottages, B&Bs, two art galleries, a pub and cafe restaurants all offering some of the best seafood in Pembrokeshire. Everyday fresh fish, crabs and lobsters are landed at the harbour and served up in a matter of hours; there are no food miles with this local produce.

Described are viewpoints of this historic harbour and quaint village, and close-by magnificent coastal views.

What to shoot and viewpoints

Porthgain means 'Chisel Port' in English, the name representing the quarrying that once took place here. From around 1850, slate, then later brick and granite were shipped from here. As you first look out onto the harbour, it is the large, red brick hoppers that will catch your gaze. When the light hits this huge wall, the red colour really pops and is exceptionally photogenic; whether used as a coloured backdrop to a wide shot or for close up and textural abstracts. For a relatively small harbour, there's a lot of photographic interest and the come and go of the tide transforms the place and, ultimately, your images.

Viewpoint 1 – Looking Back

The coast path drops straight into the harbour from both directions making Porthgain a great starting point for a coastal walk to nearby locations. Abereiddy (via Traeth Llyfn) lies to the south west and Trefin to the east. Due to the wide shape of the harbour, there's quite a lot to fit in to one shot that truly encapsulates the area; one of my favourite composition views is high up on the coast path, looking back. To reach this viewpoint, walk around to the left of the harbour, passing the vast brick wall and gated entrances of the hoppers en route to the small white building near the sea entrance. There's usually a fishing boat or two moored up and lobster pots and chandlery on the quayside to add to the coastal feel. Just in front of the harbour master's house, steps go up and around the building, then climb onwards uphill onto the headland. »

*Opposite left: Porthgain harbour (VP1). Canon 5D III, 16-35mm f/4 at 20mm, ISO 100, 1/100s at f/14. Polariser. July. **Opposite right**: Rough seas in early spring (VP2). Canon 5D III, 24-70mm f/2.8 at 33mm, ISO 50, 1/5s at f/22. Polariser & ND Grad. Tripod. Mar.*

How to get here

From Haverfordwest take the road to St Davids (A487), on reaching the small town of Solva take a right turn at the Cambrian Inn pub and follow this lane for about 3 miles towards Carnhedryn village. Take a right turn here and follow the road for just over 2 miles before taking a left after a mile signed for Llanrhian/Porthgain. Follow this lane for another mile, before going straight over at the crossroads. This lane will then take you down into Porthgain village after around one mile.

Parking Lat/Long: 51.948388, -5.1818575
Parking Postcode: SA62 5BN
OS Map Grid Ref: SM814325

Accessibility &

Most of the village and harbour is flat, with good wide pathways around the brickworks wall to the far end of the harbour wall. The start of the coast to the northern side of the harbour is flat and wide, only becoming rocky as the altitude increases. There is a large and flat slipway down to the beach. Parking is very close to the harbour walls.

Best time of year/day

Sunrise can prove fruitful with sun angles illuminating the village and harbour, especially in the summer months when the sun rises further north. Sunset will provide golden light from the left for viewpoint 1. Around midday and into the afternoon can work well here, together with a high tide for lovely sea colours. Coastal flowers peak around mid May, while stormy seas occur in late autumn.

Porthgain harbour and old brickworks at high tide. Canon 5D III, 16-35mm f/2.8 at 20mm, ISO 100, 1/80s at f/14. Polariser. July.

Porthgain harbour and moored boats at mid tide. Canon 5D III, 24-70mm f/2.8 at 33mm, ISO 500, 1/125s at f/11. May.

Porthgain harbour from top of steps at high tide (VP1).
Canon 5D III, 16-35mm f/4 at 18mm, ISO 100, 1/125s at f/14. Polariser. July.

Looking north from VP2 towards Strumble Head and Garn Fawr. Canon 5D III, 24-70mm f/2.8 at 70mm, ISO 160, 1/100s at f/14. Polariser & ND Grad. Mar.

Just as you reach the kissing gate, turn around and take in the view. The horseshoe shape of the sea wall will be more pronounced from this height, as it leads the eye back towards the village. Combine this with the foreground diagonal leading lines of the descending steps to emphasise the depth of the scene to great effect. Time of day changes the look of this shot – early morning in summer and you'll be shooting into the sun; while at late afternoon in the winter and the whole harbour will be in shade. It is really important to research the sun angles and height for the time of year of your visit. The tide will also affect your image significantly as the turquoise-blues at high tide are much more favourable than the flat, brownish sand at low tide.

Viewpoint 2 – Coastal Views

On the northern side of the harbour is a long slipway. When the tide is half-way out, the base of the slipway is a good vantage point for photographing crashing waves. When the tide is further out, you can hop off the slipway onto the rocks and the sand, venturing further round to the left and the now marooned boats. This is a great place to get down low and focus on reflections in the sand and abstract patterns, with the odd crab wandering about. Wellies are recommended for this area as the sand is

quite soft. At the top of the slipway are the remnants of an old lime kiln and adjacent to this is the start of the coast path leading northwards. Walk along the path to a small track that leads to the sea wall. In winter the sea storms can be spectacular viewed from here, and the tide has been known to breach the sea walls – take care here in inclement weather. Further up the track you will reach a ridge and a large white stone comes into view. This is one of two, conical stone beacons that mark the entrance to Porthgain harbour. You'll notice the second across the inlet, not far from viewpoint one's position. From here you can see along the coast to the north, with the occasional flash of Strumble Head light house in the far distance and the looming summit of Garn Fawr to its right. It's a wild and windblown place and a great place to watch weather fronts coming in from the sea. Usually either side of weather fronts will be magic light, so it's worth hanging around (using the beacon as a windbreak) to catch a great moment. Up here you can also see the coastal area of the quarried rocks to the south and ruined red buildings on the top of the headland which housed winding engines and weighbridges used at the brickworks in the harbour. From this position you can start to piece together how Porthgain once was.

Above: Looking from the harbour beacon (VP2). Canon 5D III, 24-70mm f/2.8 at 41mm, ISO 500, 1/400s at f/7.1. Polariser & ND Grad. Mar.
Below: Waves splash over the harbour slipway. Canon 5D III, 24-70mm f/2.8 at 21mm, ISO 100, 1/8s at f/14. Polariser & ND Grad. Tripod. Mar.

The Blue Lagoon, sandy beaches, rocks and ruins; this wild stretch of coastline is where industry and adventure combine. Like many other small coastal hamlets in this part of Wales, Abereiddy's history lies in slate mining. Today's colourful cottages at the back of the bay were once home to miners and the area would have been busy with industry in the past. A narrow gauge railway used to run into the hamlet and would cart slate off to nearby Porthgain harbour to be shipped off to wherever it needed to go. Nowadays there is little evidence of industry, except for the remains of the quarry and its buildings at what is now known as the Blue Lagoon.

The beach itself is backed by a bank of pebbles that now blend into the car park due to sea storms that over the years have reclaimed the land. The pebbles themselves and the extraordinarily dark sand of the beach is made from sea-pounded slate. Just over the headland is the same slate that gives a brilliant deep blue colour to the water in the Blue Lagoon. Once a quarry that is now breached by the tide, the lagoon is a very popular place for coasteering.

An activity born in Pembrokeshire in the 90s, coasteering is great fun and involves clambering around the coastal rocks and jumping in to the sea from great heights, the ruins and platforms at the Blue Lagoon provide a safe launching platform. The area has gained such notoriety that the Blue Lagoon has played host to RedBull Cliff Diving events. Heading up and over the headland and a short walk along the coast path drops you into a secluded bay, Traeth Llyfyn. Accessed only by a metal stairways down to the sandy bay it's a real hidden gem on the Pembrokeshire coastline. It's so remote, you'll probably be the only one there.

What to shoot and viewpoints

Viewpoint 1 – Blue Lagoon
Quite unique and extremely interesting, there are many photographic opportunities here. If you follow the main path from the car park up passed the old workers buildings and through the kissing gate you'll reach a fork in the path. Left will take you on the low path, and after a short walk you'll reach the quarry basin. Here you can get a real feel for the place as the towering cliffs surround you. »

How to get here

From Haverfordwest take the road to St. Davids (A487), on reaching the small town of Solva take a right turn at the Cambrian Inn pub and follow this lane for about 3 miles. This will just cut the corner off and put you back on the main east/west road. Take a right turn here and then a left after half a mile. Follow this lane for another 2 miles, taking a right at the end. Travel through the village of Berea and take the next left towards Abereiddy. It's a dead end road so follow this all the way to the end, taking care on the narrow downhill corners near the beach.

Parking Lat/Long: 51.936579, -5.2057868
Parking Postcode: SA62 6DT
OS Map Grid Ref: SM 797313

Accessibility   ♿

The car park is practically on the beach so with just a short walk you can paddle to your hearts content on the shore. The beach is mostly pebbles under foot until right down near the water where it's sand. There are good flat paths specifically made with disabled access in mind which will take you to the low viewpoint at the Blue Lagoon. The paths up from here and also the coast path are uneven at first and require a steep ascent, but flatten out once on the top. The stairs down to Traeth Llyfyn are quite steep and you should take your time here. Also keep an eye on the tides.

Top: View from Carn Lwyd (VP2). Canon 5D III, 16-35mm f/4 at 35mm, ISO 100, 1/125s at f/14. Tripod. Polariser & ND Grad. July.

Above: Slate patterns at the Blue Lagoon. Canon 5D III, 70-200mm f/2.8 at 200mm, ISO 400, 1/200s at f/8. Mar.

Opposite: The Blue Lagoon from above (VP1). Canon 5D III, 16-35mm f/4 at 16mm, ISO 100, 1/25s at f/13. Tripod. Polariser & ND Grad. July.

Best time of year/day

All locations can be photographed any time of day but I'd say late afternoon into the evening can result in the most dramatic images, especially in summer where the sun sets more to the north allowing for lovely sidelight and vivid skies. Tides play a big part in the scenes so opt for high tide conditions for the Blue Lagoon for maximum amount of water in the quarry. Overcast conditions work well for abstracts, especially for images of the slate colours and textures.

*Top: Slate patterns at the Blue Lagoon. Canon 5D III, 24-70mm f/2.8 at 63mm, ISO 640, 1/400s at f/10. May. **Above**: View from Carn Lwyd (VP2) looking across Traeth Llyfyn. Canon 5D III, 16-35mm f/4 at 16mm, ISO 100, 1/50s at f/16. Tripod. Polariser & ND Grad. July.*

The first thing that will strike you is the varied colour in the slates and the interesting shapes that they make. This is a great place to stick that telephoto on and zoom into some of the rocks for abstract images, the colours are truly amazing. Looking down into the Blue Lagoon you'll notice the old tram tracks disappearing into the vivid blue water. Head back up the path onto the high route and it skirts around the very edge of the cliff top. Keep back from the cliff-edge as there are often rock falls due to the structure of the slates. In spring this grass edge is awash with wildflowers and the meadow behind full of bugs and butterflies. Also keep an eye out for chough with their blood red beak and legs probing the sandy soil looking for insects. From up here, you'll have a great vantage point all around and back into Abereiddy bay to the south. To the west you can see the majestic summits of firstly Penberry and then a distant Carn Llidi near Whitesands. In the closer vicinity is Abereiddy Tower, a grade two listed building and once used as a navigational aid. It's accessible by dropping down the gully found further to the north along the path. Once down in the gap, you'll need to climb back up again and then west following the well worn tracks out to the tower.

Viewpoint 2 – Carn Lwyd

Close by the Blue Lagoon and following the coast path to the north east, you'll notice a rocky summit to your left. If you turn off the path here and ascend you'll reach Carn Lwyd summit. Fabulous 360 degree views will greet you and you'll get your first glimpse of Traeth Llyfyn beach to your east. This summit and the surrounding area is usually covered in yellow gorse flowers throughout the year making for a colourful splash to your foregrounds. It's also a nice viewpoint to see the north side of the coastline. Here's the sea swells are more prominent and you can exploit these churning seas for great interest in your images – long exposures work well here blurring the white waters. There's a naturally found composition up with Abereiddy tower on the right while the distant hills create lots of depth and layers, balancing up the left of the scene. Keep an eye out for coastal birds up here too such as meadow pipit and also stonechat with their characteristic 'clicking' calls.

Viewpoint 3 – Traeth Llyfyn

Venturing further to the east on the coast path, a relatively flat half mile or so later, the path will turn to direct you to the north. Look back on yourself and the natural positions of the aforementioned locations will neatly line up in one shot. Fantastic on a slightly hazy day when they create their own layers making for a very three dimensional scene. Taking the steep metal steps down to the bay you'll be in a world of your own on this pretty flat but picturesque sandy beach. The beach is surrounded by big cliffs, and there are smooth and shapely boulders near to the stairs, so take some time here. A good technique near to high tide, is to use a slow shutter speed to blur the water movement over the boulders. Keep an eye on the tides here though as it comes in fast and the stairs are the only way in and out.

Traeth Llyfyn beach (VP2). Canon 5D III, 16-35mm f/4 at 18mm, ISO 200, 1/6s at f/16. Tripod. Polariser, 3ND & ND Grad. July.

Pastel evening skies, the lookout tower at Abereiddy and distant headlands (VP2).
Canon 5D III, 70-200mm f/2.8 at 148mm, ISO 50, 13s at f/11. Polariser, 6ND & ND Grad. Tripod. July.

⟦10⟧ ST DAVID'S HEAD

Rugged coastline, stunning sea views and heather moorland, all steeped in Celtic history, St David's Head is a dramatic headland in the north west of the county. Home to the sweeping golden beach and rocky cliffs of Whitesands with Carn Llidi dominating the background, from whose summit boasts panoramic views over the surrounding coastline and offshore islands. This place definitely sums up the north of the county and in good conditions it can be a real experience for the senses. On a serene summer's evening you can see for miles, whilst during an autumnal afternoon rainstorm down on the beach the waves will crash, the grass will sway whilst golden light bathes the land. St David's Head is one my top places to visit in Pembrokeshire.

What to shoot and viewpoints

In a small area there are many interesting views and locations. The golden Whitesands beach has rocky cliffs and rock pools to discover. The coast path provides an infinite number of views on or across the beach towards the towering rocky summit of Carn Llidi. Venture north west from the beach to St. David's Head with its iron age burial chambers and coastal views. A circular route around the base of the Carn Llidi on well worn paths will take you through heather moorland crossed by ancient stone walls. If you've got the energy, climb up to the summit for magnificent views of the surrounding coast, You can even see the hills in Ireland on a clear day.

Viewpoint 1 – Whitesands

Whitesands Bay is one of many award-winning, Blue Flag beaches in Pembrokeshire. Backed by rocky cliffs and grassy dunes, it has been described as the best surfing beach in Pembrokeshire and one of the best tourist beaches in the world. For a good overview of the beach with the mountain as a backdrop head south from the car park and once you reach the holiday properties, join the coast path. You can get good shots here of the beach or if you want a wider view, keep walking passed the small cove at Porthselau. Anywhere along here towards Point St John are great views to the north across the beach, with various compositions using foreground rocks or seasonal flowers.

Whitesands in autumn (VP1). Canon 5D III, 17-40mm f/4 at 20mm, ISO 640, 1/2s at f/16. Tripod. Polariser & ND Grad. Oct.

Spring is best for foxgloves and other colourful wildflowers, whilst the heather flowers in early August. It's also a great place to photograph butterflies in the spring.

How to get here

All locations are accessed by foot from the main pay and display Whitesands beach car park which is a 2 mile drive north west from St David's. Follow the A487 north out of the city and take the next left at the rugby club. Follow this road for a short distance and turn left down the B4583 sign posted to Whitesands (Traeth-mawr).

Parking Lat/Long: 51.897032, -5.294231
Parking Postcode: SA62 6PS
OS Map Grid Ref: SM 73417 27174

Accessibility

There are great views from the car park of the beach, with easy access onto the sand. Those with limited mobility may be able to manage the walk to viewpoint 1 as it's generally easy going however viewpoint 2, 4 and especially 3 are quite demanding to get to and involve a bit of boulder hopping to get the best views.

Opposite: *Whitesands in summer (VP1). Canon 5D III, 24-70mm f/2.8 at 26mm, ISO 100, 1/40s at f/16. Tripod. Polariser. July.*

Best time of year/day

Photography is possible all year in this area, however the seasons bring great changes to the how the landscape looks and also the sea state. Late summer into autumn is usually my favourite time up here as the heather is in full bloom and you can experience dramatic skies and passing rainstorms. All viewpoints are very exposed to the prevailing winds (even more so on the summit) so care needs to be taken when walking along coast paths.

Late afternoon is best for viewpoint 1 with the sun giving side lighting to the scene, though morning should also yield decent results. Up on to the headland and Carn Llidi you'll generally be facing south/south west so mid-morning or evening would best suit these locations. Viewpoint 4 is an all day location but keep an eye on your own shadow intruding into compositions at mid-afternoon.

Whitesands across to Ramsey Island from Carn Llidi (VP3)
Canon 5D III, 24-70mm f/2.8 at 24mm, ISO 100, 1/800s at f/10. Polariser. Aug.

Viewpoint 2 – St David's Head and Coetan Arthur

Heading north from the car park onto the coast path, you'll first pass Porth Lleuog bay. After another climb and descent you'll reach Porthmelgan beach which can be a good place to spot seals at any time of year. Keep on going up and over the next hill and you'll reach St David's Head where you'll find Coetan Arthur. This chambered tomb is around a mile walk from the car park and is quite hidden. Unless you know what you are looking for it can be very easily missed as the area surrounding the chamber is strewn with boulders and rocks. It's a collapsed chamber of what is presumed to be a passage grave with an accompanying round barrow. The massive capstone measures approximately 6 by 3 metres. Megalithic history with a great backdrop; there's lots of scope here for images of the cromlech in the landscape or shoot close-ups of the rocky mossy textures. In the summer the heathland carpet makes a wonderful foreground for photographs during the golden hour looking back across to Ramsey Island.

Viewpoint 3 – Carn Llidi

It's a mile walk up a broad path from the car park to the summit of Carn Llidi and is worth the effort for the magnificent views from the top. Walking back up the road from the main car park take the small road to the left passing the caravan site. Head up along the track that snakes up the hillside, passed the cottages through a gate to where the path forks and take the right track to the summit.

On the hillside are the footings from a machine gun emplacement and a radar tower, not good enough for foreground composition but historically interesting. If you are prepared to hop across rocks to the summit there is a 360 degree view of the Pembrokeshire coastline.

On a good day you'll be able see Skomer and Skokholm Island to the south, following the coast around St Brides Bay up to Ramsey Island (and sometimes Grassholm Island in the far distance). The small islands of the Bishops and Clerks are close at the end of St. David's Head and sometimes, in very far distance to the north west, Ireland can be seen. To the north is nothing but sea and the north Pembrokeshire coastline with the Strumble Head lighthouse at the furthermost point. The nearest summit east is Penberry – another great location. Colourful heather and gorse are prominent here in the summer.

Viewpoint 4 – Looking East

If you head east and descend from Carn Llidi (VP3) you will find undulating heathland where wild ponies sometimes graze; they make interesting additions to any scene. Boulders and rocks here make useful focal points or do some macro work with natural textures and patterns.

Top: Heather and Gorse, looking east from Carn Llidi (VP4). Canon 5D III, 24-70mm f/2.8 at 70mm, ISO 50, 3.2s at f/18. Tripod. Polariser, 3ND & ND Grad. Aug.

***Middle left**: Carn Llidi looking to Ramsey Island (VP3). Canon 5D III, 17-40mm f/4 at 30mm, ISO 100, 0.4s at f/16. Tripod. Polariser & ND Grad. Apr. **Middle Right**: Carn Llidi looking to Whitesands & Ramsey Island (VP3). Canon 5D III, 16-35mm f/4 at 16mm, ISO 50, 3.2s at f/22. Tripod. Polariser & ND Grad. June.*

***Right**: St. David's Head looking to Ramsey Island (VP2). Canon 5D II, 24-105mm f/4 at 24mm, ISO 100, 0.6s at f/11. Tripod. Polariser & ND Grad. Sep.*

***Opposite**: Coetan Arthur and Ramsey Island (VP2). Canon 5D II, 17-40mm f/4 at 25mm, ISO 100, 0.8s at f/11. Tripod. ND Grad. Sep.*

Standing proud in the city of St Davids, on the western most tip of Wales, St Davids Cathedral is one of the jewels in Pembrokeshire's crown. Nowhere in Britain is there a more ancient cathedral settlement, it reaches back to the sixth century when Saint David; the patron saint of Wales, established a monastery here. The cathedral has been a site of pilgrimage and worship for hundreds of years; surviving several Viking plunders in the Dark Ages and it remains an active church serving the community. The cathedral lies low on a terrace of land by the river, nestled in a grassy hollow beneath the rooftops of this tiny city. From the centre of St Davids – the smallest city in the UK, the cathedral seems to appear from below ground; its bell tower poking up and reaching for the sky. As with all cathedrals, it is exceptionally photogenic inside and out, with stunningly intricate architecture.

What to shoot and viewpoints

Viewpoint 1 – Daffodils and the Cathedral

You really can't get more Welsh than a visit to the patron saint of Wales' home city cathedral, surrounded by the national flower of Wales. Maybe eating a Welsh cake at the same time would complete the patriotic experience? The rich yellows and oranges of the daffodils emerge across Pembrokeshire in late January and early February. The flowers will then peak just in time for St David's Day on the 1st of March, before dying off shortly after. There's an abundance of these pretty flowers right across the cathedral site but the best place to take in their vivid colours alongside the cathedral is at a small grassy enclosure to the south of the cathedral. Access is through an old gate just past the top of the cathedral steps, on the left. This whole stretch of around hundred yards is covered in daffodils. Choosing the right shooting spot is important. At this time of year the trees haven't quite caught up, so you will have bare branches in your viewfinder if you are too far left. Position the camera down low to fill for the foreground with flowers. Mid-afternoon works well here giving good contrast between the stone wall and the textures of the cathedral. On most days you'll see the nearby summits of Carn Llidi and Penberry in the background, both locations well worth a visit.

Clock tower viewed from nearby Bishops Palace. Canon 5D IV, 24-70mm f/2.8 at 63mm, ISO 1000, 1/160s at f/9. Aug.

How to get here

From Haverfordwest follow the one way system around the town and turn left near the garage at the bottom of Barn Street. Heading out north west on Thomas Parry Way, then take the second exit at the roundabout onto St Davids road (A487). Follow this road for 15 miles and as you enter St Davids city, turn right onto Nun Street then immediate left down 'The Pebbles'. There's a small amount of parking here, and within a hundred yards you'll be at the top of the steps. There's also a large pay and display car park to the west of the cathedral, accessed via Pit Street.

Parking Lat/Long: 51.881485, -5.2671370
Parking Postcode: SA62 6RD
OS Map Grid Ref: SM752253

Above: Springtime blooms in Mar with Daffodils. Canon 5D III, 16-35mm f/4 at 25mm, ISO 100, 1/160s at f/11. Tripod. Polariser. Mar.

Accessibility ♿

The cathedral is wheelchair and buggy friendly, to avoid the steps, head along the road down passing the coppice of trees then up the pathway towards the front door at the south west of the cathedral. There are some steps inside as you travel between rooms, but it is mostly flat and easy going.

Best time of year/day

The golden hours really work well here, with long shadows cast across the cathedral grounds and the colouration of the stonework illuminated well. Autumn through to spring can be very atmospheric with low sun angles throughout the day. For the interiors, favour a bright day as it can be quite dull inside which will affect shutter speeds, also time the sun angles right for light beams coming through the stained glass windows. Daffodils peak late February into March, while the Midnight Mass festival is very impressive on Christmas Eve with hymns, organ playing and candlelight.

Viewpoint 2 – Stairway to Heaven

After shooting the daffodils it's time to focus on the building and it's grounds, a popular viewpoint is at the top of the steps. There are some old iron gates here that have great textures for abstracts. A wide angle lens will be useful, preferably composed in portrait orientation. Try to include the foreground steps and the bell tower. Take time to fine tune your composition, make sure verticals are straight and also that the lamppost is balanced against the background. Afternoon light, with warm sunlight from the left can really help to make the scene pop, illuminating the colourful cathedral brickwork. This shot only really works in the months outside of summer due to position of the setting sun.

Viewpoint 3 – Interior Architecture

The cathedral is open every day for visitors to wander around its grand interior, free of charge. However there is a £2 charge for photography and £10 to use a tripod. Pay at the cathedral shop on arrival and receive a small sticky label telling the stewards and vergers that you have obtained appropriate permission. No photography is allowed in the Cathedral library. **»**

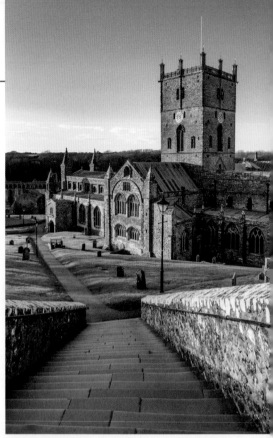

Cathedral steps near sunset. Canon 5D III, 24-70mm f/2.8 at 28mm, ISO 50, 1/2s at f/16. Tripod. Polariser & ND Grad. Mar.

The river crossing near to Bishops Palace. Canon 5D III, 16-35mm f/4 at 27mm, ISO 100, 1/60s at f/16. Polariser. July.

Above: Hall window at Bishops Palace. Canon 5D IV, 24-70mm f/2.8 at 24mm, ISO 1000, 1/400s at f/9. Aug.

Below: Stained glass windows in the Cathedral. Canon 5D III, 70-200mm f/2.8 at 148mm, ISO 500, 1/160s at f/6.3. Tripod. Jan.

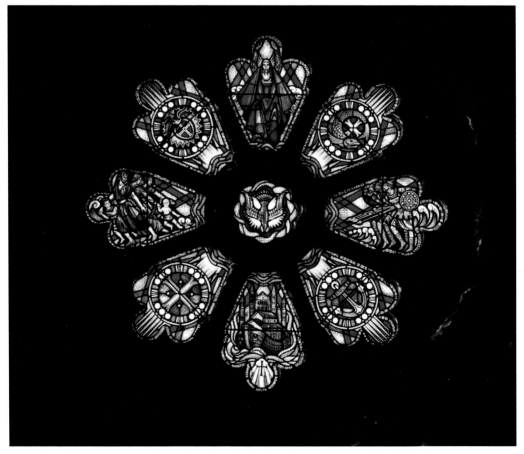

Because of Health and Safety restrictions it is, unfortunately, necessary to get advance permission in writing from the dean if you wish to use a tripod. Send an email to *info@stdavidscathedral.org.uk*

Walk through the double doors into the nave, the oldest surviving part of the cathedral, and the majesty and vastness is immediately apparent. There is so much to photograph: statues, coats of arms, stained glass windows, monuments, sepulchres and effigies. Both wide-angle and telephoto lenses are useful. If you are shooting without a tripod, you may have to increase your ISO to provide faster shutter speeds to combat camera shake, due to the limited available light. At the back of the cathedral are four separate chapels, all with their own design and styles. In the centre of the cathedral is the high altar and choir, which was constructed in the early 16th century, with medieval floor tiles displaying coats of arms, while the wooden walls are intricately carved.

Archways and stained glass windows in the Cathedral. Canon 5D III, 24-70mm f/2.8 at 59mm, ISO 400, 1/125s at f/5. Jan.

If you're lucky, there will be someone playing the organ which adds to the atmosphere during your visit. Gaze upwards to roof to the stunningly designed ceilings; especially the clock tower, with its criss-cross designs of carved wood, all painted in colourful hues. Although slightly unconventional, laying on the floor is the best way to photograph the ceilings by shooting straight up.

Looking up at the clock tower ceiling. Canon 5D III, 16-35mm f/4 at 26mm, ISO 500, 1/40s at f/5. Jan.

Chapel of Edward the Confessor.
Canon 5D III, 16-35mm f/4 at 16mm, ISO 100, 1/13s at f/14. Jan.

[12] ST NON'S CHAPEL

The Chapel of St Non is located on rocky coastline south of St Davids. According to tradition, this was the site where Saint Non gave birth to Saint David around 500 AD. St David later became the patron saint of Wales and the local city's namesake. Today, all that remains of the chapel are ruins of the walls and a stone slab inscribed with a Celtic cross. A holy well with a shrine to St Non resides nearby to the east of the chapel. The waters from the well have been used down the centuries to cure various complaints and to baptise babies.

Whatever you believe, everyone can heal their soul and mind by staring out at the waters of its stunning coastline. A modern chapel was built in 1934, making St Non's Chapel the most westerly in Wales and also one of the smallest, at only 25 feet long. Next to the chapel is St Non's retreat owned by a religious institute the Passionist Fathers.

What to shoot and viewpoints

The whole site offers fantastic views along the coastline to the offshore islands of Skomer and Grassholm and across the sea back into St Bride's Bay. Parking is free and it's a short walk to the chapel ruins and holy well. The ruins are found in a fenced off area in the field, while the holy well is on a small footpath that goes around the grounds to the retreat, in most cases the paths are easy going. Heading further along this path will bring you to the junction with the Pembrokeshire Coast Path. From here you could head westwards along the path round to the stunning small harbour of Porthclais or go left (east), eventually ending up at the lovely sandy bay of Caerfai. There's plenty of walking opportunities from here to make more of a day of it.

Back at the coast path junction and a short walk east, there's another path which will take you north, then east towards Caerfai caravan park. Walk up here for twenty paces or so and you'll ascend slightly to elevated views across the new chapel. This is my favourite view here as you gaze west along the rugged coastline, Ramsey island just popping up behind the mainland, while the stark white pyramid of the Grassholm gannet colony shines in the distance out to sea. A circular polarising filter works well here helping to enhance foliage and sea colours. Foregrounds are always important along the coast so I'd opt for a spring or summer visits as the wild flowers will be abundant. Thrift, scabious, squill and sea campion are all common along this part of the coast path and venture inland slightly to find red campion. These work as a splash of colour to your shots, later in the year the changing colours of the bracken can also work serve the same purpose.

Statue beside the Holy Well. Canon 5D III, 24-70mm f/2.8 at 59mm, ISO 100, 1/400s at f/5.6. July.

How to get here

From Haverfordwest follow the one way system around the town and head out north west on Thomas Parry Way, then take the second exit at the roundabout onto St Davids road (A487). Follow this road for around 15 miles and as you enter St Davids city follow the main road (Goat Street) for half a mile before bearing left signed for St Non's Chapel. Follow this lane all the way to the end where there's a parking area on the right before the retreat.

Parking Lat/Long: 51.872840, -5.2674709
Parking Postcode: SA62 6RR
OS Map Grid Ref: SM751244

Accessibility

Most paths around the retreat area are level, the ruins are accessed across a field through a kissing gate while the new chapel viewpoint is part of the coast path so can be uneven and rocky in places. All locations are very close to parking so walking is kept to a minimum.

Best time of year/day

Seasonal wild flowers really make the area so I would recommend a visit from May to July. Other times of the year could result in good light, especially in the autumn. Clear visibility days are preferable to view the offshore islands and coastline, time this for around a midday shot as you'll be looking west.

Above: *The chapel and wild flowers. Canon 5D III, 24-70mm f/2.8 at 44mm, ISO 100, 1/640s at f/2.8. Polariser. July.*

⟦13⟧ NEWGALE BEACH

Enormous is one of the words to describe this beach. Two and a half miles of stunning golden flat sand backed by a high pebble bank – formed after a big storm in 1859. Being one of the main hotspots for visitors to Pembrokeshire, it can get very busy in the summer. Thankfully, due to the sheer size of the expanse of sand there is room for everyone to find a spot.

Anyone who has visited the area before will remember Newgale for the breathtaking vista of St Bride's Bay as the main road plummets down towards Newgale village. There's plenty of opportunities on the beach itself for a variety of images; colourful pebbles, sand formations and rock pools are bountiful. By joining the coast path that skirts around the north and southern ends of the beach you'll gain height, where the views are even more spectacular.

What to shoot and viewpoints

The sheer size of this west-facing beach can be overwhelming so it's good to get your bearings. I'd recommend standing on top of any part of the pebble bank, looking around you and soaking it all in. Nothing but sea is ahead, slightly to the left the eye takes in the northern end of Skomer Island, then Stack Rocks (off St Brides).

Right: Looking over the beach from VP1. Canon 5D III, 24-70mm f/2.8 at 50mm, ISO 100, 1/400s at f/16. Polariser. July.

Looking north west along the coast at sunset from VP1. Canon 5D IV, 24-70mm f/2.8 at 70mm, ISO 100, 1/40s at f/16. Mar.

How to get here

Newgale is very easy to get to. From Haverfordwest take the St. Duvids / A487 road north. Follow this for around 8 miles before the road descends into Newgale village. Viewpoint 1 parking can be found at the northern end of the beach just after the bridge on the left. Viewpoint 2 parking is accessed by heading to the south of the beach on the 'Welsh Road' for around half a mile, parking by the toilets or in the national park car park.

Birds Eye View

VP 1 Parking Lat/Long:	51.857819, -5.1270559
VP 1 Parking Postcode:	SA62 6AS
VP 1 OS Map Grid Ref:	SM 847223

Pebbles

VP 2 Parking Lat/Long:	51.846450, -5.1181725
VP 2 Parking Postcode:	SA62 6BD
VP 2 OS Map Grid Ref:	SM 853210

Accessibility

Wherever you enter the beach you'll have to cross over the pebble bank, thankfully in a few areas there are large wooden boardwalks that make the going easier otherwise navigating over them could become an ankle twister. There are three car parks dotted along the stretch from north to south, as are public toilet facilities. The coast path walk is quite rugged, loose under foot in places and includes lots of steps.

Best time of year/day

Summer time will be the busiest as there's a campsite nearby that is always packed with holidaymakers. July through to September the heather will be in bloom on the coast path, as will the gorse and wild flowers. Autumn produces the best quality light and coupled with a passing rain shower the clouds can be spectacular and pick up colourful highlights from the setting sun. Winter brings wild and windy weather with sea surges and high seas bashing into the pebble bank, in some years breaching them and closing the main road, so do take care if there are weather warnings.

At the southern end of Newgale is the triangular shape of Rickets Head. To your right the coast meanders round past the Green Scar rock off Solva to the northern extremity of the bay, where Ramsey Island and the South Bishop Rock peep round the corner of St David's Head. Almost at the centre of this spectacular panoramic view is a distant Grassholm Island. It breaks the horizon like a pyramid, its northern side snow-capped with the build up of guano over centuries from its resident seabird, the gannet.

Newgale is a very popular surfing beach and is also used for sand yachting, kite surfing and windsurfing. Sea anglers fish here and groups of horses from the nearby riding school regularly are seen cantering across the beach. If you happen to get lucky on your visit, including any of these will add a human element, scale and great interest to your photos. You'll also notice supertankers out on the horizon, sometimes half a dozen or more of them. They're not the prettiest sight, but they anchor up here in the bay waiting for a free berth in one of the Milford Haven refineries. At the back of the bay the landscape is very undulating, especially towards the southern end. These hillocks are legacies of the coal industry which once flourished here. They are in fact, small slag-heaps now disguised by vegetation and wild flowers. Another more obvious sign of past coal workings on the Nolton side of the beach is the brick stack and ruined stone buildings of the Trefrane colliery. Beside the road at the mid-point of the beach is an old lime kiln, a feature which almost every cove and inlet in the county possesses as a reminder of the coastal trade in limestone to enrich the farmland.

Viewpoint 1 – Birds Eye View

One of the best views of Newgale is from up high on the coast path from the northern end of the beach. To gain access up here follow the road along the sea front, go over the Brandy Brook bridge passing the small car park then round the hill to the left. Here is the driveway to someone's garage but if you look closely the coast path peels off just to the left. Head through the gate and follow it around the hill. Lots of steps will greet you, best to take your time as the ascent is fast and steep but offers an amazing view on reaching the top. Heather and gorse flower on the banks of the path along here so include the plants in your images to help boost the overall scale

of the scene and to also help create depth by having some immediate foreground. The tidal heights range massively here so check tide times before hand to see how much beach is or isn't on show as this will affect your compositions. Heading further along, the path does descend again into a secret bay called Pwll March. This is only accessible via the coast path or the beach at a lowish tide – if you can stop to enjoy this added hidden gem.

Viewpoint 2 – Pebbles

This is one of the few beaches in Pembrokeshire that has copious amounts of pebbles that are all mostly uniformly-sized. These make fabulous focal points and foreground elements to point your lens at, and just to stand and listen to the noises made when the tide retreats through them. I'd shoot these with a slow shutter speed up to a half-a-second and time your exposures when the crashing wave reaches maximum and just as they start to retreat start your exposure. This will render lovely, shapely white trails receding back into the sea. Obviously to result in such low shutter speeds you may need to use a neutral density filter to force the camera into receiving less light – or when coupled near to sunset, the ambient low light – tied in with low ISO and medium f/stop, all should be sufficient to produce slow shutter speeds. The best time to photograph the waves crashing onto the pebbles is at high tide, if possible time your visit with a full or near full moon which will increase the tide height again.

The pebbles are set back quite a way so sometimes high tides don't always reach them. It's a game of chicken with the waves – where you want to get close enough for the incoming waves to boost your compositions but without getting your feet wet, I'd recommend some wellies as it's bound to happen. My preferred location for this is nearer to the southern end of the beach as you will have Rickets Head as immediate background interest. Autumn and winter is great for these kinds of shots, plus the setting sun will be directly in the bay producing golden side light adding reflected colour to the shiny rounded stones.

Opposite: Slow shutter speed of incoming waves. Canon 5D III, 16-35mm f/4 at 16mm, ISO 100, 1s at f/16. Tripod. Polariser, 6ND & ND Grad. Oct.

Above: Looking across to Rickets Head at sunset. Canon 5D III, 16-35mm f/4 at 17mm, ISO 100, 0.4s at f/16. Tripod. Polariser, 6ND & ND Grad. Oct. **Above right**: Waves on pebbles. Canon 5D III, 16-35mm f/4 at 16mm, ISO 100, 1/4s at f/16. Tripod. Polariser, 3ND & ND Grad. Oct.

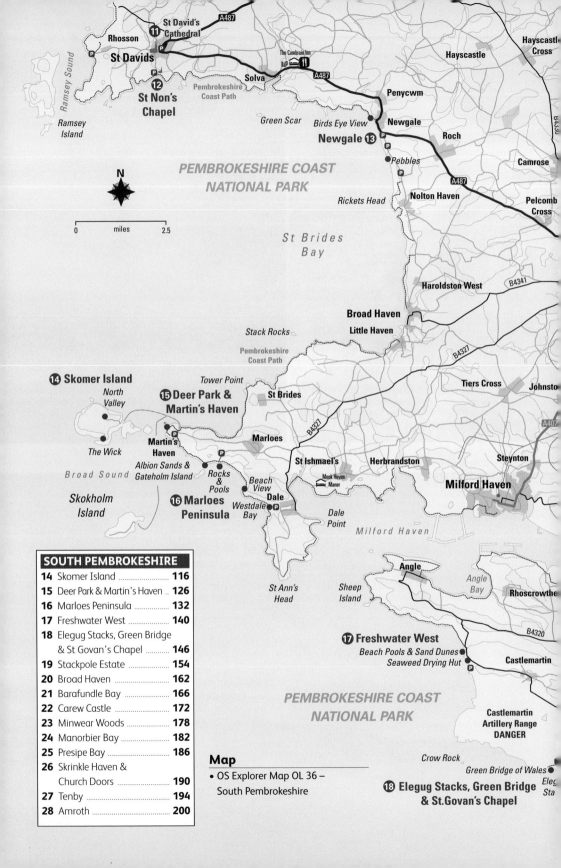

St David's Cathedral ⑪

Rhosson

St Davids

The Cambrain Inn ⑪

Solva

St Non's Chapel ⑫

Hayscastle

Hayscastle Cross

Penycwm

Green Scar

Birds Eye View

Newgale

Roch

Newgale ⑬

Pebbles

Camrose

Ramsey Sound

Ramsey Island

PEMBROKESHIRE COAST NATIONAL PARK

Pembrokeshire Coast Path

Rickets Head

Nolton Haven

Pelcomb Cross

N

0   miles   2.5

St Brides Bay

Haroldston West

Broad Haven

Stack Rocks

Little Haven

⑭ Skomer Island

North Valley

Tower Point

St Brides

Tiers Cross

Johnsto

⑮ Deer Park & Martin's Haven

Marloes

The Wick

Martin's Haven

St Ishmael's

Herbrandston

Steynton

Albion Sands & Gateholm Island

Monk Haven Manor

Broad Sound

Rocks & Pools

Beach View

Milford Haven

Skokholm Island

⑯ Marloes Peninsula

Westdale Bay

Dale

Dale Point

Milford Haven

St Ann's Head

Sheep Island

Angle

Angle Bay

Rhoscrowthe

⑰ Freshwater West

Beach Pools & Sand Dunes

Seaweed Drying Hut

Castlemartin

PEMBROKESHIRE COAST NATIONAL PARK

Castlemartin Artillery Range DANGER

Crow Rock

Green Bridge of Wales

Map

• OS Explorer Map OL 36 – South Pembrokeshire

⑱ Elegug Stacks, Green Bridge & St.Govan's Chapel

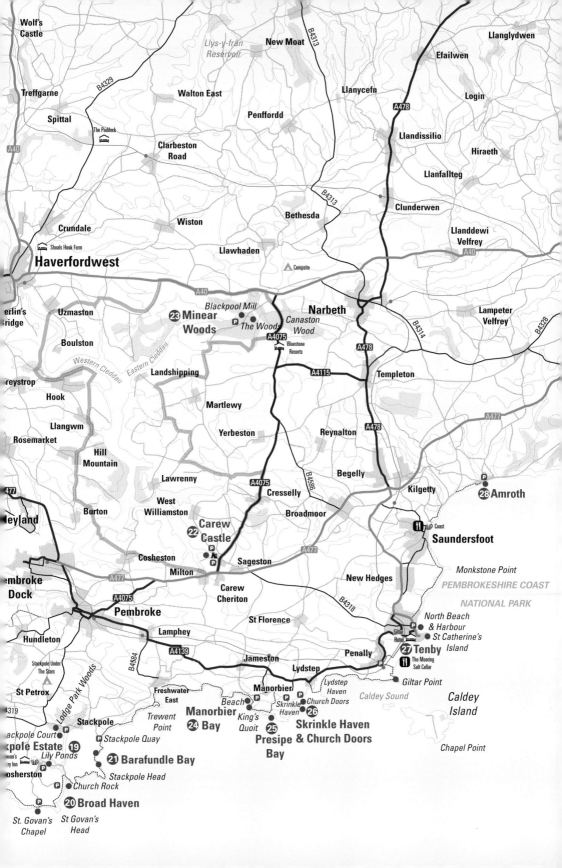

The small island of Skomer just off the Pembrokeshire coastline is home to a vast array of birds and wild flowers. The island is an extremely important breeding ground for a variety of seabirds including half the world's population of the manx shearwater and the islands charismatic summer visitor, the puffin. Whilst there's not much in the way of sea that separates Skomer Island from the mainland, taking only ten minutes on the boat, it's a world apart when it comes to the diversity of wildlife that inhabits this nature hotspot. The best time to photograph the puffins is between April and July, which also coincides with the best of the wild flowers. The island is managed by the Wildlife Trust of South and West Wales (WTSWW).

A 50-seater passenger boat transports visitors to the Island from Martin's Haven. The boat, the *Dale Princess*, runs between Good Friday or 1 April to 30 September every day, except Mondays. There is a limit of 250 people a day on the island and access is on a first-come first served basis, see 'Catching The Boat' in the grey box out.

What to shoot and viewpoints

Once finally out on open water and breathing in the fresh sea air, you will soon approach Skomer's North Haven, where the boat lands, to be greeted by not only the odd gull hitching a lift on the boat cab, but rafts and rafts of puffins, razorbills and guillemots carpeting the water. This is your first opportunity to photograph the seabirds close-up, but far from the last.

Landing on Skomer and taking the steep steps up to the greeting point you'll pass nesting burrows of puffins and razorbills giving you some very, very close-up views of these beautiful seabirds. With most wildlife and bird photography, you always feel like your lens is never long enough, but with the Skomer seabirds, it's the opposite way around. »

Opposite: *Atlantic Puffin with a beak full of sand eels. Canon 5D III, 300mm f/2.8 at 300mm, ISO 400, 1/4000s at f/4. July.*

How to get here

From Haverfordwest follow the 'Dale Road' B4327 out west, after 10 miles you'll cross a road bridge over a small river, and then take the next right signposted Marloes/Martins Haven. Head through Marloes village following the road until you reach its end at Martin's Haven. Parking is in the National Trust car park (£5 fee or free for members).

Catching The Boat

You'll need to get to the car park early in peak season. Aim for 7:30am so you can park up and head down the hill to queue for landing tickets from the little shop here (landing fee is free for WTSWW members) Boats start departing around 10am every hour and the first return boat is around 3pm. Boats do not run if the sea is rough. Once you've got your landing tickets, head down the steep hill towards the bay – don't forget to stop off at the toilets on the way. Not only to answer the call of nature, but you'll more than definitely be greeted with some of the best views of swallows and house martins you'll ever see as they nest inside the small building.

To check if the boats are running call *01646 636800* or on twitter *@skomer_boatinfo*

Visit *www.welshwildlife.org* to plan your trip, book overnight stays and read more about the island.

Parking Lat/Long: 51.734736, -5.2435631
Parking Postcode: SA62 3BJ
OS Map Grid Ref: SM 761 089

Accessibility

The jetty is up and over steps down onto the boat on a awkward slipway. There are some up and downs when landing on the island, including a steep set of steps disembarking the boat. On the island there are about 4 miles of well-maintained paths, some parts include a few elevation changes over uneven ground and some boggy sections. Other than the tricky boat embark/disembark it is generally easy going if you take your time.

Best time of year/day

Late spring – May/June – is the peak of activity on Skomer, not just for seabirds but for wild flowers. Acres of bluebells carpet the landscape together with sea thrift around Skomer Head, these flowers fading into red and sea campion in late May before the bracken takes over for the summer at the end of June. The boats sail from April through until October, and the island changes appearance and mood over the season. Best weather to photograph the seabirds is bright but cloudy conditions as it helps capture details in both the shadows and highlights as the harsh midday sun isn't flattering. If you are staying over on the island, head to the Wick for sunset for magical light that bathes the landscape in golden tones during the evening.

Guiding on Skomer

I am a registered commercial operator licensed to run day and overnight photographic workshops on the island. Check out my website for more information and to book: *www.drewbuckleyphotography.com*

A 'circus' of Puffins on a rock at the Wick. Canon 1DX, 500mm f/4 at 500mm, ISO 800, 1/1250s at f/8. June.

When you arrive at the top of the steps, the island warden or one of the great volunteers, will give a brief talk about the island explaining what to see, where to see it and also where to go and where not to go, including where the toilets are. There's only a few main footpaths on Skomer. From the air in simple terms, Skomer is like a squashed circle with a footpath going from north to south, a footpath west to east and also a coastal path that goes right around the island, with the crossing point in the middle. Here you will find the main farm building, toilets, self-catering accommodation and the only shelter on the island if there's any inclement weather.

In total it takes about three hours to go round the whole island covering around four miles of well-maintained paths. You'll need a good pair of walking boots as there are ups and downs, and some boggy sections. On any part of the island, it is easy to just sit and watch, admiring the experience of all this activity in this stunning setting; but here are some specific viewpoints.

Viewpoint 1 – The Wick

At the south west of the island is The Wick. This horseshoe-shaped, sheer cliff face is the best place to see Skomer's puffins up close and also various other seabirds making their homes on the rocky ledges. The terrain here is completely covered with rabbit burrows in which the puffins nest and in peak season, the frantic comings and goings of birds in this small area is immense. The sky is filled with birds whirling in circles catching the updrafts from the Irish Sea beneath. Thankfully there's plenty of places to stop and sit down to admire the view. Puffins land literally feet away from you diving straight into their burrows; beaks filled to the brim with sand eels trying to strive off an attack from the hungry great black-backed gulls that try to ambush them on their return. You won't regret not bringing 'that' lens with you here because whatever you have in your bag, you'll fill the frame with it – they're that close! There's so many different shots to get here: intimate portraits, close-up details, group shots and my favourite, birds in flight. I'm used to the challenge of tracking birds in flight by now but these little guys will test you to your limit, especially if it's windy. You definitely need time to get your eye in with these sea-faring missiles.

Short-Eared Owl hovering over bluebells and red campion.
Canon 5D IV, 500mm f/4 at 500mm, ISO 800, 1/6400s at f/6.3. May.

Atlantic Puffin coming into land with a beak full of sand eels. Canon 1DX, 500mm f/4 at 500mm, ISO 1600, 1/1250s at f/4. June.

Viewpoint 2 – North Valley

The island is famed for its wildlife but there's also a vast array of wild flowers that carpet the land through the spring and summer months. Bluebells cover most the most part of the island through April to June, peaking around mid-May whilst combining with freshly flowering red campion as the bluebells die off. Traveling north from the farm will take you through North Valley. You'll cross the top of an old stone wall showcasing the once farmed extremities of fields. You'll then drop into a snaking path through the bluebells, a spectacular sight and proof that the island was once wooded. Along this stretch are a few pairs of resident short eared owls that can often be seen flying to and from here and Gorse Hill, to the south of the farm. They feed solely on the endemic Skomer vole, a unique sub-species of vole only resident on Skomer. Thanks to the nearby rocky outcrop of the Garland Stone, there's some sea currents that stir up the fish here so there's a great chance of seeing feeding porpoise and dolphin.

Thrift carpets Skomer Head in spring. Canon 5D IV, 24-70mm f/2.8 at 26mm, ISO 100, 1/40s at f/13. Polariser. May.

Above: Visitors walk through carpets of bluebells in North Valley. Canon 5D IV, 24-70mm f/2.8 at 59mm, ISO 100, 1/80s at f/11. Polariser. May.
Below: The track to the farm lined with bluebells in spring. Canon 5D III, 24-70mm f/2.8 at 57mm, ISO 640, 1/160s at f/14. Polariser. May.

Staying the night

I'd recommend an overnight stay on the island, but you have to book well in advance – usually in October for the following year. Not only do you get to enjoy sunrise and sunset on this magical island but you get more time alone with the landscape and its wildlife. At night you'll hear the eerie calls of the manx shearwater. These birds only leave and return to their nests at night. You will also get more chances to see seals. They're abundant here all-year-round, but particularly August to November when they haul into the small bays to pup.

Fulmar in flight near sunset. Canon 5D IV, 500mm f/4 at 500mm, ISO 800, 1/1250s at f/5.6. May.

Young Puffin 'Puffling' at the Wick (VP1). Canon 5D IV, 300mm f/2.8 & 1.4x Extender at 420mm, ISO 500, 1/1000s at f/6.3. July.

Atlantic grey seal near the landing steps. Canon 1DX, 300mm f/2.8 & 2x Extender at 600mm, ISO 400, 1/2000s at f/5.6. June.

Razorbill perched on rocks near landing steps. Canon 5D III, 500mm f/4 at 500mm, ISO 500, 1/4000s at f/5.6. June.

Top: A Manx Shearwater illuminated in front of the Milky Way. Canon 5D IV, 24-70mm f/2.8 at 24mm, ISO 4000, 30s at f/4. Tripod. June.

Above: Milky Way in the sky and light painted SKOMER with torchlight. Canon 5D III, 14mm f/2.8 at 14mm, ISO 4000, 30s at f/2.8. Tripod. July.

The Deer Park lies just to the north of one of Pembrokeshire's best beaches, Marloes sands. It encompasses a short and generally flat circular walk around the headland, offering captivating panoramic coastal views, stunning geology and a vast array of flora and fauna.

Despite the name there aren't any deer to be found here. What it lacks in deer it makes up for in wonderful views and an abundance of wildlife, dramatic rock formations and cliff tops awash with colourful wild flowers. You'll find yourself watching charismatic choughs whirling through the air, while out at sea grey seals and porpoises play alongside diving gannets with Skomer island for a backdrop. It's a stunning place to experience island life without ever leaving the mainland.

What to shoot and viewpoints

The easiest way to gain access to the Deer Park is from Martin's Haven car park. Head through the gate at the far left end of the car park and skirt along the side of the field

towards the next gate. In summer, this field is usually full of swallows flying low across the crops feeding on insects. If you wish to make your walk longer, you can reach nearby Marloes sands by heading straight on here over the wooden bridge, however for the loop around the Deer Park you'll want to go right. This will be your first view across the short stretch of water to Skokholm Island. It's very similar to its sister island, Skomer, but much smaller and feels a lot more rugged and remote due to its tall, sandstone cliffs and wild landscape. Back on the path and below you will be your first rocky bay. This is called Renney Slip and much like many of the bays and coves around the Deer Park, it will be full of Atlantic grey seals and their pups come late summer into autumn. About 50 pups are born each year on the beaches around this peninsula and the elevated cliff top views offer a great insight into their first days at sea. Heading through the kissing gate you are now on the Deer Park. Oddly enough the headland has never been home to any deer. A walled enclosure was built for them in the eighteenth century, but they were never actually introduced. Today the Deer Park is grazed by a herd of Welsh mountain ponies and sometimes other livestock. These have helped to minimise the spread of invasive

Pair of chough on the headland. Canon 5D III, 300mm f/2.8 at 300mm, ISO 1000, 1/800s at f/4. Aug.

Top: Turquoise seas surround the Deer Park. Canon 5D III, 24-70mm f/2.8 at 35mm, ISO 100, 1/100s at f/16. Polariser. June. **Above**: Rough seas and a rainbow over Wooltack Point. Canon 5D III, 24-70mm f/2.8 at 50mm, ISO 160, 1/320s at f/10. Polariser. Sep.

Top: Atlantic grey seal mum and its pup. Canon 5D III, 300mm f/2.8 & 1.4x Extender at 420mm, ISO 640, 1/1000s at f/4. Sep. **Above**: Atlantic grey seal pup in the cove. Canon 5D III, 300mm f/2.8 & 1.4x Extender at 420mm, ISO 640, 1/1000s at f/5.6. Sep.

plants such as bramble, gorse and bracken which would otherwise cover the cliff-tops, stifling the diversity of plant and insect life.

As well as the loop walk that follows the coastline, there's an array of pathways that cross the headland through the grass, allowing plenty of access options for photography. As you reach the most western point of the headland, keep an eye out for many of the bird species that reside here. Ravens and its corvid cousin, the chough are very common in these parts. They fly around in groups stopping to feed on the short-clipped, insect rich grassland. Fulmar will be nesting on the cliff ledges below you, occasionally soaring passed at eye level on the updrafts. Northern wheatears, stonechat, whinchat and an array of pipits are all regulars on this coastal stretch. It's a favoured

spot for birds of prey, with kestrels hovering and peregrine falcon hunting along the cliffs.

The main thing you'll take away from here is being able to stand right on the edge of the mainland looking across the turbulent waters of Jack Sound towards Skomer island. With the wind in your face and the smell of the sea looking beyond Skomer westwards is the USA. Deer Park offers one of the closest feelings of being on an island, while remaining only a stone's throw from civilisation. With this western aspect, it's a fantastic place to witness the sunset all year. In winter, the sun will set to your far left between Skomer and Skokholm, while on the longest day in June the sun sets far right to the north, almost over the north Pembrokeshire island of Ramsey. I'd urge you to visit on rough weather days, as you can witness some

Long exposure at Deadman's Bay.
Canon 5D IV, 16-35mm f/4 at 31mm, ISO 50, 30s at f/20. Tripod. Polariser, 6ND & ND Grad. Sep.

spectacular seas and waves or if there's an incoming weather front, it's a superb place to watch the changing light and colours over the sea.

Turning north and skirting along the coast towards Wooltack Point, you'll pass many more rocky coves and bays which seals favour, before heading east and up towards a small hut on the highest point on the peninsula. This is the coastguard hut and it's an active coast watch point operated by the National Coastwatch Institute – a great place to sit with a picnic and take in the stunning panoramic views. To the north is the sweep of St Brides Bay and on clear days you'll spot Pembrokeshire's Preseli mountains in the distance. This high point near the coastguard lookout is very abundant with foxgloves in the summer and if you're lucky, the odd lizard or adder. You can then either head south to join the point where you started the loop, or head down the series of steps to the stone wall, where you can access via the road down to the small cove of Martin's Haven. Bear in the mind this hill is steep and the walk back up to the car park is a real lung buster. It's worth it though, Martin's Haven is a lovely and quaint, rocky beach where you can catch the boat to head over to the islands. In autumn, you'll sometimes find the odd seal pup born on the beach here. It's not always guaranteed, as they do tend to favour the quieter coves around the headland.

Top: Peregrine Falcon cruises overhead, a common sight on the coast. Canon 7D, 400mm f/5.6 at 400mm, ISO 500, 1/1250s at f/5.6. July. **Above**: Sunlight between the rain showers looking to Skomer Island. Canon 5D III, 24-70mm f/2.8 at 41mm, ISO 160, 1/250s at f/10. Polariser & ND Grad. Sep.

Top: The caves at the Anvil – low tide. Canon 5D III, 16-35mm f/4 at 18mm, ISO 200, 2.5s at f/13. Tripod. Polariser, 6ND & ND Grad. Sep.

Above: Stonechat signing with gorse flower background. Canon 5D IV, 500mm f/4 & 1.4x Extender at 700mm, ISO 250, 1/640s at f/5.6. May.

Opposite: Foxgloves on the Deer Park looking towards Skomer Island. Canon 5D III, 24-70mm f/2.8 at 70mm, ISO 100, 1/13s at f/16. Tripod. Polariser. June.

How to get here

From Haverfordwest follow the 'Dale Road' the B4327 out west, after 10 miles you'll go across a road bridge over a small river, and then take the next right signposted Marloes/Martins Haven. Head through Marloes village following the road until you reach its end at Martin's Haven. Parking in the National Trust car park (£5 fee all day or free for members)

Parking Lat/Long: 51.734736, -5.2435631
Parking Postcode: SA62 3BJ
OS Map Grid Ref: SM 761 089

Accessibility

Although most of the walk is generally flat it can be very uneven in places but nothing a good pair of walking boots can't tackle. The steeper parts are the hill down to Martin's Haven, or the steps up to the coastguard hut but the latter can be avoided by using the path heading south from the car park on a longer diversion.

Best time of year/day

The Deer Park bounces into life in spring with wild flowers such as thrift, kidney vetch, scabious and sea campion lining the paths. It's usually a great place for migrating birds and on some occasions resulting in the odd rarity. Seal pups are born in late summer into autumn and the light can be fabulous in autumn if you catch it right on the edge of the weather. Tides can change the appearance of images, so I'd recommend higher tides to hide any distracting rocks from coastal shots. Sunsets prove most popular here with the western aspect.

Another of Pembrokeshire's impressive beaches, Marloes Sands is located on the western edge of the national park. This mile-long curved stretch of golden sand is popular with visitors in the summer months. Dotted along the beach are sporadic rocky outcrops and rock pools full of life and interest. The beach is backed by tall sandstone cliffs made up of a complex mixture of rocks formed 410 million years ago. Half way along the beach are the dramatic 'Three Chimneys'.

These are layers of mudstone and sandstone which were up-ended to a vertical position by the movements of the Earth's crust. Then the soft mudstone eroded over time and left behind the harder sandstone layers protruding out from the cliff face. While it can be a very serene and calm place to be, Marloes does take the full force of Atlantic storms in winter and can be spectacular with white water stretching out to sea. Marloes and the peninsula surrounding it is also a fabulous place for flora and fauna throughout the year. With wild flowers through the spring, seals in autumn and also birds of prey such as kestrel and peregrine nesting along the cliffs. Lastly there's always a good chance to see groups of chough flying around with their acrobatic antics.

What to shoot and viewpoints

Viewpoint 1 – Rocks & Pools

From the car park take the footpath down to the coastal path and onto Marloes Sands. Marloes' trademarks scenes are its rocks and pools, make the most of the moments spent walking along the beach here backed by towering cliffs, it's a real escape from it all. Keep an eye on the tide times though, as there are only two ways out of the beach from the rear (the main path and the three chimneys steps). It is a lovely flat beach at low tide but once the tide is on the turn, it does come in fast. Towards the north western end of the beach you'll find Marloes' shapely rocky outcrops; large, angled-pointy-shapes jutting up into the air in a series of slabs. These can make great lead lines to the islands behind or go in close for abstract views and textures. Further along the beach heading south you'll come across many more rocky outcrops, some smooth and colourful; almost green in colour and also craggy, rugged rocks covered in sea creatures surrounded by vast pools. Make use of your polarising filter here and peer into the water world below.

Opposite: Large rock pool on Marloes beach with sunset coloured skies above (VP1). Canon 5D III, 16-35mm f/4 at 20mm, ISO 200, 8s at f/16. Tripod. Polariser & 6ND. Aug.

Winter sunset on the beach – VP1. Canon 5D III, 24-70mm f/2.8 at 38mm, ISO 100, 1/2s at f/16. Tripod. Polariser & ND Grad. Feb.

How to get here

Marloes Sands, Albion Sands & Gateholm Island

From Haverfordwest follow the 'Dale Road' B4327 out west, after 10 miles you'll go across a road bridge over a small river, and then take the next right signposted Marloes/Martin's Haven. Once in Marloes village take the immediate left after the first set out houses directing you towards Marloes Sands, it's a narrow single track road all the way down to the car park with few passing places so take care in peak season as it will be busy.

VP 1 & 2 Parking Lat/Long: 51.728274 -5.2164379
VP 1 & 2 Parking Postcode: SA62 3BH
VP 1 & 2 OS Map Grid Ref: SM 77973 08182

Beach View and Westdale Bay

Same directions from Haverfordwest as above but ignore any turns and head into Dale village. Go around the one way system and take the road left, after the church out towards Dale airfield. There's a lay-by here with space for a few cars, if this is full then there's another small car park further up the lane by the airfield gate that can accommodate around six cars.

VP 3 & 4 Parking Lat/Long: 51.709108 -5.1837525
VP 3 & 4 Parking Postcode: SA62 3RR
VP 3 & 4 OS Map Grid Ref: SM 80136 05952

Accessibility

All the Marloes beach viewpoints are accessed from the National Trust car park east of the beach and then down to the beach by a wide, flat path – good for those of limited mobility. At the bottom of the path where it meets the beach you will have to walk over some boulders/stones, after this it's flat sand in all directions. Viewpoint 2 is accessed either the same way down the path to the beach and then up along the coast path. But a shorter route I'd recommend is following the track down immediately found to the southern end from the car park, passing the new cafe and then turn left at the next gate. Head over the two fields and it will join onto the coast path above the beach at the northern end. Follow this path north as it winds along until you meet the corner next to Gateholm Island overlooking Albion Sands. Viewpoint 3 can be reached from Marloes car park too by heading down to the beach, then following the coast path south. Lastly Westdale Bay is a mini-Marloes just to the south, and can be walked to from Marloes if you're feeling fit, if not there's a small car park to reach it near to Dale village. From the car park, head down the pathway to get to the beach, here you can also tag on to the coast path to venture around the coast.

Best time of year/day

Thankfully there's photographs to be had here all year round due to it being a west facing beach, making it the perfect place to take in those sunsets. All viewpoints will benefit from shooting after midday as the sun will start to come round and light up the beach. Avoid viewpoints 2 & 4 over the summer as you'll be looking straight at the sun. However at peak summer time, the sun will be setting in the far north meaning viewpoint 2 will benefit from golden side lighting. Overcast days are best for abstracts and rock pooling benefiting from the lack of contrast. Keep a check on the tide times when down on the beach especially if you venture around to Albion Sands as you can easily get cut off.

The coast path snakes its way up and along the headland above the beach.
Canon 5D III, 24-70mm f/2.8 at 50mm, ISO 640, 1/80s at f/10. Polariser. Feb.

Viewpoint 2 – Albion Sands & Gateholm Island

High up on the coast path toward the most north westerly tip of the beach are great vantage points to take in the surrounding coast. In the summer along the path toward Gateholm island there are wild flowers, butterflies and insects, thrift, scabius, heather, sea campion, large daisies and gorse, to witness on your cliff top journey. Once above the rocky join between the mainland and Gateholm Island, you'll be able to see the small bay, Albion Sands. Named after the steamer, Albion, that on April 18th 1837 hit a rock in Jack Sound – the stretch of water between the mainland and Skomer Island. The captain of the vessel was able to beach his ship on the nearby sands and a cliff top rescue brought all those on board safely to Marloes. The Albion sank on the beach and was broken up by storms. Parts of the ships's engines still remain today and can be seen poking from the sand at low tide. You can make it around to this beach on foot via Marloes beach, but you will get cut off if you don't keep an eye on the tide times. There's also an unofficial pathway from the corner on the coast path down to the gap.

Viewpoint 3 – Beach View

You can reach this location from the main Marloes car park, but it's probably easier heading to the Westdale Bay parking and heading across the old airfield to the east of Marloes Sands. This walk is fairly flat – you can go the long way following the coast path but you may as well go as the crow flies across the rough grassland straight to it. On joining the coast path at the south eastern end of the beach a vast overview will be revealed of Marloes Sands, onto Gateholm Island, nearby Skokholm Island and also a slither of the Marloes peninsula behind, heading out towards Skomer Island. This is a great place to photograph sunsets in the winter when you won't have the setting sun in your face and you will be able to take advantage of the golden sidelight illuminating the sandstone cliffs.

Viewpoint 4 – Westdale Bay

Slightly to the south of Marloes beach. Slightly to the south of Marloes beach is Westdale Bay. One of Pembrokeshire's least visited beaches, it offers bags of character with interesting rock formations, rock pools and sandstone cliffs. If anything it's easier than Marloes to decide on compositions due to the limited area to play with. A popular beach with surfers, it is a good place to test out capturing series of wave images looking out to nearby Skokholm Island that frames itself neatly in the centre of the bay.

Albion Sands and Gateholm Island. Canon 5D III, 24-70mm f/2.8 at 24mm, ISO 50, 3.2s at f/18. Tripod. Polariser, 6ND & ND Grad. Dec.

Looking across the rock pools and 'Raggle Rocks' at sunset.
Canon 5D IV, 24-70mm f/2.8 at 35mm, ISO 50, 2s at f/14, Tripod, Polariser & ND Grad, Feb.

A fiery sunset on the beach at Marloes Sands.
Canon 5D IV, 16-35mm f/4 at 20mm, ISO 100, 8s at f/16. Tripod. Polariser, 6ND & ND Grad. Aug.

Undulating sand dunes carpeted with grasses; a mile long sandy beach with rock pools, shipwrecks and sand formations; a seaweed drying hut perched on a cliff top promontory surrounded by wild flowers and a fantastic place for sunset all year round – Freshwater West is one of my top five must sees in Pembrokeshire. Famous for being a location in the Harry Potter and Robin Hood movies, amongst others, there's plenty here for an extended visit with a wide variety of photographic subjects on offer. It's also one of the best places in Wales for surfing; the sea here can turn rough in a short space of time.

What to shoot and viewpoints

Viewpoint 1 – Sand Dunes

The northern half of the beach is backed by an ever shifting array of sand dunes, some over 30m high, giving you a superb vantage point of the surrounding area. Also they're a great way to keep fit, as trying to run up a massive sand hill is an achievement in itself. Scattered across all of the dunes are huge carpets of marram grass, these epitomise the look of the beach dunes along the south coast of Pembrokeshire. The grasses make lovely additions to any coastal photographs and really help you to get your creative juices flowing with compositions. Throughout the dunes there's a network of pathways cutting through the grassy clumps, these work great as leading lines to a background focal point of your choosing; most of the time, the headland to the northwest tied up with a setting sun, bliss.

How to get here

From Pembroke head south east on the A4139, after passing the school, turn left onto St Daniels Hill/B4319. Follow this road for the next 7 miles which changes to the B4320, taking in the views, then turn left after a small cottage on the B4319 down towards the beach car parks.

Parking Lat/Long: 51.654654 -5.0579703
Parking Postcode: SA71 5AH
OS Map Grid Ref: SR 88571 99526

Accessibility

Thanks to two close by car parks, access to the beach is a pleasant short stroll. The southern (main) car park has toilet facilities and a lovely local food van throughout the summer season, definitely recommend are the Pembrokeshire lobster and crab rolls. The majority of the dunes are best accessed from the northern car park. Parking is not as extensive as the south car park and there are no facilities, but it drops you in the thick of it. It is a lot quieter and provides good access to the coast path heading north towards Angle. The seaweed hut is located on the southern end of the beach and you can pull off into a lay-by along the road for easy access. It is a short walk across pretty flat grass to get there.

Best time of year/day

Late afternoon and evening are best as the beach faces west. The sun will set into the sea for majority of the year other than peak summertime. In the summer it can be serene and peaceful here, with pastel skies. However Atlantic storms smash head first into this corner of Wales. Expect spectacular waves and windswept grassland. Any time of the day is good for abstracts, especially overcast days which will keep contrast low when photographing the rock pools revealing more details in the shadows. This location is a dark sky site, thanks to there being sea to the west and south, and it is an excellent place to try out some night sky photography. The Milky Way should be in the south west during late summer.

Opposite: Rough seas, rain showers and golden light at sunset. Canon 5D IV, 16-35mm f/4 at 20mm, ISO 100, 1/5s at f/14. Tripod. Polariser & ND Grad. Mar.

Looking across the dunes at sunset. Canon 5D III, 24-70mm f/2.8 at 24mm, ISO 320, 4s at f/16. Tripod. Polariser & 6ND. Mar.

The Seaweed Drying Hut (VP3). Canon 5D IV, 16-35mm f/4 at 31mm, ISO 100, 30s at f/14. Tripod. Polariser, 6ND & ND Grad. Mar.

*The dunes at sunset (VP1). Canon 5D III, 24-70mm f/2.8 at 24mm,
ISO 100, 0.4s at f/13. Tripod. Polariser, 3ND & ND Grad. June.*

Viewpoint 2 – Beach Pools & Ship Wrecks

Due to strong sea storms this beach is ever changing.
Usually at the beginning of the year, large storms transit
across the Atlantic toward Britain bringing strong winds
and huge waves that reveal hidden features on the beach.
Every year the area of the pebbles that back the beach,
change shape and increase in numbers. Shipwrecks, anchor
chains and old mechanical parts are unearthed briefly
and countless pools and sand formations are created by
strong swells churning up the sand. All these interesting
photographic subjects are usually situated half way
along the beach.

*Sand formations created after winter sea storms.
Canon 5D III, 24-70mm f/2.8 at 35mm, ISO 100,
1/15s at f/10. Tripod. Polariser. Mar.*

Ship wreck exposed after winter sea storms.
Canon 5D III, 16-35mm f/2.8 at 16mm, ISO 100, 0.8s at f/18, Tripod, Polariser & ND Grad. Mar.

Seaweed Drying Hut at sunset. Canon 5D III, 17-40mm f/4 at 17mm, ISO 800, 2.5s at f/16. Tripod. Polariser & ND Grad. July.

Viewpoint 3 – Seaweed Drying Hut

There's so much to photograph at Freshwater West but I'd definitely recommend a visit to the seaweed drying hut. Situated on a cliff top overlooking the beach it was built by the Pembrokeshire Coast National Park Authority some years ago to reproduce an example of one of the many huts that would have once occupied this site. Built by the local womenfolk from driftwood with a marram grass thatch and turf ridges the huts were used to dry laver, a seaweed that grows in abundance at Freshwater West. Out of the laver they collected and dried, they would make laverbread or bara lawr, a vegetable puree, to sell in local markets.

Laverbread is traditionally eaten fried with bacon and cockles as part of a Welsh breakfast. In 2009 when part of the Robin Hood film was filmed on this beach, they constructed many more dummy huts on this cliff top as a base for some of the characters, while over two hundred horses battled on the beach, it was quite spectacular to watch.

Opposite: Sand dunes and grasses at night with Milky Way overhead. Canon 1DX, 14mm f/2.8 at 14mm, ISO 6400, 30s at f/2.8. Tripod. Aug.

With its varied terrain, stunning coastal views and spectacular sea cliffs, stacks and arches, this stretch of the south Pembrokeshire coast path is my favourite. Not only is it a stones throw from my front door, but it encompasses everything I love about the coast. It is one of the more level sections of the coastal path with lots to see in a short distance. From the large car park, it is easy walking to all of the viewpoints, all the way east to St Govan's Chapel.

What to shoot and viewpoints

Here you'll find the stunning Green Bridge of Wales natural sea arch and the equally impressive Elegug Stacks. Not only do you need to plan for tides and sun angles here, but this stretch of coastline is used by the MOD for military training on some weekdays, and there's usually a very limited window of access down the small road to the viewpoints. The same restrictions apply for the St Govan's Chapel to the east (see below for details).

Viewpoint 1 – Green Bridge of Wales

From the car park, head to the right down the grassy pathway to the main viewpoint platform of the Green Bridge. The Green Bridge is a limestone arch that was formed when the sea wore away the rock underneath. It's likely that a cave was formed in each side of the spur. As the sea gradually washed more rock away, the two caves joined together to make an arch. Use natural cut outs along the cliff line to photograph the whole arch, this works best at high tide when the distracting base rocks are covered.

NOTE: You may notice that the Green Bridge looks different on your visit than the photos in this book. On the 16th October 2017, ex-hurricane 'Ophelia' blasted into the south west of Great Britain causing gale force winds and sea storms with huge waves smashing into the coastline. The following day it was discovered that part of the 'nose' of the Green Bridge had been lost by the power of the sea. Then, the following weekend 'Storm Brian' again caused large waves, taking a further chunk of rock away from the base of the Green Bridge, changing the shape of it.

How to get here

Green Bridge of Wales and Elegug Stacks
Viewpoints 1 & 2 are a short walk from the car park. To get to the car park, from Pembroke, take the A4139 to the south of the town then a left up St Daniel's Hill on the B4319. Follow this road for 4 miles and take the next left after the 'Castlemartin MOD Range' sign at Merrion. This should take you down and past Flimston Chapel with the car park at the end of this road.

VP 1 & 2 Parking Lat/Long: 51.612515 -4.9977587
VP 1 & 2 Parking Postcode: SA71 5EB
VP 1 & 2 OS Map Grid Ref: SR 92542 94668

St Govan's Chapel
Viewpoint 3 is either accessible via the car park above, then a 3 mile coast path walk east along flat terrain. It also has its own car park. Use the same A4139 road out of Pembroke and turn onto the B4319 towards Stackpole. After 2.5 miles take the next left sign posted Bosherston. After a mile, drive through Bosherston village then follow the road out towards St Govan's Chapel car park.

VP 3 Parking Lat/Long: 51.599640 -4.9372709
VP 3 Parking Postcode: SA71 5DP
VP 3 OS Map Grid Ref: SR 96672 93066

Accessibility

There's great coastal views to be hand from both car parks, and all three viewpoints are accessible via level paths. Those with limited mobility will be ok for viewpoints 1 & 2 and the cliff top viewpoints for viewpoint 3 but you have to descend many steep steps to get down to St Govan's chapel.

Best time of year/day

Access to the Castlemartin MOD Range is generally available on all weekends and public holidays, with limited access on weekdays. Check the Ministry of Defence 'Castlemartin Firing Times' website or call 01646 662367 for firing times to find out when the roads are open. Firing times are also published in local newspapers and at entrances and exits to Range East. Best times are at sunrise and sunset for side lighting and best during autumn and winter months. This is a good location for night time and milky way photography. With St Govan's Chapel, as it's nestled in the cliff edge, direct light is available around the middle of the day, otherwise there will be cliff shadows casting across it.

Opposite: Milky Way in the sky above the Green Bridge of Wales. Canon 5D III, 14mm f/2.8 at 14mm, ISO 3200, 30s at f/2.8. Tripod. May.

Long exposure of the Green Bridge at high tide.
Canon 5D IV. 16-35mm f/4 at 16mm, ISO 100, 30s at f/14. Tripod. Polariser & 6ND. Aug.

Viewpoint 2 – Elegug Stacks

The Elegug Stacks are situated just to the east of the
Green Bridge. These two prominent limestone sea stacks
stand proud of the cliffs in a boulder-strewn bay. In spring
and summer, the stacks, Green Bridge and surrounding
cliffs are covered in nesting sea birds. The word Elegug
means guillemot in Welsh, and along with razorbills and
gulls, thousands of them cram together battling for the
best nesting plateaus in which to raise their chicks; while
more raft out to sea in the surrounding turquoise blue
waters along the coastline catching fish. You can
photograph the stacks either from the Green Bridge side,
or better is to head through the gate east to the top of
the bay. Use the natural curvature of the cliffs to frame
your shot, use the foreground cliff edge to improve the
scale of the scene so you'll need a wide angle lens here,
around 16-20mm. This is a great place to test out your
long exposure filters.

*The Elegug Stacks with moon above. Canon 5D IV, 16-35mm f/4 at
16mm, ISO 400, 30s at f/8. Tripod. Polariser & ND Grad. Mar.*

*Guillemot comes into land at the seabird colony on top of
the stacks. Canon 5D IV, 500mm f/4 & 2x Extender at
1000mm, ISO 1600, 1/4000s at f/10. June.*

Evening light shines across the headland above Elegug Stacks.
Canon 5D IV, 16-35mm f/4 at 16mm, ISO 50, 75s at f/16. Tripod. Polariser. 10ND & ND Grad. Mar.

The entrance to the chapel from inside. Canon 5D III, 24-70mm f/2.8 at 50mm, ISO 1250, 1/160s at f/3.2. Mar.

Viewpoint 3 – St Govan's Chapel

Perched precariously in a cliff-lined cove at St Govan's Head, the tiny 13th-century St Govan's Chapel is a spectacular sight. It was built on the site of a holy well that once attracted pilgrims. After a short walk from the car park it is reached by 52 steep steps that lead down to it. Count the steps down and up again – legend has it that the number of steps are never the same. The best views are to be had at the base below the chapel, you can use side lighting to your advantage here emphasising the textures of the brickwork and stonework.

St Govan's Chapel nestled among the cliffs. Canon 5D III, 16-35mm f/4 at 16mm, ISO 100, 1/125s at f/10. Tripod. Dec.

The Stackpole Estate is home to some of the most dramatic coastline and idyllic beaches anywhere in the UK. While the estate has been shaped by man over the years, the coastline has definitely been shaped by nature. Wild, rugged and windswept; Stackpole's coast is the jewel of south Pembrokeshire.

Inland the Estate has several freshwater lakes hugged by rich woodland, home to a rich array of bird and wildlife. Water lilies flourish on the lakes, wild flowers bloom and dragonflies dance around the pools through the summer months. It truly is a fabulous place to escape for a day's exploring with your camera.

What to shoot and viewpoints

There are lots of walking and photographic opportunities thanks to the network of well-maintained footpaths that criss-cross the estate all of which take in fabulous views of the surrounding lakes and woodland. You will also be in close proximity to two of the finest sandy beaches in Pembrokeshire; Broad Haven (page 162) and Barafundle Bay (page 166). There are two National Trust car parks that allow access to the estate's woodland and lake pathways, with a third and forth parking areas at each of the beaches.

Viewpoint 1 – Stackpole Court

I'd recommend visiting Stackpole Court to begin with. This will start your walk off at the top of the eastern arm of the lakes in the stunning Lodge Park Woods. There's a map and information board at the parking area, which will show you where you are and places of interest in the immediate area. From the car park head east following the path until you reach the large lawn area, where the magnificent Stackpole Court building once stood. The parkland here was established by the Cawdor family as a scenic backdrop to their grand home. Whilst the house is long gone (it was demolished in 1963), there's still plenty to look at, all hinting at the area's lavish past. There are a few remnants visible which depict its history and grandeur, mainly the remaining footings and outbuildings. Walking past this site to the top of the steps will give you a

fabulous view down and along the eastern arm of the lakes. Head down the steps and go through the small gap in the wall to your left. In recent years the National Trust have cleared weeds and bushes to reveal vast amounts of snowdrops and daffodils. This whole hillside shines golden yellow with daffodils from February to April. You can descend down the path here to join the footpath below, but I'd recommend skirting along the wall to your immediate left. Here is perfectly suited for a shot down

How to get here

Stackpole Court and Lodge Park Woods
From Pembroke head out south on the A4139 and turn onto the B4319 towards Stackpole. After 2 miles you'll drop down through the woods and take the next left signposted Stackpole/Freshwater East. Follow this lane for another half mile, before turning right at the chicane in the road and enter the Stackpole Court site. The Parking area is up the track in the woods.

VP 1 & 2 Parking Lat/Long: 51.628494, -4.9256435
VP 1 & 2 Parking Postcode: SR976962
VP 1 & 2 OS Map Grid Ref: SR 92542 94668

Lily Ponds
From Pembroke head out south on the A4139 and turn onto the B4319 towards Stackpole. After 2.5 miles take the next left sign posted Bosherston. After a mile, drive into Bosherston village and the National Trust car park is on your left.

VP 3 Parking Lat/Long: 51.615618, -4.9380031
VP 3 Parking Postcode: SA71 5DW
VP 3 OS Map Grid Ref: SR966948

Accessibility
The pathways around the eastern arm and lodge park woods are lovely and flat, so it's perfect for all levels of mobility. There are some hills and also steps if descending from the court site down to the lake, however there are other routes to avoid this. The central and western arm paths are still decent underfoot, however some are uneven and rocky in places. The footbridges across the lake require a good level of balance including steps at either ends. Paths can become flooded and muddy on rainy days. Also if the water levels are high, sometimes the footbridges are impassable.

Best time of year/day
Spring into summer is when Stackpole is at its best for wildlife, pond life and the fantastic array of colourful flowers. Dawn is a favourite time of mine here as the woodland wakes up with bird song and life. You'll probably find that you're the only one there if you visit early, however it's a big place so it never feels busy even on sunny days and holidays. If there's been heavy rain the lakes turn a muddy brown from field runoff so avoid these days if you're hoping to see some fish.

View of the eight arch bridge from below the court site.
Canon 5D III, 24-70mm f/2.8 at 67mm, ISO 100, 1/50s at f/11.
Tripod. Polariser & ND Grad. Oct.

the eastern arm of the lake with the famous Eight Arch bridge filling your view in the distance, creating an interesting background focal point to any image. The Eight Arch bridge was built in the late 1700s and constructed with small dams and sluices beneath each archway helping to control and regulate the water level of the lakes. You'll see a path below that follows the lake to the bridge and if you're feeling energetic you can take the road across the bridge and over the fields toward Stackpole Quay, with its lovely small pebble beach. This is also the parking area for Barafundle Bay (page 166). This whole area can be explored by linking up various paths.

The eight arch bridge from the pathway. Canon 5D III, 24-70mm
f/2.8 at 28mm, ISO 400, 1/50s at f/16. Polariser. June.

Viewpoint 2 – Lodge Park Woods

The parking area is situated in Lodge Park Woods from where a network of paths cut through the woodland including a circular walk around the edge of the woods. About half-way round the circular walk is a wider snaking path that goes uphill to the walled gardens. You can find wild garlic in and around most of the woodland at Stackpole but this section is particularly photogenic due to the curve of the path. The green leaves will become most prominent in early March, before the flowers bloom mid-April onwards. I've seen this wood change shape over my life and have been walking these paths since I was young. Through great management of the wood floor over the years swathes of this delicate star shaped white flower carpet this deciduous woodland at this time of year. Underneath these little white globes are large green parasol leaves. Couple this with the sprouting lime-green tree canopy above and any compositions here have great colour contrast. After the wild garlic die off the bluebells will take over. These vivid green trees turn a lovely golden orange in autumn and fill the floor with leaf matter. There's plenty of birdlife on offer: nuthatch, jay, great spotted woodpecker, along with the usual tits and robins. You'll notice around the estate how very tame the robins are, you can even get them perching on your hand if you're patient enough and tempt them with some seed.

Top: Winding pathways through the wild garlic (VP2). Canon 5D III, 24-70mm f/2.8 at 35mm, ISO 320, 1/6s at f/13. Tripod. Polariser. May.

Above: Blue Tit on a lichen covered branch. Canon 5D III, 300mm f/2.8 + 1.4x Extender at 420mm, ISO 1600, 1/2500s at f/6.3. Jan.

*Golden hour sunlight shines through the woodland onto wild garlic flowers (VP2).
Canon 5D IV, 24-70mm f/2.8 at 24mm, ISO 200, 2s at f/16. Tripod. Apr.*

Winding pathways through the wild garlic (VP2).
Canon 5D III, 24-70mm f/2.8 at 50mm, ISO 100, 1/5s at f/10. Tripod. Polariser. May.

Viewpoint 3 – Lily Ponds

Parking at the car park in nearby Bosherston village is the best place to witness another great floral display, water lilies. Bosherston Lakes or the Lily Ponds are known for their spectacular display of water lilies and their resident otters. This is the place to watch wildlife and enjoy the pond side walks. The Cawdors built the lakes in the 19th century by blocking off three narrow limestone valleys, the ponds now form part of a nature reserve, and the best time to see the flowers in bloom is in the late spring and throughout the summer. From the parking area it's just a short walk down the path to the lakeside. The lake is split into three arms all merging into one in the middle as it meanders its way south towards the sand dunes to the rear of nearby Broad Haven beach and in to the sea beyond. The western arm and central arm are the best places to see the water lilies.

There's a circular path that encompasses all three of the lakes, including two foot bridges that cross the western and central arms. These bridges only have a hand rail on one side, so take care when crossing. They do however offer superb close-up views down into the water and thanks to the clarity of the ponds' fresh water, it's easy to spot a shoal of passing fish or large pike lurking in the shadows. Keep an eye out along the sides of the lake for herons perching – you'll need a mid-sized telephoto lens for these. Moorhens, coot and countless species of ducks reside on the lakes, especially over winter with migrating wildfowl. There's plenty of ornithological interest to keep the twitcher in the family entertained. The stars of the show here though are the otters. Keep an eye out for the classic v-shaped line of bubbles on the water surface as this indicates an otter swimming beneath. They can't hold their breath for long, so if you're lucky you'll be greeted with the pop-up of the otter surfacing, hopefully with a fish. I've seen them in any weather here, and at any time of day on the stretch between the Eight Arch Bridge, Grassy Bridge and also near the western arm footbridge. A visit earlier in the day is definitely a better bet as the lakes are a beautiful and serene place to walk at dawn. The golden sun rising and reflecting off the lake with the cacophony of birdsong above you in the trees is truly magical.

Above: Water lilies on the western arm of the lakes. Canon 5D III, 24-70mm f/2.8 at 31mm, ISO 500, 1/80s at f/13. Polariser. June.

Opposite left: Grey heron on the middle footbridge. Canon 5D III, 300mm f/2.8 at 300mm, ISO 500, 1/2000s at f/4. May. *Opposite middle*: Otter fishing among water lilies. Canon 5D III, 500mm f/4 & 2x Extender at 1000mm, ISO 800, 1/640s at f/11. June. *Opposite right*: Moorhen walking across water lily pads. Canon 5D III, 500mm f/4 & 1.4x Extender at 700mm, ISO 1000, 1/500s at f/7.1. Sep.

Top: Water lilies grow around the middle lake footbridge. Canon 5D III, 24-70mm f/2.8 at 30mm, ISO 640, 1/160s at f/13. Polariser. June.

Above: Close up of water lily flower and pads. Canon 5D III, 24-70mm f/2.8 at 70mm, ISO 640, 1/125s at f/13. Polariser. June.

Sometimes confused with its northern Pembrokeshire counterpart, Broad Haven (south) is a hugely impressive wide and sandy bay found on the south Pembrokeshire coastline. It's backed by an impressive grassy dune system that leads inland towards the Lily Ponds and idyllic woodland of the Stackpole Estate. The beach is sheltered either side by towering limestone cliffs that are covered in a whole host of sea life including limpets and barnacles, with many rock pools along the shore where you can discover sea snails and crabs.

There's plenty of bird life that call this place home. Nesting fulmar, kittiwakes and house martins all reside on the cliffs, while gannets dive out to sea and porpoise dance in the waves at the foot of the stunning Church Rock sea stack. It's a mighty stretch of coastline with bags of character, serenity and photo opportunities.

What to shoot and viewpoints

All viewpoints can be accessed from the National Trust beach car park at the cliff top or via a longer walk from the Stackpole Estate. Also, the beach can be reached via the coast path from nearby Barafundle Bay or St Govan's Head so there's plenty of walking opportunities available.

Viewpoint 1 – Church Rock views & Dunes

Most great landscape photographs require a strong focal element and you don't get much better than Church Rock. Named due to its resemblance to a submerged church at high tide; from most angles, however, it appears as a large pyramid. But if you venture along the beach and around the coast, its appearance changes with every new view. Side on, it's an exceptionally long and narrow rock with a prominent end stack. If you catch the light at the right angle, it looks like a gorilla's face at the top of the rock, but maybe that's just me. On low tides, the beach always holds water on the sand so it's perfect for reflections. Capturing a reflection of Church Rock depends on the tide state as to how the angles work out, but you will mostly need to have the camera very low to the sand and shoot towards the waves. »

Milky Way streaks over Church Rock at low tide. Canon 5D IV, 14mm f/2.8 at 14mm, ISO 4000, 30s at f/2.8. Tripod. May.

How to get here

From Pembroke head south on the A4139 and turn onto the B4319 towards Stackpole. After 2.5 miles take the next left sign posted Bosherston. After a mile, drive into Bosherston village passing the tea rooms on your left. Just after the residential area there is a left turning signed towards Broad Haven. Follow this road for a further mile and you'll reach the National Trust car park.

Parking Lat/Long: 51.607437, -4.9250829
Parking Postcode: SA71 5DR
OS Map Grid Ref: SR975938

Opposite: Telephoto long exposure of Church Rock. Canon 5D III, 70-200mm f/2.8 at 153mm, ISO 50, 15s at f/22. Tripod. Polariser & 10ND. Sep.

Accessibility

From the car park access to the beach is down a wide pathway then down a series of steps to the sand. Walking across the sand at the top of the beach and the dunes especially, can be tiresome, but once down on the flat, it's quite hard and compacted. The walk up the valley to the dunes is on a gravel track which is level but uneven in places.

Best time of year/day

Broad Haven is superb for sunrises all year round, with the sun appearing out of the sea behind Church Rock. The mere pool area comes to life with plants and insects in the spring and summer. The night skies are great here, with the beach being a fabulous location to witness the Milky Way rising at dusk. Choose a moonless night for star filled skies. Winter storms bring spectacular waves to the coastline and also driftwood gets washed up on the beaches providing good foreground interest.

The dunes are a good place to use a telephoto lens by shooting through the grasses towards Church Rock, this will add a colourful green splash to the foreground of the shot. It may take a few attempts to get the 'look' right and the corresponding depth of field, but it can be quite effective in the right light.

Big waves

Due to its Atlantic aspect, Broad Haven can experience big waves whipped up by stormy weather. The sea storms usually occur in winter, and in extreme circumstances, the wave's spray can clear the tops of the cliffs. Powerful waves always make for fantastic photo opportunities if you don't mind being out in some inclement weather. Time your visit on a high tide as then large rollers will smash into Church Rock firing the waves upwards into the air. This is best viewed from the safety of the cliff tops on the wide and flat plateau just east of the beach car park. To get here follow the pathway passing the toilet block and towards the stone seat. Continue walking this way keeping the beach on your left, go through the gate then across the field. Head through a gap in the gorse and the plateau is in front of you. This viewpoint offers a great elevated view right around and along the coast, down towards the beach, Star Rock is below and Church Rock out to sea. Also, there is a small cove to your right, which is a great explore with its rock pools and sea life, access this via the coast path and turn off just before the military checkpoint.

Waves crash into Church Rock (VP1). Canon 5D III, 70-200mm f/2.8 at 200mm, ISO 640, 1/1250s at f/13. Dec.

Viewpoint 2 – Mere Pools

As you wander away from the beach and up the valley behind, the sound of the waves and the hustle and bustle disappears creating a more serene atmosphere. It's very sheltered, so expect temperatures to increase. This makes it the perfect habitat for all kinds of flora and fauna that prefer a drier, warmer climate. Plants such as sea kale and sea holly thrive here including a large array of orchids such as early purple orchids and autumn ladies' tresses. Look out for bee and pyramidal orchids in the dunes, and marsh orchids in the damp sandy areas by the mere pools. The pools themselves harbour amazing wildlife through spring and summer: frogs spawn, while dragon and damselflies dance in air to air dogfights. Common hawker and darter, four-spotted chaser and the magnificent emperor dragonflies are all found here. The pools are relatively small, if you sit patiently you'll be rewarded with fantastic close up views of the insects. Try to photograph them in flight which is challenging. Keep an eye out for adders, slow worms and lizards as they love this terrain and thrive in the dry and sandy soils.

Viewpoint 3 – Changing Coasts

I'd only recommend heading to this viewpoint if you don't mind a bit of a scramble using your hands. It's not as bad as it sounds, but worth a word of caution. Towards the back of the beach where the Bosherston Lily ponds drain out into the sea a small stream goes under a footbridge. This small river sometimes backfills from incoming high tides, carving shapes into the sand as it goes. This is a really interesting way of seeing this part of beach change shape over time. Sometimes the river is constant, sometimes it forms massive sand cliffs and at other times there's just a separated pool. At the footbridge, take the path heading west towards the Bosherston Lily Ponds car park. After a couple of paces, you'll see a worn path heading up a stony mound to your left. Follow this as it snakes up the hillside to the top. You'll ascend over sixty feet in no time and it will provide an elevated viewpoint down towards Church Rock in the distance. Take extra care on the way down and don't attempt it if it's been raining as the ground will be very slippery.

Emperor Dragonfly resting at the mere pools (VP2). Canon 5D III, 300mm f/2.8 at 300mm, ISO 1600, 1/8000s at f/4. Aug.

The snaking of the river at the back of the beach (VP3). Canon 5D III, 24-70mm f/2.8 at 63mm, ISO 400, 1/250s at f/13. Polariser. June.

Sunlight across the dunes after the rain (VP1). Canon 5D III, 24-70mm f/2.8 at 24mm, ISO 50, 1/6s at f/16. Tripod. Polariser & ND Grad. Jan.

Wow, is probably the best way to describe this secluded beach. Barafundle is a crescent bay backed by grassy dunes and pine trees. Accessible by a short walk from the car park across the headland, the beach features swathes of golden sand and crystal clear turquoise waters.

Barafundle has been voted many times as one of the best beaches in Britain and even the world. This pristine beach is quite isolated compared to the rest of Pembrokeshire's beaches, which is a good thing as even though it's popular you can sometimes be the only one there, magic.

What to shoot and viewpoints

The walk to the beach used to seem so long when I was little, especially with all of the family walking over the cliff top in flip flops carrying deck chairs, our picnic and the

obligatory inflatable boat. These days it takes under ten minutes to walk from the car park to the beach without breaking a sweat. The first thing you see as you approach the bay is a stone wall with a picturesque archway framing the view to the beach. Here you can grab a shot of the Barafundle Bay National Trust sign and coastline beyond.

Before you go down into the bay via the stoney steps, head up the hill to your right staying the field side of the wall, taking you to a high viewpoint. This isn't visited much but is probably my favourite view of the bay. Here you can photograph everything that makes this little beach special: the shapely limestone rocks on the headland, golden sands, a curved tide that takes your eye to the lush woods and onto the coastline opposite. Looking across the bay and using a telephoto lens you can zoom in to photograph 'Griffith Lorts Hole'; a craggy natural sea arch that is a regular haunt of touring kayakers – time this at high tide for nice contrast with the turquoise waters. **»**

Overlooking the beach by the top of the steps. Canon 5D III, 24-70mm f/2.8 at 24mm, ISO 800, 1/125s at f/18. Polariser. July.

Opposite bottom: *Above Stackpole Quay from the beach footpath. Canon 5D III, 17-40mm f/4 at 17mm, ISO 100, 25s at f/20. Tripod. Polariser, 3ND & ND Grad. Jan.*

Above: Looking across Barafundle. Canon 5D III, 24-70mm f/2.8 at 50mm, ISO 800, 1/160s at f/14. Polariser. July.

Above: To the north of Stackpole Quay. Canon 5D III, 16-35mm f/4 at 18mm, ISO 50, 8s at f/22. Tripod. Polariser & ND Grad. Dec.

A vivid rainbow above the coastline near Stackpole Quay.
Canon 5D IV, 70-200mm f/2.8 at 75mm, ISO 400, 1/40s at f/9. Polariser. Nov.

Backlit waves along the shoreline. Canon 5D IV, 70-200mm f/2.8 at 200mm, ISO 250, 1/320s at f/10. Polariser. Feb.

This is also a great viewpoint as the headland opposite is slightly lower than the horizon, showing about 270 degrees of sea around you and on clear days Lundy island is visible to the south east.

Heading down to the steps into the bay and reaching the beach, take any of the criss-cross pathways to your right into the dunes and through the marram grass which can add a splash of green to your images; most effectively used as foreground interest. Lookout for lizards and the odd adder in here on hot sunny days. If you're feeling fit, continue across the beach towards the steps into the woods. In peak summertime this is some welcome cooling shade, it also offers a good viewpoint using the natural tree boughs and branches to frame any photos looking back into the bay. Follow the steps up through the trees and head through the kissing gate and take an immediate left. This little track will terminate on the cliff edge offering a similar elevated viewpoint but from the opposite direction. This is a great location in the morning and evenings as golden sidelight bathes the craggy cliffs and long shadows are drawn across the sands.

How to get here

From Pembroke head south east on the A4139, after passing a school, turn left onto St Daniels Hill/B4319. Follow this road up until the road levels off, here is a turning left signed for the A4139. Turn left and follow this road for 1.5 miles then take the left junction signed towards Stackpole/Freshwater East. Continue down this road taking care on the blind corners until you reach a T-junction after Cheriton. Turn left here and after around a quarter of a mile, turn right down to Stackpole Quay. This road leads down to the National Trust car park.

Parking Lat/Long: 51.624891, -4.9029440
Parking Postcode: SA71 5LS
OS Map grid ref: SR 991957

Accessibility

The beach is accessed by a half-mile walk over the cliff top headland from Stackpole Quay car park. Although the paths are well worn and flat across the fields, there are steps near the car park and at the descent to the beach, including some boulder crossing. Therefore this location is not suitable for wheelchairs or for those with limited mobility. The Quay at the car park has a slipway down into the sea for a more sedate descent to the coast.

Best time of year/day

Barafundle is one of those places that can look great whatever the weather. With the beach facing east, sunrise is a lovely time to photograph this serene bay, particularly through the autumn to spring months when the sun illuminates the rocky cliff and sand textures. Head down onto the beach where the sun will rise out of the ocean. Late afternoon into the evening is best for the elevated viewpoint as you'll have soft side lighting from the right. This helps to light up the dunes and beach giving a good colour to the sky. Summer is the busiest time here but it's also a great opportunity to photograph the vivid blue, almost tropical sea.

Above: Beach views from the headland outcrop. Canon 5D III, 24-70mm f/2.8 at 35mm, ISO 800, 1/160s at f/16. Polariser. July. **Below**: South side of the beach on coast path looking back. Canon 5D III, 16-35mm f/4 at 19mm, ISO 100, 1/13s at f/16. Tripod. Polariser & ND Grad. June.

Probably the most photogenic castle in Pembrokeshire, Carew is a stunning sight whatever the weather. Even though largely in ruin, it is still imposing with its high walls and huge mullioned windows reflected spectacularly in the placid waters of its surrounding mill pond. The castle is one of the most architecturally diverse in Wales; from the west a Norman fortress, from the north a splendid Elizabethan mansion.

To the western end of the mill pond is an old tidal mill – the only restored tidal mill in Wales and one of just five in the UK. Though the water mill is no longer in operation, it now hosts a great museum tour demonstrating how it produced flour using two large mill burr stones. The site also features an eleventh century Celtic cross, a medieval bridge and a picnic area, all linked by a mile-long circular walk and with every stride, magnificent views over the mill pond.

What to shoot and viewpoints

Described is a circular loop walk around the castle, mill pond and the tidal mill.

The most favourable conditions usually happen at high tide, or when the mill pond is full of water. Calm days will produce mirror-like reflections and can really boost your shots, adding another dimension to your compositions. Parking at the south car park, you'll be next to the path that takes you to the entrance of the castle. If you head left and down the tarmac road this is the start of a circular loop walk. En route you'll be passing the stone walls that surround the castle's grounds. In the trees here you may see blue tits, robins, wrens and the odd thrush all feeding on the insects and berries. If you visit in the early dawn or late evenings there may be a barn owl that frequents the area around the castle hunting across the grassland. As you continue, the road snakes around a bend and at the western end of the castle you can look over the wall at the large Norman turrets which become nicely textured with some side lighting.

If you're feeling adventurous, there is a small pathway down through the trees opposite the toilets where you can gain access to the mill pond. Here is an unusual view looking back to the castle, but be careful along the shore line as it's quite muddy and slippery under foot. Continuing down the road it will take the right fork which will pop you out next to the tidal mill. »

Cold and frosty morning in winter. Canon 5D II, 17-40mm f/4 at 17mm, ISO 100, 1/13s at f/13. Tripod. ND Grad. Tripod. Jan.

Winter Milky Way and Orion reflected in mill pond at night. Canon 5D III, 14mm f/2.8 at 14mm, ISO 3200, 30s at f/2.8. Tripod. Jan.

How to get here

From St Clears, head west for 12 miles on the A477 before taking the second exit at the Kilgetty roundabout signed for Pembroke Dock. Follow the A477 for a further 5 miles, over the roundabout then take the third exit at the next one signed towards Carew. Parking for the castle can be found on your left after a few hundred yards or alternatively continue over the bridge, turning immediate left. Another car park can be found at the end of this lane on your left.

Parking Lat/Long: 51.697639, -4.8283142
Parking Postcode: SA70 8SN
OS Map grid ref: SN 046036

Accessibility ♿

The circular walk around the mill pond is fairly flat, well maintained and suitable for buggies and wheelchairs. Both car parks are free and usually empty. The route described takes you down by the castle, across the bridge by the tidal mill, back up the other side and over the main road bridge so you can photograph the castle from most angles.

Best time of year/day

Carew can be spectacular at sunrise, especially after a cold clear night, when misty conditions may greet you at dawn creating a atmospheric location that time almost forgot. Evenings throughout the summer can have lovely warm soft side-lighting giving great contrast across the stoney textures of the castle walls; best photographed from across the water on the northern side. Undoubtedly I prefer it when the mill pond is full of water for mirror like reflections so time your visit when the tide is in and the wind calm. Sometimes the mill pond sluice gates are closed holding the water in so you may get lucky. Outside of high tide times the pond turns into a bit of a sorry looking mudflat, however this is a great time to photograph wading birds.

Opposite: Tidal Mill and Castle from the river side at high tide. Canon 5D III, 24-70mm f/2.8 at 30mm, ISO 50, 10s at f/16. Tripod. Polariser & 6ND. June.

Evening light on the castle reflected in a calm mill pond.
Canon 5D III, 24-70mm f/2.8 at 33mm, ISO 50, 0.8s at f/16. Tripod. Polariser, 6ND & ND Grad. Sep.

The best angle to photograph the characterful old mill is to head down the slipway and onto the banks of the river. This area can get flooded on super high tides which is something to watch out for. As this area is by the Pembroke river it's a great spot for bird watching and is a hive of activity in the summer. Look out for wading birds such as curlew, redshanks and godwits along with kingfishers, herons, and swallows nesting in the areas at the back of the tidal mill building. Also this little slipway is one the best places to fish for crabs, with bait and line available in the tidal mill shop. Heading north across the dam bridge offers a great view back towards the castle with a large expanse of water in front of you, perfect to test out those high-value neutral density filters blurring any water or cloud movement with long exposures. There's a small bridge over a waterfall here where water exits the mill pond if it's too full.

Walking around and through the car park offers another great viewpoint of the castle, preferably in late evening when an orange glow from the setting sun could create lovely contrasting light and shade on the castle walls, along with reflections to add content to your images. Keep on walking east along the small road that will arrive back on the arched bridge. This is one of the main A road's in Pembrokeshire that cross the Pembroke river so watch out for large lorries and traffic crossing and keep to the wall along the indicated footpath area. There are spots on the bridge where you can stand out of the way and set up a tripod. Here is a great viewpoint to photograph both the castle and tidal mill in the same frame – ideally in the early morning when the tidal mill will be illuminated by the rising sun, time this with a cold morning for mist hanging over the water. To complete the loop keep walking south and up the hill slightly where you can turn back into the castle grounds and the car park.

Opposite: The Milky Way streaks over the castle at night. Canon 5D III, 14mm f/2.8 at 14mm, ISO 3200, 30s at f/2.8. Tripod. July.

Top: The castle viewed from the mill pond sluice. Canon 5D III, 24-70mm f/2.8 at 35mm, ISO 50, 13s at f/22. Tripod. Polariser, 6ND & ND Grad. June.

Above: The castle in evening light reflected in the mill pond. Canon 5D III, 24-70mm f/2.8 at 24mm, ISO 50, 1s at f/16. Polariser & ND Grad. Sep.

Pembrokeshire is famed for its stunning beaches, rugged coastline, castles and inland waterways but there's also plenty of woodland to explore. One woodland in particular, Minwear woods, by the southern bank of the Cleddau river, is a great place to witness the come and go of the seasons. Minwear woods are found at the centre of the county near to Canaston bridge and offer good photo-opportunities over tens of acres of deciduous and coniferous woodland.

These woods have many places that are easily accessible thanks to an abundance of pathways and bridleways that criss-cross the site. Together with nearby Canaston wood, Minwear has been thickly wooded for centuries making it a very quiet and peaceful place to explore. From the high ground there are stunning views over the estuary and a derelict mill with a picturesque stone bridge spanning the calmly flowing river. It's a haven for wildlife, the woodland canopy is filled with sound of bird song, and squirrels, owls, kingfishers and dippers are all regularly seen here all year-round. Come autumn time, the woods are a hotspot for a wide variety of fungi, so pack that macro lens in the camera bag.

What to shoot and viewpoints

Viewpoint 1 – Woodland
From the main car park, the path heads west along a wide flat track. Most paths in the area have a solid stony base to walk on, sometimes covered in seasonal leaf mulch and mud, so it can become soft and slippery under foot in wet weather. A good recipe for pleasant woodland photography are nicely spaced out trees, and this first part of the wood is perfect for that. This area has been a site of special scientific interest (SSSI) since 1968 in an attempt to protect its fragile species including ancient specimens of sessile oak, hazel and downy birch. The majority of the wood is made up of deciduous trees with many varieties of oak, beech, chestnut, birch and more recently plantations of larch and conifer. All of the native deciduous tree species make Minwear a fantastic place to visit in autumn, a time when their leaves turn to the characteristic reds and oranges. Thanks to the northern part of the wood

descending down towards the river, this allows for any setting sunlight to enter the woodland without being blocked out by any other land. Time this right and you'll be in for a treat as golden light shines through the canopy and across the woodland floor with spectacular effect. Keep an eye out for fungi on the floor, as this time of year is the peak season for many fungi species and Minwear holds an impressive selection. Bird life is abundant in this area with many woodland species present including great spotted woodpecker, nuthatch, treecreeper, tawny owl and springtime migrants like cuckoo and wood warblers.

Further along to the west there's a path that takes you slightly north towards a lookout point over the estuary below. In the winter months this is a great place to watch

How to get here
From Carmarthen head west on the A40. After nine miles, take the second exit signed Haverfordwest/A40 and continue for a further four miles, going straight over the roundabout. After 1.5 miles there'll be another roundabout, take the second exit continuing on the A40 for 5 miles. Straight over at this roundabout and head west for two miles, taking the second exit at the next roundabout. After a mile, take the first exit signed for Pembroke Dock/A4075 and then 300 yards later, turn right signposted for Blackpool Mill. Follow this lane, passing the mill on your right and after a short distance the car park will be found on your right in the woods.

Parking Lat/Long: 51.793086, -4.8168960
Parking Postcode: SA67 8AA
OS Map grid ref: SN058142

Accessibility
Pathways across the majority of woodland are generally easy going and flat, however it is mainly gravel/mud so in wet weather and winter the tracks do become muddy and slippery. There are many places and lay-bys to park up at throughout the area so the woodland and it's bird life can be enjoyed from the car.

Best time of year/day
Undoubtedly as it's predominately a woodland environment, the cycle of the seasons bring the biggest changes here. Fresh growth on the trees in spring create a lovely colour splash of vivid greens while in autumn, striking oranges flow through the wood like wildfire thanks to the mainly deciduous tree species. Autumn being the preferred time of year for many species of fungi too. Starlings murmurate and roost in the river reed beds over winter, while migrant birds such as redstart nest near the mill in summer. The golden hours can provide spectacular lighting conditions as the sun shines through the leafy canopy onto the forest floor, while foggy weather can create amazing atmospheric shots, especially where woodland clearings can be found, helping to isolate single trees.

Great spotted woodpecker in winter. Canon 5D III, 300mm f/2.8 &
1.4x Extender at 420mm, ISO 2000, 1/800s at f/5.6. Feb.

Dipper with food, stood on river falls. Canon 7D II, 300mm f/2.8 & 1.4x Extender at 420mm, ISO 1000, 1/4000s at f/5.0. May.

that nature is starting to take over, with many of the paved areas and walls becoming overgrown. It is however to the benefit of wildlife in the area. Over the spring months, many birds use the nooks and crannies in the stone walls of the mill and the stone outbuildings to rear their young. Redstarts are a colourful visitor to the area, along with blue and great tits busy flying back and forth feeding their youngsters. The archway under where the mill wheel is a hive of activity too, with swallows and house martins whirling around and along the river catching insects, a real soundtrack to summer.

Walking over the stone bridge to the right of the mill are views down the river in both directions. Continue north from the bridge down the track and after a short distance there's a field on the right that you can wander into which gives access to riverside views upstream towards a series of weirs. Here the Cleddau river reaches its tidal limit, and the combination of sea and fresh water provide a varied habitat for wildlife. Look out for waterside birds like herons, dippers, grey wagtail and the charismatic kingfisher flying by. From here you can either continue west via a gravel road towards Slebech Park or north to Llawhaden village via Toch Lane. Alternatively go back to the road and travel east for a short distance before crossing the road onto the main track that runs through the eastern part of Minwear Wood. Right at the end of this it crosses the main road into Canaston woods, another huge woodland site with many pathways creating miles of possible routes, the entire area rich in flora and fauna. Most woodland paths in early spring are edged with the bright yellow flowers of lesser celandine and delicate white wood anemones. Both make fantastic macro subjects along with the bountiful fungi found in autumn.

the swirling murmurations of starlings as they dance and flock in their thousands, before finally descending down into the reed bed on the opposite side of the river. From here too you'll able to spot herons, redshank, little egret and other wading birds feeding along the mudflats. Back on the main track there's another clearing and also a series of paths which head south up steps. These go up towards a grassy picnic area and further on, crossing the road to join onto other pathways which loop around the southern parts of the wood. This route will eventually come back around to the parking area, or you can head eastwards down the road towards the mill.

Viewpoint 2 – Blackpool Mill
You can either park in the wood and take the short walk down the road to the mill, or alternatively park in the lay-by (SN060144) next to the mill gates. Blackpool Mill was built on the site of an earlier Iron Age forge, constructed with four huge millstones to grind grain. The waterwheel completed almost a century of milling before being replaced in 1901. After World War Two the mill fell into disuse, but was restored in 1968 as a museum. In recent years it was used as a tea room, but in the last few years has closed up and is now dormant. You can start to see

Opposite top: Late afternoon light in autumn. Canon 5D III, 24-70mm f/2.8 at 24mm, ISO 500, 1/200s at f/6.3. Polariser. Nov.

Opposite middle left: Fungi on decaying mossy tree stump. Canon 5D III, 24-70mm f/2.8 at 24mm, ISO 500, 1/80s at f/4.5. Polariser. Nov. Middle right: Golden colours in autumn. Canon 5D III, 24-70mm f/2.8 at 50mm, ISO 400, 1/50s at f/7.1. Polariser. Nov.

Opposite bottom left: Blackpool Mill, now derelict and bridge over river. Canon 5D III, 16-35mm f/4 at 16mm, ISO 400, 1/250s at f/13. Polariser. Apr. Bottom right: Grey wagtail on rocks in the river. Canon 5D III, 300mm f/2.8 at 300mm, ISO 400, 1/1600s at f/4. May.

With its magnificent cliff top castle and historic Norman church, an idyllic sandy beach backed by pebbles and a series of grassy dunes Manorbier is a beautiful small coastal village rich with photographic opportunity. Its wide, sandy bay faces south west and is reasonably sheltered from the worst of the weather thanks to headlands on either side.

Significantly, to the north of the bay is a geological marvel, an extensive wave-cut rock platform and at low tide this seaweed covered, rock strewn landscape is revealed in all its glory. Vast, parallel rocky lines of red sandstone, reach out towards the nearby headland. The platform, around half-a-mile long, is dotted with rock pools, rich with marine and plant life. To the south of the bay on the coast path is a Neolithic burial chamber while out to sea it's not uncommon to see gannets diving in the fish-rich waters.

Whilst it is an uneven descent down to the beach over large bedrock paths, it is the quickest route to reach the shoreline and easy enough for most people. An interesting focal point along the beach is undoubtedly the shapely piece of coastline to the north west. This works as a background element in most of the shoreline compositions, but also as a silhouette when under exposing for sunset-filled skies. The wave-cut platform and rock pool system should keep you busy for hours, it is such a compelling area. Most of this area is covered in seaweed so take care as it can be very slippery and some of the rock pools are quite deep, so watch your footing. The pools are full of crustaceans, and marine life and are great features to zone into for abstract images. Overcast days work best for this as you won't be contending with any contrasted light from the sun. Also pop on a circular polariser filter to help reduce any surface reflections and allow you to see through the water to the colourful stones and plant life below. >>

What to shoot and viewpoints

Like many sandy beaches in south Pembrokeshire, Manorbier is very family friendly and it can be exceptionally busy in the summer months with holidaymakers soaking up the sun. It's won various beach and coast awards for its cleanliness and thanks to nearby parking and reasonably calm waters, it is a very popular visitor destination. However, it is not as congested as some of the other larger, more well known beaches. Outside of the 'busy' hours is the best time to visit when not only will the light angles be more favourable for photography – around the golden hours – but also you're more than likely find yourself to be the only one on the beach.

Beach & Rock Pools

The beach is split into two halves by a gentle stream that flows across the pebbles down to the sea from Manorbier village. It's just that little bit too wide to jump over, especially after heavy rain but thankfully there's a concrete walkway at the back of the beach if you need to cross it. You'll either access the beach from the main car park to the east which will bring you straight onto the sand, or my preferred approach, parking on the hill to the north of the beach.

How to get here

From Tenby head out west on the A4139 and follow this for around 5 miles, before turning left signed for Manorbier/B4585. Head down this road and through Skrinkle village before entering the narrow streets of Manorbier village. As the road descends down passed the stone walls, take a left (straight on) down the hill with signs pointing towards the beach. The pay and display car park is on your left after a short distance, the hill parking area is another half mile further.

Parking Lat/Long: 51.644402 -4.8052365
Parking Postcode: SA70 7SZ
OS Map grid ref: SS060976

Accessibility

From the pay and display park there is a flat and wide, wheelchair-friendly gravel path down to the beach. There's another parking area just up the hill from here too, with free parking and a couple of disabled bays to enjoy the view into the bay. The path from here down to the beach is via a gully in the bedrock. Both parking areas are close by, and you'll be on the beach in under a minute.

Best time of year/day

Low tide is the optimum time to explore all the rock pools and shoreline marine life along the wave-cut platform. Midday sun can work well here due to the shooting angles along the coast, although sunsets are my favourite as it'll either be above the sea or setting behind the headland. It's a popular surfing beach so there are some larger waves whipped up during winter storms for images of dramatic seas.

Above: Drew's brother fishing at sunset on the rock pools. Canon 5D IV, 24-70mm f/2.8 at 42mm, ISO 400, 1/60s at f/11. ND Grad. Mar.

Below: View from the hillside parking area across the beach. Canon 5D III, 24-70mm f/2.8 at 50mm, ISO 100, 1/6s at f/14. Polariser. Apr.

Manorbier Castle viewed from the dunes that back the beach. Canon 5D III, 24-70mm f/2.8 at 53mm, ISO 640, 1/250s at f/13. Polariser. June.

This area works great as a foreground to a wider image, though be mindful as to how much of it you include as the random shapes can become quite messy and distracting. A good option is to use the parallel strata of the rocks as leading lines, out towards the headland to boost you compositions. Shoreline photography can be good too, positioning yourself on the tide line, perhaps using a slightly longer shutter speed of around half a second to blur any waves rushing up the sand or around the pebbles at high tide.

King's Quoit

At the south east corner of the beach you can access the coast path and explore to the west. Heading up the steps and about half way along the headland, you'll find the King's Quoit, a Neolithic burial chamber dating back to 3000 BC. As views for cromlechs go across Wales, this one is pretty impressive. It is beautifully perched in a dramatic location above the bay, with views across Manorbier Bay towards the beaches of Freshwater East and Barafundle. The tomb consists of two small side stones that support an enormous capstone, which points back in to the bay towards the castle. It's a great place to sit for a picnic stop and watch the world go by. The most common compositions here use the rule of thirds, with the tomb in the bottom left and the headland and distance beaches in the top right third. Also keep an eye out for diving gannets just offshore and other wading birds on the rocks below such as oystercatchers and redshank.

*Top: Pastel colours near sunset across the rock pools. Canon 5D III, 16-35mm f/2.8 at 24mm, ISO 100, 2s at f/16. Tripod. Polariser, 3ND & ND Grad. July. **Above**: King's Quoit chamber to the south of the bay. Canon 5D IV, 24-70mm f/2.8 at 24mm, ISO 100, 1/20s at f/16. Tripod. Polariser. May.*

Incoming waves at sunset on the beach.
Canon 5D IV, 24-70mm f/2.8 at 35mm, ISO 50, 1/2s at f/16. Tripod. Polariser & ND Grad. July.

A true hidden gem in the Pembrokeshire Coast's crown, Presipe Bay is so secluded, you are unlikely to find it touched by any other footprints other than your own. Vast, fossil-rich, red sandstone strata surrounds the bay, with towering rocky pillars thrusting upwards out of the beach. From the coast path at the top of the bay, you'll descend down to the beach via 160 steps finishing with a small scramble over boulders onto pristine golden sands. A real serene escape, even on the busiest of days in summer.

What to shoot and viewpoints

After parking on the road, to access the beach you'll want to head west along the coast path which skirts around the RAF base. Go over the stile following the RAF fence line, then over another stile before entering the large field. The path heads down towards the coast. **»**

How to get here

From Tenby head out west on the A4139, passing though Penally and Lydstep villages en route. After around 5 miles, take the left turning signed towards Manorbier. Follow this road down for a further quarter mile, then take the left turning towards Skrinkle Haven/Youth Hostel. Head down here, going straight over the mini-roundabout and travel towards the RAF base. You'll see the road will go round to the left taking you down towards Skrinkle Haven but all you need to do here is stop in the lay-by on the right side. Access to the footpath then is back towards the RAF base, with the stile on your right. This footpath takes you to the steps that lead to the beach.

Parking Lat/Long: 51.642573, -4.7810362
Parking Postcode: SA70 7TT
OS Map grid ref: SS 076974

Accessibility

Because of the steps down to the beach, plus some scrambling over rocks and boulders this is not a great location for those with limited mobility. However, there are great views of the beach from the cliff tops.

Best time of year/day

The best time to visit is when the tide is low, otherwise the beach will be submerged with water. Not a bad thing, as you can photograph wave patterns and the glorious view from the cliff tops. In late autumn and winter, afternoon visits should see lovely side lighting of the setting sun directed into the bay, emphasising the red tones of the sandstone rocks. Overcast days would be best for rock pool and stoney abstract images.

Golden sands and rock pools at sunset. Canon 5D III, 24-70mm f/2.8 at 24mm, ISO 100, 0.3s at f/14. Tripod. Polariser & ND Grad. Nov.

At the next gate the path down to the beach will be on your left. There are 160 steps down plus some scrambling over rocks and boulders. Presipe for me, is akin to Marloes Sands in miniature. Marloes is a much larger beach found on the west coast of Pembrokeshire over 25 miles away, but there are many similarities. Presipe has the same sandstone and distinctive vertical strata structures as Marloes with similar large rock pools and sand formations.

However Presipe has utter seclusion, on most days you'll be the only one here. It is located in an unusual setting behind a RAF artillery range and access to its beach is limited to low tide, at other times of day the waves will be lapping at the base of the cliffs. That in itself can be quite spectacular, especially if a sea storm is rolling in off the Atlantic, but the star of the show here is the pristine golden beach and the crystal clear rock pools.

Watch your steps

Timing your visit as the tide is going out should give you many hours to explore this small bay. Once you've descended the steps down and clambered over the boulders that back the beach, the first thing to do, before stepping on the sand, is look around for possible photo-opportunities. There's nothing worse than finding a great composition only to see your own foot prints in the shot. It's an easy mistake to make and I've done it countless times.

There are interesting rock shapes jutting out of the sand, rock pools and sand formations to use as your main foreground interests, with the towering cliffs as a back-drop. The colours of the rocks differ; there are smooth, greenish-grey rocks found in the centre of the beach and old red sandstone. Towards the eastern end of the beach trace fossils (tracks left by animals) can be found on the surfaces of bedding planes within certain rock strata especially large, tennis ball sized, red coloured circles, which have been interpreted as in-filled burrows of a millipede-like animal. Also present are large dehydration cracks and current bedding, showing that the strata containing the trace fossils were laid down on land.

The amazing strata viewed from the coast path. Canon 5D III, 24-70mm f/2.8 at 50mm, ISO 100, 0.3s at f/14. Tripod. Polariser. Nov.

Another secret gem on the south east coastline of Pembrokeshire is Skrinkle Haven, a collection of sandy bays or coves backed by huge towering cliffs. Access is down a series of stone then metal steps onto the large boulder strewn beach.

When the tide is out, you can walk around the cliff to the larger bay to the south, all of which have lovely golden sands. The first bay is aptly named Church Doors Cove because of the two high-arched caves that resemble the doors of a church. Views out to sea include nearby Caldey Island and on clear days, the Gower and South Wales beyond.

What to shoot and viewpoints

Viewpoint 1 – Cliff top

The best way to view the coves below is from the second cliff top car park. Follow the old concrete road from the first parking bay to the second parking area. A popular viewpoint is just up on the bank by the second parking area where there are great views looking west over the headland down toward both coves. From here you can see the tall cliffs that surround the bay and the promontory of rock that

How to get here

From Tenby head out west on the A4139, passing though Penally and Lydstep villages. After around 5 miles, take the left turning signed towards Manorbier. Follow this road down for a further quarter mile, then take the left turning towards Skrinkle Haven/ Youth Hostel. Head down here, going straight over the mini roundabout and towards the RAF base. You'll see the road go round to the left taking you down towards the youth hostel, continue down this road a short distance before parking in either of the larger areas.

Parking Lat/Long: 51.643120, -4.7725108
Parking Postcode: SA70 7SD
OS Map grid ref: SS082974

Above: *Morning light illuminates the bay from VP1. Canon 5D III, 16-35mm f/4 at 22mm, ISO 100, 0.4s at f/14. Tripod. Polariser & ND Grad. Oct.*

Opposite: *Sun rises shining into the Church Doors aperture. Canon 5D III, 16-35mm f/4 at 20mm, ISO 100, 1/8s at f/16. Polariser & ND Grad. Nov.*

Accessibility

The access road and parking areas are all flat with great coastal views in both directions without too much walking. To reach the cove and beach there is a short walk over even ground then down steep steps onto boulders and rocks: you need to be fairly mobile. If you can't manage the descent, on the coast path in either direction are fantastic views and photo-potential.

Best time of year/day

The tides are the most important factor here as they dictate how much of the beach is accessible on foot. If you want to walk through the archway or round to Skrinkle Haven then you need a low tide. On extreme high tides, the waves are at the base of the steps covering the beach completely. If photographing near the parking area I'd opt for a high tide visit as the cliffs and land will stand out more against the contrast of the sea. Early morning is best for light.

divides the beach. In spring your foregrounds will be rich with wild flowers with seabirds whirling below. Sun angles are quite important here because you'll be looking down on the sea, time your visit so the sun isn't in front of you, otherwise you'll end up with blown-out reflections in the water. Opt for a morning visit when the sun is in the southeast to benefit from a turquoise blue sea and an illuminated beach and sandstone cliffs. A circular polarising filter would be useful here to cut down the glare and boost the beautiful colours.

Viewpoint 2 – Church Doors

From the second parking area head through a gap at its edge and down a path as it crosses the grassy field to the west. Follow this for a short distance before it turns left through the hedgerow. This descends downhill with the hedge either side of you, before emerging at the top of the steps that lead to the cove. From here you'll get a first glimpse of the' Church Doors'. Take care descending the steep concrete steps then metal steps to the beach. Most of the beach is composed of boulders that decrease

in size the closer you get to the shoreline, finally turning into pristine golden sand. A mid-tide is perfect here as you'll be able to photograph the waves lapping against the boulders. Try this with a slightly longer shutter speed, to blur any water movement as the surf swirls around the rocks to great effect. A wide-angle lens will help you to include the full height of Church Doors. Move around to try and get a contrasting background behind the window of the arch to make the archway stand out. Keep an eye out for sea life especially on low tides when starfish and anemones are left exposed. Bring a macro lens for these interesting coastal subjects. When the tide is right out, you can venture through the archway to the small cove the other side or around to Skrinkle Haven to the south and enjoy your very own private beach. **Keep an eye on the tides here, as the only way out is via the metal steps In Church Doors cove**.

Opposite: Sunrise at Church Doors cove – VP2. Canon 5D III, 16-35mm f/4 at 16mm, ISO 100, 1s at f/16. Tripod. ND Grad. Nov.

Star trails and full moon at high tide – VP2. Canon 5D III, 14mm f/2.8 at 14mm, ISO 1600, 120x30s at f/2.8. Tripod. Mar.

Tenby is a place I absolutely adore and never get tired of visiting, even on the most rainy of days. It's absolutely packed in the summer months being a highly-regarded holiday destination with the whole town geared up for tourism. It truly is a classic British bucket and spade location. It's also a mecca for artists and painters, the view of the harbour is extremely beautiful with many buildings differing in pastel hues creating a colourful tapestry.

Tenby's North beach (where the harbour is situated) is a great spot for sunbathing and building sand castles in the summer, but in my opinion Tenby's other beach, South beach, is very special. Its golden sand spans over nearly two miles from St. Catherine's Island to Giltar Point and is backed by a stunning sand dune and grassland landscape. From here, you'll get a great view across the sea to nearby Caldey Island, best known for its Cistercian monastery and the monks which reside there. You can experience

The harbour at low tide. Canon 5D III, 24-70mm f/2.8 at 24mm, ISO 800, 1/125s at f/14. Polariser. June.

island life there for yourself via regular boat trips from Tenby Harbour. All in all this small little fishing town has so much potential whatever the weather.

What to shoot and viewpoints

Viewpoint 1 – North Beach & Harbour

I'd expect that most people in Britain have either visited Tenby on holiday, or at least seen a photo of its picturesque harbour. It's one of the more popular seaside destinations in Wales and attracts over three hundred thousand visitors to this corner of Pembrokeshire each year; that's a lot of fish and chips, and ice cream. North beach itself is a golden

How to get here

North Beach & Harbour

From Carmarthen take the main A40 road west until your reach the St. Clears roundabout then follow the signs for the A477 'Pembroke Dock/Tenby'. Continue for a further 12 miles before taking the first exit at Kilgetty roundabout signed A478 for 3 miles then over the roundabout continuing towards Tenby town centre. There's various pay and display car parks in the town offering short walks to the viewpoints. If you can try 'The Croft' street for free roadside parking or the Esplanade where you can sometimes be lucky in finding a space.

VP 1 & 2 Parking Lat/Long: 51.674598, -4.7021672
VP 1 & 2 Parking Postcode: SA70 8AA
VP 1 & 2 OS Map Grid Ref: SN 132007

Giltar Point

For Viewpoint 3 follow the same directions towards Tenby, but when near the town (by the large arched train bridge) take the roundabout south signposted Pembroke A4139. This will take you along Marsh Road out of the town, passing the caravan park and up a hill onto the main road. After a mile you'll enter Penally village and as you enter the 50mph zone, lookout for the Penally Train Station car park to your left. It's free to park here and close to the footpath that heads towards the coast path or beach, crossing the golf course.

VP 3 Parking Lat/Long:	51.659223, -4.7217795
VP 3 Parking Postcode:	SA70 7PS
VP 3 OS Map Grid Ref:	SS 118991

Boats in the harbour at high tide. Canon 5D III, 24-70mm f/2.8 at 33mm, ISO 800, 1/1000s at f/10. Polariser. July.

*Opposite top: North beach. Canon 5D III, 24-70mm f/2.8 at 24mm, ISO 800, 1/400s at f/10. Polariser. July. **Middle**: Tudor Square. Canon 5D III, 24-70mm f/2.8 at 24mm, ISO 800, 1/320s at f/10. Polariser. July. **Bottom**: Quaint cottages, Cob Lane. Canon 5D III, 24-70mm f/2.8 at 45mm, ISO 800, 1/250s at f/10. Polariser. July.*

stretch of sandy beach, dotted with occasional rock pools and the prominent Goscar Rock standing proud in the middle of the beach. The whole beach is overlooked by the promenade and town of Tenby, with richly coloured houses extending around the harbour. The beach has great views over Carmarthen Bay and is accessed by the North Cliff steps or through the harbour down to the beach. The most popular views are taken from the public gardens on 'The Croft' road opposite the Fourcroft hotel. From here there are great unobstructed and elevated views across the beach towards the harbour and town. It is a great place to test out your long exposure filters smoothing out the tide and blurring passing clouds. >>

Accessibility ♿

Tenby is a great place to explore, it is mostly paved and there are many ways to get down to the harbour. The quick way is via many stepped routes from North Cliff or if you don't fancy lots of stairs, follow Crackwell Street or the main road (St Julian's street) down to the harbour for a more sedate descent, then follow the slipway at the bottom by the fishing huts for access to the beach. There's many more routes and paths around this area so you should be able to access any compositions you desire. St. Catherine's island is accessed via Castle Beach which is down the slipway to the east of the harbour, and only when the tide is out. Here you can also get the boat over to nearby Caldey Island. For Giltar Point viewpoint the path is from Penally train station car park and then across a flat wide path towards the golf course, from there however the path resembles more of the coast path that it joins after a steady ascent to the cliff top. Once on the headland it's easy going over well-worn paths with some sandy sections near the viewpoint.

Best time of year/day

Tenby is perfect for those summer sunrises with rich morning side lighting, casting an orange glow across the boats and buildings. Best shot here on a high tide providing you with mirror like reflections. You can also photograph similar at sunset, but the main colour in the sky will be behind the majority of the buildings so you'll need to head down to the harbour itself and shoot back. It's also worth photographing in and around the boats once the tide has gone out as there's superb ripples, textures and patterns in the sand; together with small pools of sea water that help reflect the colourful boats. Over the summer holidays every Sunday in August is the Summer Spectacular event, expect live music and street food in the harbour, culminating at 10pm with a large fireworks display. A great chance to capture some colourful scenes with your camera. All the viewpoints around Tenby are best shot on a mid or high tide as the water adds another interesting element to your photographs. Giltar Point view works best either in the morning or evening, catching sunlight across the beach, dunes and the town's church spire.

Full moon rises behind the harbour at high tide.
Canon 5D IV, 24-70mm f/2.8 at 63mm, ISO 400, 30s at f/14. Tripod. 6ND & ND Grad. Apr.

High tide at the harbour in summer. Canon 5D III, 24-70mm f/2.8 at 44mm, ISO 100, 1/100s at f/8. Polariser. June.

Heading down various pathways you'll reach Tenby's heart – its harbour, with an abundance of colourful moored boats and all sorts of interest to point your camera at: chains, ropes, lobster pots and many types of chandlery. Just before the bridge walkway, there's a slipway on the left which gives access down to the shoreline (or beach) depending on the tide state. My preferred time of shooting the harbour is on a calm day when the tide is right in; this is the time when Tenby turns its most tropical, with signature turquoise seas and a backdrop of multicoloured houses. When the tide is out and the boats are stranded is a great time to wander around them looking for possible shots. Boat reflections in the sand pools are a popular subject, as are the many sand formations and abstracts you will find.

St Catherine's Island at high tide. Canon 5D III, 24-70mm f/2.8 at 38mm, ISO 640, 1/200s at f/11. Polariser. July.

The summer spectacular, fireworks over the harbour. Canon 5D III, 24-70mm f/2.8 at 30mm, ISO 800, 3.2s at f/10. Tripod. Aug.

Viewpoint 2 – St Catherine's Island

St Catherine's Island is the small island just off Castle Beach in Tenby, being a tidal island access to the island is limited to around low tide. There was once a chapel on the island, dedicated to St Catherine (hence the name) but this was replaced by the Normans by a castle (Dinbych meaning fortress thus explaining the name Dinbych-y-Pysgod meaning little fortress of the fishes).

Viewpoint 3 – Giltar Point

Giltar Point is a bit of a secret spot. It's a superb vantage to view Tenby town without the hustle and bustle of the busy streets, and you'll probably be alone with the sea almost completely surrounding you. From here you'll get the best viewpoint to nearby Caldey Island in what looks like a stone's throw across the sea. If you're feeling a bit adventurous you can scramble down to the edge and back up the other side to the last piece of land that juts out for a real sense of being on the end of the mainland. Around to the north side of the headland are a small series of dunes adding interest to your foregrounds when shooting towards the town. Evenings and mornings are great here with soft side lighting illuminating the south beach. Look out for chough and other coastal birds. Lizards and adders are spotted up here too in the sandy dune grasses.

Above: *Flowers in bloom above the harbour. Canon 5D III, 24-70mm f/2.8 at 42mm, ISO 100, 1/100s at f/8. Polariser. June.*

Grassy dunes at Giltar Point. Canon 5D III, 24-70mm f/2.8 at 61mm, ISO 100, 1/25s at f/16. Tripod. Polariser & ND Grad. June.

The starting point of the world renowned 186-mile Pembrokeshire Coast Path, Amroth is a long, flat sandy beach overlooking Carmarthen Bay. Backed by a large pebble bank along its mile long shore, the beach is intersected by wooden groynes that jut out into the sea.

Amroth is a very tranquil and picturesque place in the summertime as the eye gazes out across the sea to the recognisable locations of nearby Caldey Island, Pendine Sands or across towards the Gower and Worms Head. Come the winter time, large sea storms can whip up spectacular waves that crash into the sea walls.

What to shoot and viewpoints

Amroth is all about the sea and the aspect. Other than at either end of the beach, there's not much in the way of cliffs or a dominating backdrop. One thing Amroth does do well though, is minimalism. Look out to sea most days and there'll be nothing there, just a pin sharp watery horizon. To the left is Pendine sands snaking around towards the Gower and to the right is Monkstone Point, then on to Tenby and Caldey island, but for the majority of your gaze, they'll be nothing but sea and sky. Combine this minimalism with the shapely boulders for foregrounds and textured, directional wooden groynes and it is a long exposure photographers' heaven.

Amroth is split into two halves, the western end is the tourist part of the beach. Here there are eateries, pubs, ice cream sellers and some parking. There's also a slipway down to the beach and the pavements are very wheelchair friendly. The beach is dotted with rock pools, sand

Pebble bank and the seafront properties. Canon 5D III, 24-70mm f/2.8 at 47mm, ISO 100, 1/50s at f/16. Polariser. June.

formations and a pebble bank at the rear. As you head east the bustling sound quietens, and the wooden groynes start to appear. These weather-beaten fences stick out at right angles to the beach. They are function over form, counteracting the movement of beach material along the coast by long shore drift. However they are now an integral part of the beach and, over time, the wood has been weathered and shaped by the sea. The nuts, bolts and metal poles that hold the groynes together are rusted with all kind of textures and colours making them the most interesting photographic subjects along this beach. »

How to get here

The nearest big town is Carmarthen. Staying on the main A40 head out west for 9 miles, and then take the first exit at the St Clears roundabout signed for A477 Pembroke Dock/Tenby. Continue down this road for another 8 miles and after driving through Llanteg just before the national speed limit signs, take a left turn signed for Colby Woodland Garden. Follow this lane down for a short distance then turn right and follow this road all the way down to meet the beach. Here you'll be in the centre of the beach road so you can park up here in the lay-by, or head either to the eastern or western ends of the beach. All parking places require little walking into the beach.

Parking Lat/Long: 51.733085, -4.6546774
Parking Postcode: SA67 8NN
OS Map grid ref: SN167071

Accessibility &

Although the three parking areas are very close to the beach, there's only a few places that allow those who are less mobile to access the sand. There is the slip way in the centre of the beach and also at the western end where paved ramps are provided, together with a small seating area and toilets. Elsewhere will require some up/down steps over the sea wall to gain entry into the pebbled areas and the sand. One thing to point out is that the groynes divide the beach up into sections, as such, when the tide comes in it will enclose you in an area. Not all of these areas have steps to exit them so it's very important to keep an eye on the tide times. It'll only be on very high tides or windy days when the water will reach the sea wall.

Best time of year/day

Thanks to its south east aspect, sunrises here can be a great way to start the day with the sun rising over sea. In winter months the setting sun will be just off to the right allowing many opportunities to shoot here right through the day. Other than the surrounding countryside the beach doesn't really change its look through the seasons, offering almost timeless views. On low tides the beach is very large and can offer superb reflections on the sand. Time your visit after a sea storm or high tides for spectacular waves crashing against the coastline.

Above: Three minute exposure of the tide and groynes. Canon 5D III, 24-70mm f/2.8 at 35mm, ISO 50, 180s at f/4. Tripod. Polariser, 10ND and ND Grad. Jan. *Below*: Close up of various sized pebbles. Canon 5D III, 24-70mm f/2.8 at 63mm, ISO 320, 1/500s at f/4. Jan.

They're also an instant help for composition, providing easy to follow lead lines directly into the water. While not necessarily leading the eye to a background focal point as such, they create a harsh man-made form in a naturally organic setting. With a high tide and a heavy neutral density filter, you'll be able to create dreamy smooth water images, while the incredibly textured wood panels stand out in the frame.

Travelling further onwards, there's another large slipway covered in the vivid green and yellow algae, then from here on there's a large stepped sea wall which has fantastic stony textures. There's many abstract images to be had along Amroth: beach from the stonework of the walls, a multitude of coloured pebbles and wooden textures to the shapely sand formations and rock pools, so keep an eye out for all of these. Nearing the eastern end of the beach the colourful cliffs loom and there's a fabulous wave cut platform just beneath a very interesting strata lined rock face. Bountiful rock pools are found here with sea creatures and plant life.

Top: *Crepuscular rays shine through rain clouds looking across to Tenby. Canon 5D III, 70-200mm f/2.8 at 73mm, ISO 500, 1/1600s at f/9. ND Grad. Dec.*

Middle: *The ebb of the tide on the beach. Canon 5D III, 24-70mm f/2.8 at 24mm, ISO 100, 0.6s at f/10. Tripod. Polariser. Jan.*

Bottom: *Pebbles trapped in the wooden groynes by waves. Canon 5D III, 24-70mm f/2.8 at 70mm, ISO 320, 1/640s at f/4. Jan.*

Minute long exposure of the slipway.
Canon 5D III, 24-70mm f/2.8 at 24mm, ISO 50, 60s at f/16. Tripod. Polariser, 10ND & ND Grad. Jan.

Pre-dawn pastel skies from Pen y Fan (p.256). Looking at Cribyn and west to Sugar Loaf. Canon 5D IV, 24-70mm f/2.8 at 47mm, ISO 100, 1/50s at f/14, Tripod, ND Grad, Sep.

BRECON BEACONS
NATIONAL PARK

Home to mountains and moorland, waterfalls and lakes, rolling hills, canals, caves and castles and an array of wildlife, the Brecon Beacons extend for 42 miles from Llandeilo in the west to the English border in the east. It is one of three national parks in Wales and straddles three counties; Carmarthenshire, Powys, and Monmouthshire, covering 520 square miles.

The national park is divided up into four areas. The vast, open terrain of the Black Mountain (singular), is the most remote area in the west of the park; punctuated by craggy peaks and hidden upland lakes. To the east of this wilderness Fforest Fawr forms miles of grassy moorland that drops down into a rocky landscape of tree-lined rivers, deep caves and tumbling waterfalls around the village of Ystradfellte. This is Waterfall Country, aptly named as it has the greatest concentration of cascades, waterfalls, and gorges anywhere in Britain, including the tallest waterfall in South Wales, Henrhyd Falls.

To the north east across the Taff Fawr valley is the area that defines the park, the centrally located Brecon Beacons; home to some of the highest mountains in southern Britain. Four of these peaks form a horseshoe shaped ridgeline, the highest two are Corn Du (873m) and Pen y Fan, standing at a lofty 886 metres. These shapely mountains dominate the landscape for miles around and the views from their summits offer magnificent panoramic views. To the east of Brecon town, the Black Mountains (plural) begin stretching towards the English border and here is the park's most varied of scenery, from rolling upland wilderness to the gentler slopes of Vale of Ewyas. This region is home to the Sugar Loaf mountain, with its characteristic triangular shape and also Llangorse, the largest natural freshwater lake in South Wales.

Traversing the eastern half of the park is the Monmouthshire and Brecon Canal, that meanders its way through 35 miles of fine countryside, linking up many of the area's towns and villages. It was once an important transport route but today is mainly used for leisure, a place for an easy stroll while watching boats pootle past. Rural and peaceful, with a flavour of a bygone era, it's often voted Britain's prettiest canal. For further walking opportunities, try out a section or even all of 'The Beacons Way'. This long distance footpath snakes for 95 miles from Llangadog to Abergavenny showcasing some of the best views the national park has to offer. Taking a recommended eight days to complete; some sections are more challenging than others, the route follows the ridgelines and steep ascents of all the Brecon Beacons' highest peaks.

Early morning sun breaks through rain clouds at Llangattock Escarpment (p.282). Canon 5D IV, 24-70mm f/2.8 at 33mm, ISO 100, 1/40s at f/16. Tripod. Polariser & ND Grad. Oct.

The weather can make a real difference to your experience in the park. The countryside is generally a lush green and the waterfalls are always flowing – the area gets its fair share of rain. Like much of Wales, the weather here can be unpredictable and can change quickly, even more in the mountains, so keep an eye on the forecasts. The likes of Pen y Fan may be easily accessible, but it's still a mountain environment, and sometimes when it's calm at the bottom there can be gale force winds on the summit. Due to their altitude the Brecon Beacons are always the first place for snow to fall in winter in South Wales so expect to encounter other visitors, all hitting the hills and enjoying the onset of winter.

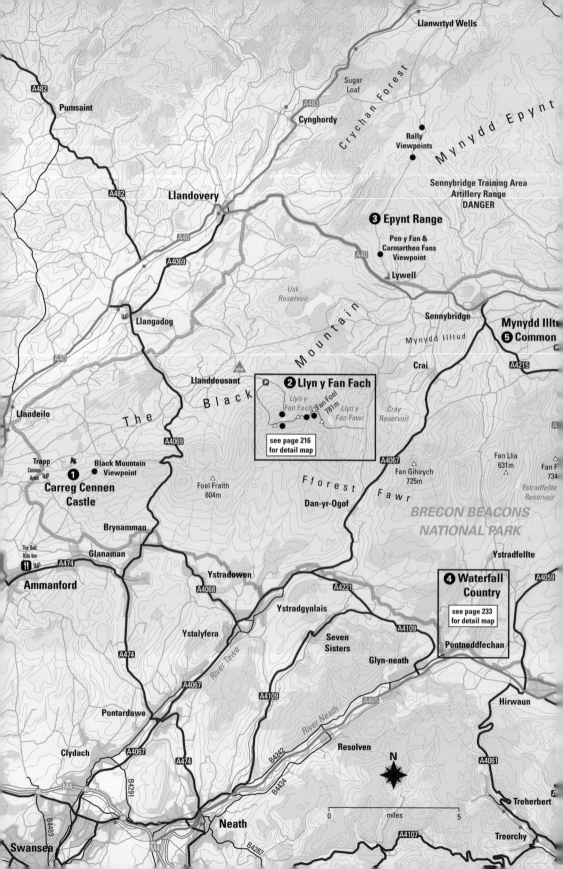

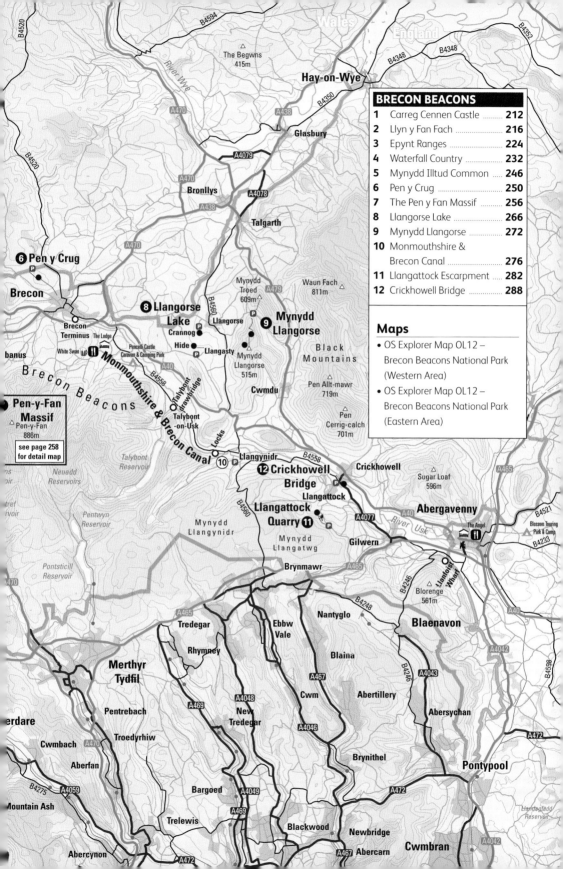

Maps

- OS Explorer Map OL12 –
  Brecon Beacons National Park
  (Western Area)
- OS Explorer Map OL12 –
  Brecon Beacons National Park
  (Eastern Area)

*Dusting of snow covers the landscape at Carreg Cennen.
Canon 5D III, 70-200mm f/2.8 at 200mm, ISO 100,
1/100s at f/6.3. Jan.*

Carreg Cennen is a haunting, atmospheric castle in a spectacular setting. Surrounded by rolling hills, it sits atop a limestone crag guarded on its south side by a 100m cliff face. You could easily imagine Carreg Cennen in a fairytale or legend. Described is an elevated photographic viewpoint that captures the castle in its surroundings.

The castle is a few miles south east of Llandeilo overlooking the Carmarthenshire countryside in the western area of the Brecon Beacons national park. 'Carreg' is Welsh for stone, and 'cennen' is the name of the small river that winds around the limestone outcrop. This dramatic setting was formed by an unusual wedge of hardy limestone, surrounded by softer Devonian sandstone. As the sandstone eroded, the limestone remained, resulting in an isolated cliff, the perfect place for a castle.

The castle was built by John Giffard and his son in the late 13th century and was in English hands for much of its history. It was damaged by Owain Glyndwr's rebellion (1400) and during the Wars of the Roses in 1461. Though quiet and peaceful place today, the castle was a hive of activity back in medieval times. There would have been stables, workshops and kitchens keeping the castle going day to day with banquets being prepared, the clang of the blacksmith, the clatter of the horses and music drifting from the Great Hall, together with the shouts and chatter of the people that lived and worked here.

What to shoot and viewpoints

Black Mountain Viewpoint

Today, Carreg Cennen is privately owned and run as a tourist attraction, managed by Cadw. For a small admission, you can walk the corridors, explore the great rooms and even head down into the secret cave via an underground tunnel that lies underneath the castle. The best views are not at the castle itself however but from nearby viewpoints looking back towards the castle. The way the ruins sit aloft in the landscape really adds an immense scale factor to any photo; a scene that is almost timeless.

My favourite views are from a track on the lower slopes of the Black Mountain, found to the south east of the castle. Singular in name and not to be confused with the better known Black Mountains to the east of the national park; the Black Mountain range is a wild and remote upland area of the western Brecon Beacons, that stretches from Ammanford to Sennybridge.

Top: *Afternoon light across the grassland to the castle.*
Canon 5D III, 24-70mm f/2.8 at 65mm, ISO 400,
1/125s at f/9. Polariser & ND Grad. Jan.

Above: *Snow covers the landscape in the valley below near sunrise.*
Canon 5D III, 24-70mm f/2.8 at 44mm, ISO 100, 1/50s
at f/9. ND Grad. Jan.

Opposite: *Wild pony on the Black Mountain.*
Canon 5D III, 70-200mm f/2.8 at 160mm,
ISO 800, 1/2000s at f/2.8. Jan.

Using the single road south of the castle, the road climbs
up onto a very desolate upland environment. At a cross
roads take a left, so as to head in an easterly direction.
Up here you'll be eye level with the castle with swathes
of grassland in front of you. Venturing further to the east
you'll climb up to nearly 350 metres in altitude, passing old
quarry spoil heaps now covered in grasses. You've only to
scour the OS maps for remnants of yesteryear; pillow
mounds, hut circles and druids graves are all listed in this
small area, adding to the character of the terrain. It can be
exceptionally windy up here, ever reminded by the bent

over windswept trees. After driving up to the highest point, the road crosses another cattle grid and levels out. From the road here are the best views of the castle and you should be able to make the most of the available light angles.

This elevated viewpoint also provides a superb vantage point over the surrounding farmland and countryside, so use this to great advantage when shooting with a long lens, cherry picking compositions of distant fields. Keep that telephoto lens handy as the wildlife really starts to make itself known as you venture into the upland landscape. I counted six buzzards, 15 ravens and four red kites on one short visit, not to mention a variety of other small birds and the majestic wild ponies that roam these uplands.

How to get here

From Swansea exit the M4 at junction 45 and take the A4067 in a northerly direction. Over the next few miles there is a series of roundabouts but go straight over these keeping on the A4067. On reaching Pontardawe take the second exit at the roundabout signed for A474. Follow this road for 7 miles and when entering Garnant take the right turn onto Folland Road, then the next right on Heol Felen before travelling for a further 1.5 miles and turning left onto Llandeilo Road. This road will climb up the mountain, passing a cattle grid before arriving at the crossroads. Here you'll spot your first glimpse of the castle and by turning right and following the road along the mountain you'll reach the old quarry and the viewpoint.

Parking Lat/Long: 51.849817, -3.9126885
Parking Postcode: SA19 9RU
OS Map grid ref: SN683185
Map: OS Explorer Map OL12 – Brecon Beacons National Park (Western Area)

Accessibility &

Other than if you want to walk up to the castle itself which is a steep climb from the car park, most of the photography from the mountain road can be shot near or next to the car; and even out of the car window if the weather's not the best. Your car will work as a great makeshift hide too, should you come across any birds or wildlife up here, including the obliging ponies.

Best time of year/day

I'd always try to time my visit with the sunrise if possible, as you'll get some lovely side lighting and the skies behind may colour up nicely. In autumn the valleys will often fill with mist, and the trees will be in their seasonal colours. In most winters due to the elevation you can experience snow up here that together with the bare trees can work well. In high summer when the sun sets far to the north west you can even shoot the castle backlit, silhouetting it against an orange sky.

Top: Moon rising over the pillow mounds. Canon 5D III, 24-70mm f/2.8 at 70mm, ISO 800, 1/125s at f/5.6. Jan.

Middle: Snow covers the single track road across the Black Mountain. Canon 5D III, 70-200mm f/2.8 at 135mm, ISO 100, 1/250s at f/6.3. Jan.

Bottom: Sheep fields covered in snow below the castle. Canon 5D III, 24-70mm f/2.8 at 70mm, ISO 100, 1/800s at f/7.1. ND Grad. Jan.

Above: Wild ponies on the Black Mountain. Canon 5D III, 70-200mm f/2.8 at 173mm, ISO 800, 1/400s at f/4. Jan.

Below: Snow covered landscape. Canon 5D III, 70-200mm f/2.8 at 70mm, ISO 100, 1/400s at f/9. Jan.

Llyn y Fan Fach is a secluded and picturesque lake, backed by a stunning mountain ridgeline with summit views that would rival anywhere in the world. Aptly named the Carmarthen Fan it is nestled just inside the Carmarthenshire county border at the western extremities of the Brecon Beacons National Park.

This mountain range is also known as the Black Mountain and the llyn is synonymous with Welsh folklore including the medieval story of the Lady of the Lake – where a 13th century young farmer agreed to marry a beautiful girl he saw emerge from the lake. There's no denying this is truly a magical location. As the lake and ridgeline are over 600 metres above sea level the area catches the first snow in winter which transforms the landscape creating an amazing spectacle of terrain and textures. It's tough going in snow, especially through the drifts on the final ascent to the ridgeline, but the photography is worth it.

What to shoot and viewpoints

Viewpoint 1 – The Lake
Distance 1.5m/2km, elevation gain 1220ft/67m, time 40 minutes

After what seems like driving down a lane to the middle of nowhere you'll reach the small car park at its end. From here walk up the road to the south, which turns into a gravel track. Heading up through the valley you'll walk alongside the start of the river Sawdde to a small trout farm and fish ladder. Follow the path around it as it's private property; a place to stop and admire any jumping fish. Heading further up the track you'll notice small waterfalls and the odd pool in the river which have great photographic potential. If you line your composition up you can capture the majestic shape of the Picws Du summit reflecting in the pools. Keep on ascending and you'll reach a turn in the track near the lake. »

Opposite: The lake viewed from above. Canon 5D IV, 16-35mm f/4 at 16mm, ISO 100, 15s at f/18. Tripod. Polariser, 6ND & ND Grad. Sep.

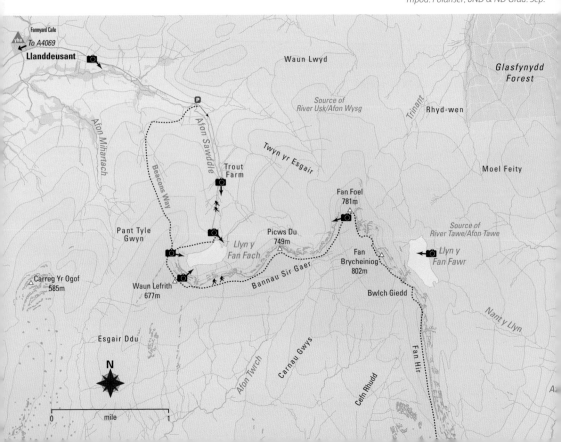

How to get here

From Llandovery, head south east on the A40 towards Maes-Y-Coleg then turn right into Waterloo Street. Follow signs towards Myddfai then head towards Llanddeusant. Once in Llanddeusant, turn left signed Llyn y Fan. This is a dead end road and after a mile and a half, you'll reach the car park. The track continues, but access is only on foot.

Parking Lat/Long: 51.899883, -3.7455775
Parking Postcode: SA19 9UN
OS Map grid ref: SN 79997 23809
Map: OS Explorer Map OL12 – Brecon Beacons National Park (Western Area)

Accessibility

Although it's easy to access the lake, this is a mountain environment. Other than the gravel track up to view the lake, elsewhere it's tough going and can be loose and slippery under foot in places; especially after heavy rain and worse in winter, when everything feels twice as hard with ice and snowdrifts impeding your progress. The two lakes and ridge line can be reached from the north west (described here) and east, however, the eastern access parking is only a lay-by on a local road and also requires a fair bit of boggy moorland to cross, perhaps one for summer visits. For straightforward visits, I'd recommend the car park to the north west of the Llyn y Fan Fach.

Best time of year/day

Any time of day can be great for photography, even on an overcast day the landscape can be magic but only with the addition of great light will it truly sing. You'll be on top of the world up here so it's important to check the weather forecast. Sunset can be great in the summer when it sets in the north west, making the most of side lighting illuminating the slope contours. This is a great place for night photography as light pollution is low. However, a visit in winter is something I'd strongly recommend, especially a snowy sunrise for a truly magical experience.

Drew in winter on the ridgeline above the lake. Canon 5D III, 16-35mm f/4 at 16mm, ISO 640, 1/25s at f/16.
Tripod. Polariser & ND Grad. Feb.

A snow covered landscape and frozen lake.
Canon 5D III, 24-70mm f/2.8 at 24mm, ISO 50, 30s at f/16. Tripod. Polariser, 6ND & ND Grad. Feb.

Countryside views looking up to the summits from the road.
Canon 5D IV, 24-70mm f/2.8 at 50mm, ISO 400, 1/125s at f/7.1, Polariser, Sep

*Telephoto views of the countryside from the ridgeline.
Canon 5D IV, 70-200mm f/2.8 at 200mm, ISO 400,
1/40s at f/1. Tripod. Polariser. Sep.*

*Lone sheep on the flanks of the hills. Canon 5D IV, 70-200mm
f/2.8 at 70mm, ISO 800, 1/250s at f/7.1. Sep.*

Viewpoint 2 – Picws Du
**Distance 3.2m/5km, elevation gain 1552ft/473m,
time 1 hour 30 minutes**

The second highest peak of the Carmarthen Fans, Picws
Du stands at 749m/2457ft jutting out high above the
eastern end of Llyn y Fan Fach lake. It falls within the
Fforest Fawr Geopark and its prominent summit is marked
by a large, Bronze Age round barrow. Like many of the
Brecon Beacon summits and ridgelines, this glacial area
has a flat top summit with sheer cliff escarpments on one
side, intersected by horizontal strata of hard sandstone,
the softer rocks having been eroded away.

Onward to the summits

From here you can either head around the western side
of Llyn y Fan Fach and up to the top of the cliffs. However,
you may prefer to follow the path towards the lake itself,
before ascending and following a path that traverses along
the northern escarpment of Bannau Sir Gaer (meaning
Carmarthen Fans in Welsh) with its stunning curving cliffs.
These cliff bands are characterised by horizontal strata of
old red sandstone and millstone grit and enclose Llyn y Fan
Fach, which lies over five hundred feet below the ridgeline.

Scree (fans of loose rocks) run down the escarpment and
in good light conditions produce some great shadows and
textures. Most of the classic images of this location can
be photographed from the western end of the ridge line,
from above the lake. However for a change of composition
– if the sun angle allows – it is also possible to head further
east and photograph Picws Du and the lake from the
summit of Fan Foel (4 miles/6.3km from the de-scribed
parking). Venture to the east again to reach the lesser
photographed and larger lake of Llyn y Fan Fawr.

*Opposite: Snow drifts carved by the wind, looking down to
the lake. Canon 5D III, 16-35mm f/4 at 24mm, ISO 200,
1/13s at f/14. Tripod. Polariser & ND Grad. Feb.*

Mynydd Eppynt, also known as the Epynt Ranges, is a vast upland area in the western Brecon Beacons. This ancient Welsh mountain plateau is wild and bleak where sheep roam freely and red kites soar. In 1939 this area was acquired by the Ministry of Defence and is now an artillery range, the Sennybridge Training Area. Although much of the area is off limits, there's a circular path that skirts this 30,000 acre range called the Epynt Way. Open to walkers, horse riders and cyclists, this permissive bridleway consists of open moorland, enclosed agricultural pastures, river corridors and large areas of woodland and forestry.

This location, on a road that crosses the moor, is all about views and compositions to be had from it. With an average altitude of around 400 metres and at its highest; 478 metres, this largely treeless moorland plateau is a great vantage point across the surrounding countryside. To the north are the Cambrian mountains, distinctively rolling away towards mid Wales and to the south are the Brecon Beacons, with their characteristic flat tops.

Mynydd Eppynt is also home to regular car rallies for the photographer who enjoys shooting motor sports.

What to shoot and viewpoints

Viewpoint 1 – Pen y Fan & Carmarthen Fans

Situated on the western extremities of the Brecon Beacon National Park, this viewpoint allows you a first glance not only at the nearby Carmarthen Fans but also into the central Beacon summits of the Pen y Fan massif. It couldn't be an easier location to shoot from either, right by the car.

Leaving the main A40 road at the small village of Llywel you'll pass a quaint church before ascending up on a dual carriageway towards the range. After a short climb and after a mile the road levels off where there are a few lay-bys in between the carriageways to pull over in.

From the roadside here you can shoot to the south west looking towards the Black Mountain and Carmarthen Fans across the rolling hills or south-east, framing Pen y Fan and Corn Du in your viewfinder.

Gazing towards the Black Mountain is the main shoulder of Fan Brycheiniog (802m) before the ridge snakes westwards along the Carmarthen Fans descending through Fan Foel onto Picws Du; a truly stunning shapely ridgeline. It's not uncommon to find these peaks shrouded in clouds, creating an exceptionally moody scene. From west to east there's a panoramic view and looking south eastwards reveals even more interest with the most iconic ridgeline in South Wales taking centre stage, the Pen y Fan massif. »

The Black Mountain ridgeline shrouded in clouds.
Canon 5D IV, 70-200mm f/2.8 at 170mm, ISO 200, 1/4s at f/10. Tripod. Polariser. July.

A slightly different angle of these summits to the other viewpoints in this book, here we're looking at Corn Du and Pen y Fan square on, creating an unmistakable outline of these flat topped peaks; the countryside in foreground creating shapely curved layers as the hills recede away. Both compositions will benefit from a variety of focal lengths, long telephotos allowing you to compress perspective and bring the distant mountains into the scene; hopefully in their white winter coat. Due to the abundance of sheep in these parts it's tricky to not include them in your scenes, however they do work as a great scale factor. Red kites are very common soaring overhead on these upland hills so keep an eye out for them.

Viewpoint 2 – Rally

If you are a motorsport fan like me, the Epynt Ranges have something else to offer other than fantastic views – rallying. In its early days as a military training area the Ministry of Defence gave the Builth Wells and Carmarthen Motor Clubs permission to run the Mainland Tourist Trophy Motorcycle race on the Epynt. It was Britain's largest mainland mountain circuit and the race ran every year between 1948 and 1953. An estimated 35,000 spectators congregated on the mountain to watch each weekend that it was held. Later on rally events made Epynt even more well known, with cars competing on the tarmac and gravel of the military roads. Although the military encourages low impact, environmentally-friendly activities in and around its lands, such as walking, horse riding, mountain biking and bird watching, the tradition of motorbike and car rallying does continue. Epynt is host to a few rallies through the year with the main tarmac rounds being the 'Tour of Epynt', the 'Harry Flatters Rally' and also part of the 'Nicky Grist Stages' too among others. The stages are fast and undulating with a many big jumps and junctions. **»**

Top: Red kites are a common sight. Canon 1D IV, 300mm f/2.8 & 1.4x Extender at 420mm, ISO 1600, 1/4000s at f/6.3. Mar.

Above: Close up of abstract snow patterns. Canon 5D IV, 70-200mm f/2.8 at 135mm, ISO 200, 1/1000s at f/9. Polariser. Dec.

Opposite: Huge snow drifts looking towards Pen y Fan & Corn Du. Canon 5D IV, 70-200mm f/2.8 at 115mm, ISO 200, 1/250s at f/13. Polariser. Dec.

Colourful clouds at sunset, looking towards Pen y Fan & Corn Du across the countryside.
Canon 5D IV, 70-200mm f/2.8 at 130mm, ISO 100, 0.8s at f/14, Tripod, ND Grad, July.

Flocks of sheep on the range. Canon 5D IV, 70-200mm f/2.8 at 123mm, ISO 200, 1/5s at f/10. Tripod. Polariser. July.

There's always the danger of a wandering sheep to avoid and the range holds no prisoners if any driver puts a wheel wrong, having witnessed some spectacular crashes here in the past. It has also hosted a stage of the Wales Rally GB, part of the World Rally Championship, until recent years. There are many good locations from which to spectate and photograph, the best places being Deers Leap cross-roads jump for tarmac rounds or Route 60 for gravel events, as the cars come up the valley towards Llandeilo'r Fan. This is great motorsport action with a stunning landscape in the heart of Wales.

More information about these events
can be found at the websites of:
the Port Talbot Motor Club – *www.ptmconline.com*
the Epynt Motor Club – *www.epyntmc.co.uk*
and at: *www.itsmymotorsport.co.uk*

Opposite top: Mk2 Escort, Wales Rally GB. Canon 7D, 70-200mm f/2.8 at 200mm, ISO 100, 1/320s at f/5. Nov.

Opposite middle left: Mk2 Escort, Tour of Epynt. Canon 30D, 70-200mm f/2.8 at 200mm, ISO 100, 1/200s at f/5.6. May.
Middle right: Mk1 Escort, Tour of Epynt. Canon 7D, 70-200mm f/2.8 at 200mm, ISO 100, 1/200s at f/5.6. Mar.

Opposite bottom: Citroen C4 WRC, Wales Rally GB. Canon 50D, 70-200mm f/2.8 at 200mm, ISO 5100, 1/250s at f/2.8. Sep.

How to get here

From Merthyr Tydfil, take the A470 north-west and follow this road up and over the main mountain road for 13 miles, before turning left just before the town of Libanus signed A4215/Sennybridge. Follow this road for 5 miles then turn right onto the A4067 and after half-a-mile turn left onto the A40. Head west down the A40 for 4 miles then turn right at Llywel passing the church and going up the hill to the viewpoint.

Parking Lat/Long: 51.966613, -3.6550865
Parking Postcode: LD3 8RG
OS Map grid ref: SN863310
Map: OS Explorer Map OL12 – Brecon Beacons National Park (Western Area)

Accessibility &

The main views are from the roadside lay-by so access couldn't be easier for all, but if you're venturing onto the Epynt Way or footpaths expect them to be boggy all-year-round and tough going in places. This is a live firing range so beware of sudden gunfire/noise. Keep to the way marked path and otherwise observe the military signage. Do not touch or pick up any objects.

Best time of year/day

Although easy to get to this is still a mountain environment and the weather up here can be awful. There's not much shelter and rain, low cloud and fog are common. It can snow here in winter. Late spring into summer produces the best countryside views when all the fields are lush and green. Autumn brings misty valleys and colourful foliage. Evening and morning light is preferable as the sunlight first hits the surrounding mountain summits and you'll have a front row seat from up here.

Nestled on the southern slopes of the Fforest Fawr massif west of Merthyr Tydfil, Waterfall Country is one of the most beautiful and popular parts of the Brecon Beacons National Park. Amongst steep, tree-lined gorges there is an abundance of tumbling water, with over ten waterfalls in a relatively small wooded area. The most famous waterfall is Sgwd-y-Eira (Falls of Snow) on the river Hepste, where a path leads behind the curtain of water, a truly magical experience. Waterfall Country, within a triangle formed by the villages of Hirwaun, Ystradfellte, and Pontneddfechan is one of the best places for waterfall photography in the UK.

What to shoot and viewpoints

Red sandstones and a long belt of limestone have created a highly distinctive environment of wooded gorges, large caves, swallow holes and waterfalls. The rivers Mellte, Hepste, Pyrddin and Nedd-Fechan; all tributaries of the river Neath, wind their way south through Waterfall Country via steep-sided and tree-lined gorges. This area contains two Sites of Special Scientific Interest and a Special Area of Conservation with fine specimens of sessile oak and ash trees together with over 200 species of mosses, liverworts, and ferns. Although the main attractions are the waterfalls this is a great place for woodland photography.

The waterfalls are accessed by two trails. The **Elidir trail** starting from Pontneddfechan, covers four waterfalls on a relatively flat route for most of the path. To the north east is the **Four Falls Trail**, which you've guessed it; also features four waterfalls on its wooded walk.

Out of the two, the **Four Falls Trail** requires a higher level of fitness to follow, mainly due to the steep descent down to Sgwd yr Eira via lots of steps.

Water Flow

Different times of year affect the look of the waterfalls. They are most spectacular after a heavy spell of rain, with thousands of gallons travelling through them every minute. However, if there's too much water falling, you'll just end up with white water overload on your photos and also probably have to clean your lens every minute due to the amount of spray generated. In high summer, it's the opposite, with some of the falls reduced to a minuscule trickle, meaning the resulting photographs aren't that interesting; so something in between would be ideal. Coupled with the amount of water falling, the seasons play a big part.

Seasons

In mid April through to June, the surrounding foliage and tree cover colours will be a vivid green as new leaves spring into life. Through the summer months, the tree canopy becomes very dense allowing less light into the more wooded falls, reducing available light and affecting shutter speeds further. The best time of year, in my opinion, is in autumn. Vivid russet tones will frame the falls in the characteristic orange tones. Fallen leaves will be found in the water swirling around, plus leaves will rest delicately on moss covered boulders, adding a nice contrast with the greens. It never gets very cold in South Wales so it is only during prolonged cold snaps that the falls freeze over. Hoar frosts and icicles are possible and at these times walking poles, micro-spikes on your footwear and good balance are essential.

Be Prepared

Although the paths accessing the falls are generally well managed and maintained, a good pair of walking boots or preferably, wellies that you feel comfortable covering some miles in, are recommended. It's a very wet climate and there's always boggy and muddy sections to traverse, and although the paths usually follow a drier route, the ground can get churned up, especially in autumn and winter months. When down at the falls, choosing wellies will allow you to reach a few viewpoints that aren't accessible normally and with some careful walking into the shallow river, can result in some interesting compositions. It is not advisable to walk into a raging river or carry loads of kit with you in the water, as the rocks under the water can be like sheet glass offering very little grip. Tread carefully, walk slowly and you'll remain nice and dry. Lastly, don't forget your circular polarising (CPL) filter when visiting. This is a superb place to use them to full effect, boosting natural tones, reducing reflections and surface glare. If there's one place I couldn't be without a CPL filter it's a waterfall, they will really transform your image.

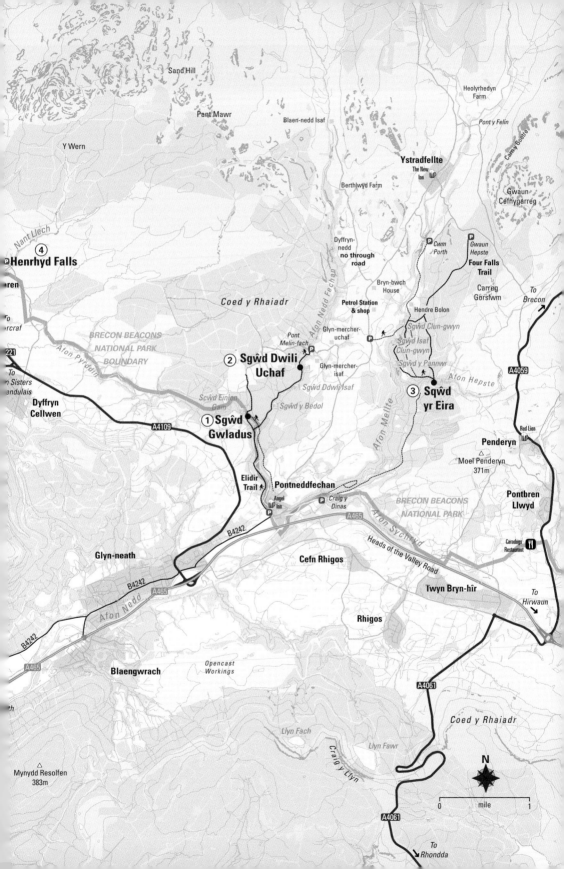

Keep Dry

Waterfalls are notorious for producing lots of spray, even standing near the foot of relatively calm falls can result in spray on your lens or filters, and yourself. There's nothing more annoying than out of focus water drops on your images come processing time. Bring plenty of lens cloths and a towel to wipe your lens and camera. If the spray is unavoidable, use a wider aperture (low f-stop number) to minimise drops, albeit with a decrease in depth of field.

• Bring a waterproof jacket.
• Wear wellingtons with a good sole and if you have
  them micro-spikes for extra traction.
• Bring plenty of lens cloths and a towel to dry your
  lens/filters and camera.
• Constantly check and clean your lens/filters for water droplets.

Reducing Glare — Polarising Filter

A circular polarising (CPL) filter reduces reflected glare from wet rocks, shiny leaves and water highlights and increases colour saturation. They also act like a neutral density filter blocking the incoming light by two stops and hence increasing shutter speed to blur any water movement.

Long Exposures – Slowing Your Shutter Speed – Neutral Density (ND) Filters

The most effective part of any waterfall image is the appearance of the water itself, and choosing the right shutter speed is important. The controlling factors that determine which shutter speed to choose are the amount of water present, the speed of it falling and the amount of ambient light.

If you decide that you want a long exposure that smooths the water, shutter speeds can range from half-a-second right up to thirty seconds or more depending on the flow, so it's important to experiment to get the desired effect. Neutral Density (ND) Filters reduce the amount of light reaching your sensor and increase the shutter speed.

For each composition take several shots and review your images.

• Using a sturdy tripod for long exposures is essential.
• Use a cable release/self-timer to reduce camera shake.
• Set your camera to ISO 100
• Switch on your level tool in your viewfinder.
• Compose your shot then focus without the filter on
  (with some ND filters on you wont be able to focus effectively).
• Take a photo without the filters as a test shot to check
  the composition, exposure length, and natural colour,
  in case of any colour cast caused by your filter.
• Attach your chosen ND filter.
• Take your photograph and review the results.
• Change your shutter speed by changing the aperture/f-stop
  to get the desired effect you are after. You may also have
  to change your ISO.
• Check your filter for spray.

Aperture

Using a small aperture/higher f-stop will also reduce the amount of light on your sensor slowing your shutter speed to blur water. This can be used in conjunction with an ND filter to increase your exposure time, or without an ND filter.

Waterfalls naturally cause localised breezes and wind, so if you have a plant or flower as your foreground subject, the slightest movement will cause it to blur throughout the exposure, take this into account when choosing your shutter speeds.

Avoid the sky

Generally, I'd always photograph waterfalls on overcast days, as it creates global illumination with no harsh highlights or shadows to contend with, lighting the scene evenly. In these situations as well try to exclude any sky from your compositions, as this area will tend to blow out. Even if you do manage to retain sky detail by underexposing, exposure blending, or on occasion when it's blue, it will still create a unattractive brighter triangle that just won't sit right with the overall lushness of the falls and its surroundings. Shooting tight will help to make a much more intimate scene, dedicating the frame to what is best about that particular composition and location.

Composition

• Use prominent foreground subjects such as a big mossy boulder
  or fallen leaves to add some impact and scale to your images.
• In shallow, calm rivers at the base of waterfalls, shoot from a low
  position just above the rushing water for a unique perspective.
• The falling water in most cases, will be the brightest part in the
  image that your eye is drawn to, so remember to have some
  breathing space around it, keeping a good margin either
  side of the falls.
• Lookout for leading lines to take the eye through the image
  ending at the falls – the main subject. A fallen log, a series of
  smaller rocks or even the blurred, sweeping lines made by water
  bubbles on a long exposure, are all effective ways of creating
  a journey for the eye.
• For wider shots it can be effective to see where the water
  is coming from and/or where the water flows to.

Opposite: Sgwd Ddwli Uchaf in autumn (VP2). Canon 5D III, 24-70mm f/2.8 at 24mm, ISO 50, 30s at f/18. Tripod. Polariser & 6ND. Nov.

The Falls

I've focused on four of the more popular falls in this area, each with their own distinctive character. You could combine two trails in one long walk which could be done in a day at a push. However it is better to opt for a more sedate approach, taking your time and exploring and exhausting all of the photographic opportunities before moving on to the next. In case you haven't had enough waterfalls also included is Henrhyd Falls found slightly to the west. It's southern Britain's highest waterfall, plunging 27 metres into a wooded gorge.

Viewpoint 1 – Sgwd Gwladus (Lady's Falls)

One of the easiest falls to access in this area is Sgwd Gwladus. Park in Pontneddfechan near the old Waterfalls Centre then head through the metal kissing gate and down the path into the woods. On your left after a short distance is Farewell Rock, a band of thick sandstone. Miners called it this because they knew it lay at the base of South Wales' coal bearing rocks, therefore when they reached this, they knew it was time to down tools and bid farewell to any more mining activity. Another hundred or so metres down the track head through the wooden gate keeping the river on your right, this a fabulous place for wild garlic in springtime. Further along, you'll come across lines of stones in the path that have holes drilled into them. These are remains of the old tramway from the 19th century, when ponies were used to draw carts transporting silica

Wild garlic on the banks of the river near VP1. Canon 5D III, 24-70mm f/2.8 at 41mm, ISO 50, 10s at f/16. Tripod. Polariser. May.

from the mine upstream to be manufactured into firebricks. After another gate you'll come across the old silica mine. Dinas silica bricks were a prized product back then, in demand not just locally but worldwide. Follow the path as it bends around to the right near the picnic tables. This area is mostly alder trees, the damp and boggy environment is ideal for them. Shortly after this you'll come to a bridge, if you continue on the same path you'll come close to Sgwd Gwladus but be on the western side of the river with limited views, so I'd recommend crossing over the bridge and turning left (north).

Finally the sound and sight of Sgwd Gwladus will come into view. If the river height allows you can stand quite easily in the river here; the undercurrent will still surprise you though. This naturally shady amphitheatre is a lovely setting and there's also some nice boulders to the right of the falls or a shapely tree trunk to help frame your shots. A steeper path to the right of the falls allows access up to the top of the waterfall before it plunges ten metres down into the water below.

This is where the rivers Nedd Fechan and Pyrddin meet and if after photographing Sgwd Gwladus your taste for waterfalls has not been satisfied, you can follow the path to the right up the Nedd Fechan that takes in three more waterfalls, this route however is steep in places and uneven so to access **Viewpoint 2 – Sgwd Dwili Uchaf** I've added an easier route and different starting point.

How to get here

Viewpoint 1 – Sgwd Gwladus

From Swansea take junction 43 exit and head north on the Heads of the Valley' road/A465. After 8 miles go straight over two roundabouts then turn left down the A4109 towards Glynnearth. At the crossroads take a right and after a few hundred metres, turn left. Follow this road for a mile into Pontneddfechan village. You'll find parking either to the right of the Angel Inn or in the large parking area to the left of the pub. The start of the walk is through the metal gate.

Parking Lat/Long:	51.756626, -3.5938530
Parking Postcode:	SA11 5NP
OS Map grid ref:	SN 900076
Map:	OS Explorer Map OL12 – Brecon Beacons National Park (Western Area)

Sgwd Gwladus (Lady Falls) in autumn.
Canon 5D III, 16-35mm f/4 at 16mm, ISO 50, 10s at f/22. Polariser & 6ND. Oct.

Viewpoint 2 – Sgwd Dwili Uchaf (Upper Gushing Falls)

This waterfall can be reached via the same route from Pontneddfechan village, however, to save some time and a lot of muddy ups and downs this is a more direct approach. Parking at Pont Melin Fach car park, head into the woods via the only path leaving the car park. The falls are about two thirds of a mile from the car park. Keeping the river on your left, look out for the many small tumbling falls on the way, which are worth a stop to photograph. There are a few board walks on ascent changes here so take your time as they can get slippery in wet weather. The path starts to climb up and before long you're high above the river. The autumn colour is spectacular here; one tree, in particular, goes a very vivid yellow. After descending down over a few stone steps, the sound of rushing water will fill the air. From here you can head to the top of the falls to your left where there is a large rocky plateau area, this area will be flooded if river levels are high. Alternatively, continue down the path passing the falls keeping an eye out for a small opening in the foliage to your left. Once you find it, follow this route down back on yourself arriving at the base of the falls in the small wooded area. From here you can walk along the river's edge almost to the base of the falls or stay back at a distance, photographing the falls with a telephoto lens. Again there are many boulders, smaller falls and pools to photograph so I'd budget a good two hours here at least to make the most of it.

How to get here

Viewpoint 2 – Sgwd Dwili Uchaf

As for viewpoint 1 but drive straight through Pontneddfechan and up the steep hill out of the village on the B4242. Follow this road for 2 miles then a left turn by the large rocky boulders. This narrow road goes steeply downhill to the valley base, go over a small bridge and the car park will be on your left.

Parking Lat/Long: 51.782209 -3.5844927
Parking Postcode: SA11 5US
OS Map grid ref: SN 907104
Map: OS Explorer Map OL12 – Brecon Beacons National Park (Western Area)

Top: A turbulent Sgwd y Bedol, in-between VP1 and VP2. Canon 5D III, 16-35mm f/4 at 25mm, ISO 50, 2.5s at f/16. Tripod. Polariser & 6ND. Oct.

Above: A near frozen waterfall and huge icicles at Sgwd Gwladus (VP1). Canon 5D IV, 16-35mm f/4 at 20mm, ISO 50, 13s at f/16. Tripod. 6ND. Mar.

Sgwd Dwili Uchaf (VP2) in autumn.
Canon 5D III, 24-70mm f/2.8 at 61mm, ISO 50, 30s at f/16. Tripod. Polariser & 6ND. Nov.

Sgwd yr Eira (waterfalls of snow) on the River Hepste.
Canon 5D III, 24-70mm f/2.8 at 35mm, ISO 50, 1s at f/13. Tripod. Polariser. Sep.

Viewpoint 3 – Sgwd yr Eira (Falls of Snow)

This is the most photographed of the all the waterfalls in the area because you can walk behind the fifty feet curtain of thundering water. To get to the falls follow the Four Falls trail. From the small car park, follow the track to the right going through a small ford then through a couple of gates. There's a bench to the right here to enjoy the views prior to entering the wooded area. Most of the walking on this stretch is pretty even under foot. As the path starts to descend you'll hear the first sounds of the river. To your right are the large falls called Sgwd Isaf Clun-Gwyn (Fall of the White Meadow), a Niagara-like waterfall with multiple levels of tumbling water. Down to your immediate right is a path down to the waterfall, which later rejoins the main path further along at a sign pointing towards Sgwd yr Eira. The path then heads along the river before crossing a wooden bridge. The route then heads south (keeping the river on your right) as it climbs up through woodland, with interestingly shaped bare tree roots and a boardwalk section through the forest. From here is another path to your right where you can take to view Sgwd Isaf Clun-Gwyn from the other side at slightly a higher viewpoint on a rocky slab. There will be some trees obstructing your views of the falls. Back on the main path it now climbs and falls over a few steeper ups and downs before levelling out high above the gorge below. This is a lovely open plateau to catch the sunlight in the late afternoon through the summer. After some more walking you'll reach a bench on your left (you'll be very thankful for this bench on your return up!) and the sign to Sgwd yr Eira to your right. From here it's a series of zig-zagging steps all the way down the gorge. You'll eventually reach the river and the waterfall is found upstream to your left.

If your ability allows it (and also the river flow) you can walk along the small rocky path on the left side of the river and round behind the falls, coming out of the other side. Sgwd yr Eira means Falls of Snow, named after the feeling of looking at falling snow as you stand behind the wall of cascading water. The path was once used by sheep farmers and today it's a designated footpath that forms a loop around back to the wooden bridge you crossed. The rocky ground is exceptionally slippery here and you will probably get wet from the spray, but it's a very invigorating experience.

The path towards Sgwd yr Eira (VP3). Canon 5D III, 24-70mm f/2.8 at 35mm, ISO 100, 1/13s at f/11. Tripod. Polariser. Sep.

How to get here

Viewpoint 3 – Sqwd yr Eira

As for Viewpoint 2 but rather than turning left on the road from Pontneddfechan, carry on going along the B4242 where you'll find the parking area immediately before the cattle grid on your right.

Parking Lat/Long: 51.783399, -3.5689761
Parking Postcode: SA11 5US
OS Map grid ref: SN 918105
Map: OS Explorer Map OL12 – Brecon Beacons National Park (Western Area)

Macro of icicles at Sgwd Gwladus (VP1). Canon 5D IV, 100mm f/2.8 at 100mm, ISO 400, 1/125s at f/5.6. Tripod. Mar.

Henrhyd waterfall in autumn (VP4).
Canon 5D IV, 16-35mm f/4 at 30mm, ISO 100, 3.2s at f/16. Tripod. Polariser & 6ND. Oct.

Viewpoint 4 – Henrhyd Falls

Famed as the highest waterfall in South Wales, Henrhyd Falls plunges into a small wooded gorge from a height of 27 metres. Film buffs may recognise it as the Batcave in a recent Batman film, The Dark Knight Rises. It's also another waterfall that you can stand behind, but as always with places like this, it can be very slippery under foot. From the car park (National Trust – free) you pass through two small kissing gates and follow the footpath down into the gorge. It's quite a steep descent but the path is very well maintained. After a few hundred metres the path levels out and you'll need to double back crossing over a wooded bridge, then head up the wooden staircase. I find the steps on this staircase largely spaced and steep, so those with limited mobility may find them tricky. From here it's onwards for a short distance to reach the falls. The path to your right will take you round and down to stand behind the falling water, or to the left will offer views close to the river. If water levels are low you can access the left side of the river bank enabling you to walk into the river and right up to the falls base, a spectacular view looking straight up.

Opposite: *Long exposure of Henrhyd waterfall up close. Canon 5D III, 16-35mm f/4 at 16mm, ISO 100, 30s at f/11. Tripod. Polariser & 6ND. May.*

Henrhyd waterfall in spring (VP4). Canon 5D III, 16-35mm f/4 at 17mm, ISO 50, 25s at f/20. Tripod. Polariser, 6ND & ND Grad. May.

How to get here

Viewpoint 4 – Henrhyd Falls

From the Glynneath crossroads head straight across on the A4109 towards the High street. Follow this road for 4 miles before turning right onto Camnant Road. Head down here for a mile-and-a-half and as the road starts to climb the National Trust (free) car park is on your left. Go through the kissing gate at the southern end of the car park to commence the walk down to the falls.

Parking Lat/Long: 51.795521 -3.6642898
Parking Postcode: SA10 9PG
OS Map grid ref: SN 853120
Map: OS Explorer Map OL12 – Brecon Beacons National Park (Western Area)

Accessibility

As you can imagine with what's effectively a rainforest climate, the going under foot is always going to be tricky, especially after heavy rain. Winter can bring ice and snow impeding progress. Add in undulating, rocky and slippery terrain and you do need to take care when walking the paths and algae covered rocks in the river can feel like sheet ice. All in all, you need a good level of mobility to explore this area, especially **Viewpoint 3 – Sgwd yr Eira** where the descent down and back up the steps are enough to make even the fittest person need time to catch their breath. The easiest to see is **Viewpoint 1 – Sgwd Gwladus** as the path for most of it is generally flat and well maintained. There's also a few smaller falls along the way to keep your interest.

Best time of year/day

Spring and autumn are the best times to visit. In spring the trees will be a vivid green and autumn is when the native woodland comes to life with vibrant red and orange tones framing the falls. In prolonged cold snaps the waterfalls can freeze over with huge icicles hanging down from them, making any visit a spectacular experience. Sunlight directly hitting the falls will differ throughout the year as the season's change, which can cause harsh shadows or unevenly lit scenes making exposure difficult. My favoured weather for photography here is bright, but overcast.

Mynydd Illtud is an extensive area of high-elevation common land located just outside the village of Libanus near Brecon and is a fabulous place to visit for a wander and to photograph the panoramic views of the surrounding countryside and mountains. Near to the Brecon Beacons National Parks' visitor centre (aka the Mountain Centre) and covering over 250 hectares, the common land here is a designated SSSI (site of special scientific interest) for its unique saucer-shaped pools and marshy areas, scoured out of the bedrock in the last ice age. As well as a great place for landscape photography there is much here for those interested in wildlife and floral photography.

What to shoot and viewpoints

The common is criss-crossed with paths with the protected pools and bog (sphagnum) vegetation near to the visitor centre. It's a great place to bring your macro lens for the flora and fauna that inhabit the pools. In the summer months, cotton grass blooms and waves in the breeze, quite a rare sight these days and this plant is only found at a few upland areas in South Wales. The area is biologically diverse with 11 different species of dragonflies and damselflies, along with 18 different beetles, over 50 species of spiders together with up to 70 different mosses and lichens; in all 129 types of plants have all been recorded here. The plants are abundant in summer but starting in the autumn when the foliage starts to die down and the weather becomes wet, the pools grow to substantial sizes attracting countless species of wintering water fowl such as teal, wigeon and pochard. Short-eared owls are not uncommon and can be seen quartering the marshy areas.

The Grand Views

As well as wildlife there are superb views to photograph of the Brecon Beacons summits. The main national park summits of Pen y Fan, Cribyn and Corn Du stand proudly on the horizon to the south, while Sugar Loaf and the Black Mountains are visible to the east. A variety of focal lengths can be used up here, even a long telephoto as it will allow you to hone in on distant views of the peak; hopefully in their snowy winter coat. Wide angle lenses will be perfect for getting down into some of the pools with the wildflowers, really emphasising the foreground interest with the summits positioned in the far distance.

How to get here

From Llandovery head out east on the A40 and follow it for 12 miles. On entering Sennybridge, take the right turn signed A4215. After half-a-mile join the A4067 and follow this for 2 miles before turning left back onto the A4215. Head down this road for a further 2 miles before turning left at the crossroads. Follow this lane for about a mile and you'll arrive at the cattle grid that indicates the start of the common. The pools will be just on your right a few hundred yards further along the road, with the visitor centre at the next right junction.

Parking Lat/Long: 51.927966, -3.4910452
Parking Postcode: LD3 8ER
OS Map grid ref: SN 975265
Map: OS Explorer Map OL12 – Brecon Beacons National Park (Western Area)

Accessibility ♿

You can access the common via the minor road that runs across it, there's a cattle grid at either end and occasional lay by parking areas along the route. Most of the paths are made up of short grass, compacted mud tracks so it's easy going and even those with limited mobility should be able to explore the area with ease. There's also plenty of parking at the National Parks Visitor Centre and an adjacent tea room.

Best time of year/day

As with most landscapes, early morning and late evening will provide the best light with golden tones and long shadows thanks to the low angle of the sun. Summertime is best for wild flowers and the beautiful cotton grass that grows across the pools. Being 335m above sea level, snow is a regular sight across the common in winter and this location offers a safe and accessible outing to photograph snowy scenes. The afternoon light is best to help illuminate the distance summits of the Pen y Fan massif giving scenes a great sense of depth and scale.

One of the pools reflecting passing rain clouds. Canon 5D IV, 24-70mm f/2.8 at 28mm, ISO 50, 1/20s at f/10. Tripod. Polariser & ND Grad. July.

Frozen pools in winter with snow on the Beacons.
Canon 5D III, 24-70mm f/2.8 at 31mm, ISO 320, 1/800s at f/10. Tripod. Polariser & ND Grad. Jan.

Cotton grass in summer looking towards Pen y Fan & Corn Du summits.
Canon 5D III, 24-70mm f/2.8 at 31mm, ISO 200, 1/125s at f/11. Tripod. Polariser. June.

Wide view across the Beacons countryside towards snow capped summits. Canon 5D III, 24-70mm f/2.8 at 50mm, ISO 160, 1/160s at f/8. Tripod. Polariser & ND Grad. Jan.

As with many hill locations in the Brecon Beacons, it is the elevated views across the neighbouring countryside that make them so attractive to visit and Pen y Crug (331m) is no exception. Standing on the summit of this hill (aka The Crug), situated above the Usk Valley, is one of the most impressive iron age hillforts in the Brecon Beacons National Park. Its ramparts, which today are rounded earthwork banks and ditches, would once have been impressive stone and earth revetments with a wooden defensive palisade built on top.

Little survives of the round houses, stock pens and granaries that once occupied the interior of the hillfort. During the Iron Age, Pen-y-Crug would have been a very busy place; where people lived, worked, farmed and traded. It is clear to see why our ancestors chose to build a settlement here. The hill has extensive views of the central Brecon Beacons summits, with views to a number of neighbouring hillforts including Coed Fenni Fach on the adjacent hill and to Twyn-y-Gaer on Mynydd Illtud on the other side of the valley, as well as 360 degree views across the rolling countryside – a great place to spot any approaching raiders, and these days for us to take panoramic photographs.

Opposite: Looking across the Brecon Beacons countryside covered in the snow at sunset. Canon 5D IV, 24-70mm f/2.8 at 24mm, ISO 100, 1/125s at f/11. Tripod. ND Grad. Dec.

Telephoto view, looking down on the fields near sunset.
Canon 5D III, 300mm f/2.8 at 300mm, ISO 250, 1/320s at f/8. Jan.

What to shoot and viewpoints

Approach: 0.5m/0.7km, 299ft/91m, 20 minutes

After a short walk you will be on top of the world gazing across the Brecon Beacons National Park. There are some very shapely windswept trees here that make for interesting photos, especially in winter with their stark branches. . However the main subjects for photos are the expansive vistas that greet you on reaching the trig point around the summit. Here are views far to the eastern Black Mountains, west and north across the countryside and also south across the picturesque Usk Valley towards the main backbone of the Pen y Fan massif. Pen y Crug is definitely on the must do list when visiting the area for these panoramic views.

Pack a variety of lenses, a long telephoto if you have it will allow you to cherry pick your compositions and choose distant views, such as isolated trees on hills, the snaking of the field hedges or just simply zooming in on the rugged summits of Pen y Fan, Corn Du and Cribyn, hopefully with a dusting of snow to really make them glow in the light. In late afternoon, look out for long shadows from nearby trees and don't be afraid to shoot into the light for atmospheric backlit lighting conditions and sun rays if it's misty. There's an array of blackthorn and hawthorn trees up here so keep an eye out for birds feeding on the berries, especially fieldfare in autumn and red kites soaring overhead.

How to get here

From the A470 roundabout by Brecon, head into the town and at the first roundabout take the second exit onto the B4601, then shortly after take the second exit and head down here for half a mile. Turn right onto the Struet/B4520 before taking the next left onto Priory Hill. Follow this for around 2 miles before turning left signed towards the golf course. Half a mile down here there is a large lay-by on your right, park here then walk over the road to access the hill fort via the bridleway.

Parking Lat/Long: 51.968811, -3.4163873
Parking Postcode: LD3 9LW
OS Map grid ref: SO 027309
Map: OS Explorer Map OL12 – Brecon Beacons National Park (Western Area)

Accessibility

The best views are from the near the trig point. The footpath up can get very muddy near the start in most seasons other than summer. Following the track there is some loose ground to walk over, the least strenuous route is to skirt around the left side and come up the south side of the hill. Near the top, there's quite a few up and downs, as you cross over the now grassy ramparts.

Best time of year/day

Late afternoon or early morning can see spectacular conditions, sometimes mist hanging in the valley but mainly the soft sunlight that will bathe across every undulation in the landscape below you. It can snow here in winter due to its altitude and it offers a great vantage point over the Usk valley towards the main snowy summits of the Brecon Beacons.

Opposite top: Telephoto of Cribyn mountain, taken from Pen y Crug. Canon 5D III, 300mm f/2.8 at 300mm, ISO 400, 1/320s at f/8. Tripod. Jan.

Opposite middle: Late sun backlights fields and trees below Pen y Crug. Canon 5D III, 70-200mm f/2.8 at 140mm, ISO 250, 1/160s at f/8. Tripod. Jan.

Opposite bottom: Wide view across the snowy landscape towards the main Beacon summits. Canon 5D IV, 16-35mm f/4 at 16mm, ISO 100, 1/40s at f/16. Tripod. Polariser & ND Grad. Dec.

Wild pony and a robin in the snow with Black Mountains in the distance. Canon 5D IV, 70-200mm f/2.8 at 182mm, ISO 500, 1/200s at f/6.3. Dec.

⑦ THE PEN Y FAN MASSIF

The Pen y Fan massif is the crowning glory of the Brecon Beacons National Park. At 886 metres (2,907 ft), Pen y Fan is the highest mountain in South Wales. Along with its neighbour Corn Du (873m/2,864 ft) both peaks have very distinctive flat tops, a characteristic of many summits in South Wales caused by the soft brownstone rock being eroded away leaving the harder plateau rock behind.

Below Corn Du, is Cwm Llwch, a deep hollow or cirque that was scooped out by grinding glaciers during the last ice age and at its base is a small glacial lake, Llyn Cwm Llwch. The Pen y Fan massif is an accessible place for mountain photography with a relatively short approach, and anywhere along the ridge that connects the peaks (known as the saddle) and on their summits are fabulous places to spend time photographing beautiful mountain scenery and panoramic views.

What to shoot and viewpoints

Pen y Fan Summit via the Beacons Way (aka the Motorway)
1.9m/3.1km, elevation gain 1,383ft/422m, 1 hour+
You can get your mountain fix here without too much effort. The main path from Pont ar Daf car park is nicknamed The Motorway with many thousands walking up this route every year to the summits – it will be busy at weekends especially in the summer. I'd recommend this path for a first time visit as it's nigh on impossible to get lost and will give you a good idea of the terrain and views to be had. It is a well-maintained path, easy under foot, with a gradual incline and takes around 45 minutes in good conditions to reach the ridgeline.

The path starts from the southern end Pont ar Daf car park. There's usually a burger van here on busy days and an interpretive map of the area. This path is part of the Beacons Way which runs across most of the national park. Heading over the small river crossing via a bridge, the path winds its way up to the Bwlch Duwynt ridge (meaning windy pass in Welsh). From here head north east along the ridge line to ascend first over Corn Du, then down and up onto Pen y Fan summit.

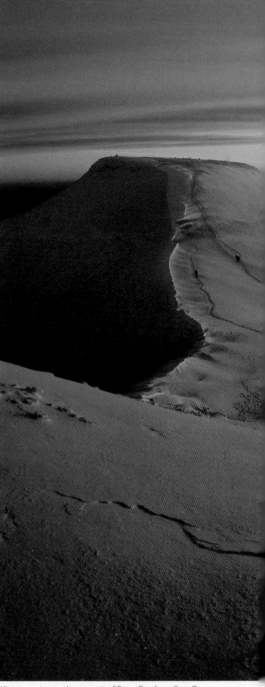

Wintry sunrise on the summit of Pen y Fan from Corn Du. Five image stitch. Canon 5D III, 24-70mm f/2.8 at 24mm, ISO 100, 1/50s at f/13. Tripod. ND Grad. Jan.

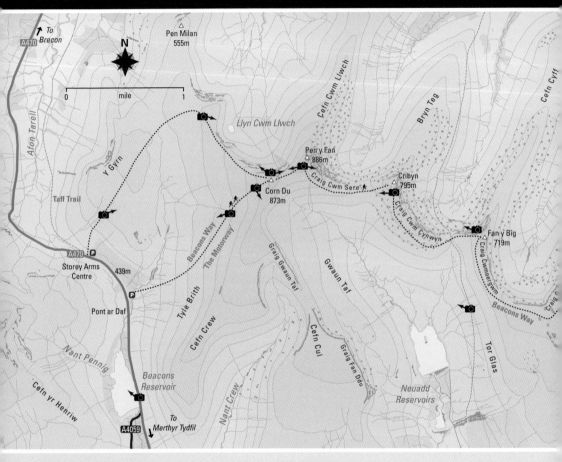

How to get here

From the Severn Bridge, head west on the M4 and turn off at junction 32 and head north on the A470. You'll meet some roundabouts en route north, but keep following signs for Brecon/A470 and it will bring you to the Storey Arms, 30 miles from M4. The most popular parking spots are located just off the A470 near to the Storey Arms outdoor education centre. Both are free, either park opposite the centre itself or slightly to the south at a car park called Pont ar Daf. Paths to the peaks start from both car parks. The main path, the Motorway starts from Pont ar Daf car park.

Parking Lat/Long: 51.869277 -3.4728545
Parking Postcode: LD3 8NL
OS Map grid ref: SN 98690 19993
Map: OS Explorer Map OL12 – Brecon Beacons National Park (Western Area)

Accessibility

Although accessible and popular, this location is a mountain environment and it is important to be correctly dressed for mountain weather – a hat and gloves as well as a rain jacket – with a pair of good boots and if you use them, walking poles. Even if it is a sunny day, it can be cold on the tops and rain showers can blow in. Bring a packed lunch and a hot drink if you plan on an extended stay on the tops.

Best time of year/day

Any time of day can be profitable for photography but it is important to check weather conditions to benefit your photography. Sunset can be great in summer due to it setting further north, making the most of side-lighting illuminating slope contours. Make sure to give yourself plenty of time to get up high – be on the summit at least an hour before sunset – and bring a head torch for a dark descent or stay for some night photography. However being on the summit for sunrise is something I'd recommend everyone putting on their list – even better in winter with a snowy sunrise for a truly magical experience. Again, set off early.

The morning sun rises at Pen y Fan looking across the path towards Cribyn.
Canon 5D IV, 16-35mm f/4 at 16mm, ISO 100, 1/60s at f/16. Polariser. Sep.

Early walkers on Pen y Fan summit before dawn. Canon 5D IV, 24-70mm f/2.8 at 70mm, ISO 1250, 1/100s at f/4. Sep.

Once on the ridgeline and looking out to the vastness of the environment in front of you, it is important to remain conscious of working on composition and capturing scale. Use natural elements to create interesting foreground and also focus in on any aspects that are unique to this region, especially the summit plateaus and sweeping ridges. Including fellow walkers in a composition adds a sense of scale to the landscape. The name Pen y Fan roughly translates to 'the Top Peak or the Beacons Summit' and 360 degree views greet you from the summit on a clear day when you can see the Bristol Channel, round to Carmarthen Bay and the Gower Peninsula to the south west. While to the west and north will be the Black and Cambrian Mountains, the town of Brecon and much of Mid Wales and the South Wales valleys'; even as far as Exmoor and South Shropshire can be seen. At the summit, I'd thoroughly recommend perching on the cairn to grab a selfie, a great way to celebrate all that effort on the climb. The bragging rights are not to be sniffed at; this is, after all, one of the highest points in southern Britain.

Looking back at Corn Du summit and distant hills. Canon 5D IV, 24-70mm f/2.8 at 70mm, ISO 320, 1/100s at f/14. Tripod. Polariser. Sep.

The 'Diving Board' at Fan y Big. Canon 5D IV, 16-35mm f/2.8 at 20mm, ISO 500, 1/80s at f/14. Tripod. Polariser. Sep.

If you're still feeling energetic keep going east. Continuing beyond the Corn Du and Pen y Fan summits is Cribyn (795m/2608ft) with its pyramid shape and steep sloping sides reaching the valley floor. Both Cribyn and Pen y Fan summits are marked by the remains of bronze age burial cairns. There are few more points of interest along the Beacons Way, one in particular is the summit of Fan y Big (719m/2,359 ft) giving you a great panorama back towards the major peaks of Cribyn, Pen y Fan and Corn Du; with its multiple ridges, cwms and summits. Here you will also find a well-known plinth of rock known as the diving board. It projects out over Cwm Cynwyn and features in many a dramatic photograph.

Early morning mists and clouds envelop the Brecon Beacons, from Pen y Fan summit. Canon 5D IV, 70-200mm f/2.8 at 200mm, ISO 100, 1/60s at f/10. Tripod. Polariser. Sep.

A lone walker makes their way through the snow towards Pen y Fan.
Canon 5D III, 24-70mm f/2.8 at 28mm, ISO 100, 1/40s at f/13. Tripod. ND Grad. Jan.

Above: *Looking over Llyn Cwm Llwch and the valleys. Canon 5D IV, 24-70mm f/2.8 at 30mm, ISO 200, 15s at f/10. Tripod. 6ND. Sep.*

Below: *Abstract of snow textures at sunrise. Canon 5D III, 24-70mm f/2.8 at 24mm, ISO 100, 1/500s at f/13. Tripod. Jan.*

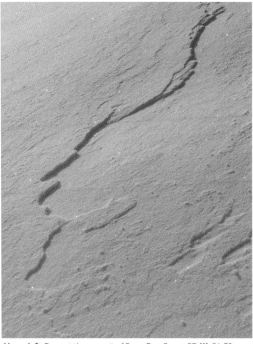

Above middle: *Hill runners at sunrise on Pen y Fan. Canon 5D III, 70-200mm f/2.8 at 200mm, ISO 100, 1/50s at f/11. Tripod. Jan.*

Above left: *Drew at the summit of Pen y Fan. Canon 5D III, 24-70mm f/2.8 at 24mm, ISO 100, 1/80s at f/11. Tripod. Polariser. Jan.*

A hill walker stands on the summit of Cribyn at sunrise – photographed from Pen y Fan. Canon 5D IV, 70-200mm f/2.8 at 150mm, ISO 100, 1/6s at f/11, Tripod, Polariser, Sep.

East of Brecon town, between the Central Beacons and the Black Mountains, is the largest natural lake in Wales. Llangorse Lake is a mile long and not only has fantastic mountain views and is home to a diverse amount of wildlife but also features a Crannog; an ancient lake dwelling. Llangorse is surrounded by a patchwork of green hills, fields and meadows, much of it common land with a network of footpaths to explore. This area is a beautiful place for photography and to just spend time.

What to shoot and viewpoints

Viewpoint 1 – Crannog

The Crannog that stands on the lake shore today is a reconstruction of what these island homesteads once looked like. They were built upon layers of stone, earth and brushwood held in place by oaken palisades to form an artificial island, with a gangway for access to a roundhouse dwelling. Common in Scotland and Ireland, the Crannog at Llangorse is the only one found in Wales and England and is thought to have been constructed in 916 AD by the King of Brycheiniog .

From the car park head down towards the boat hire centre and beyond to access the floating jetty. This is a good viewpoint to capture the Crannog in its environment with a distant Pen y Fan and the surrounding summits in the background; a good place to try out some long exposures using neutral density filters to blur any water movement. Back near the car park, walk down through the trees to access the roundhouse itself. As well as photographing the building, there's also a balcony around it providing another viewpoint of the surrounding hills and any passing wildlife. This area is very popular with wild fowl birds, especially migrants in the autumn and young chicks learning to swim in the spring. Lastly back near to the wooded entrance head around to the right where there's a slipway and moored boats. This allows access close to the Crannog itself, depending on the water level. Water lilies and wild flowers grow abundantly here in the summer months which add a splash of colour to the scene.

How to get here

If approaching from Merthyr Tydfil, head north east on the main A465 'Heads of the Valleys' road for around 5 miles, then take the exit towards A4281. Follow this road for about a mile or so, then take the B4560 roundabout exit towards Llangynidr. Head down here for 3 miles, then take a right turn signed Llangattock. After a further 3 miles go through Llangattock village and out the other side, coming to a T-junction. Take a left turn then a right over the bridge into Crickhowell town. Follow this road then take a left to get on the main A40 road. After 6 miles you'll reach the village of Bwlch, then take the right turn (B4560) signed to Llangorse. After 4 miles, take the left turning towards to lake and the parking is found at the end of the road.

Parking Lat/Long: 51.935246, -3.2709405
Parking Postcode: LD3 7TR
OS Map grid ref: SO 127270
Map: OS Explorer Map OL12 – Brecon Beacons National Park (Western Area)

Accessibility &

The main lakeside area and jetty are all easily accessible from the car park. Access to the Crannog is only during working hours however you can manage a photo when it is closed from around the sides of the entrance without too much problem. The pathways around the western side of the lake round towards the bird hide are over uneven common land, including some boardwalks and stream crossings; one of which has a few steps up and over a bridge. Parking for both viewpoints is free and offer good views within a short walk. The path towards the bird hide from the church includes access through farmland so close gates as you cross fields and keep dogs under control if livestock present.

Best time of year/day

The lake is a great place to visit all-year-round. Arrive in autumn or winter on cold clear mornings and you may be greeted by swathes of mist hanging over the lake's surface, sometimes combined with frosty reed beds. Visit in the winter time and you may be lucky enough to have snow on the surrounding countryside and summits making great backdrops to your images. In spring and in to summer the lake is at its best for wildlife and birds, wildflowers, reed beds, irises and water lilies. Water levels change here with the rainfall throughout the year so expect the paths that lead around the common to be boggy or flooded in some months, a good pair of boots or wellingtons is advisable if walking through these areas.

***Opposite**: The Crannog and water lily pads in summer. Canon 5D III, 24-70mm f/2.8 at 24mm, ISO 400, 1/125s at f/10. Tripod. Polariser & ND Grad. June.*

Morning sun illuminates reed bed and the Crannog at Llangorse Lake.
Canon 5D IV, 24-70mm f/2.8 at 70mm, ISO 320, 1/20s at f/13. Tripod. Polariser & ND Grad. Oct.

Beautiful stained glass window in the bird hide. Canon 5D III, 24-70mm f/2.8 at 70mm, ISO 400, 1/250s at f/5. June.

Viewpoint 2 – Bird Hide

Llangorse lake bird hide is a fabulous place to spend an early morning or late afternoon when birds will be most active. Found at the south of the lake, it's accessed by pathways across the common land. The easiest way to get to it is from the small car park at Llangasty village hall then by walking down the lane a short distance and turning down a farm track heading north. After a few hundred metres take a right before the yard and through the gate into the field. Follow the field down into the woods and the bird hide is found straight on after a short walk. There's a small jetty here allowing water level photography, a popular area for swans and home to wild flowers.

The bird hide is a work of art, constructed with a roof of Welsh water reeds it also features stained glass windows. The lake is home to twenty-three plant species that are rare to Wales and is an important stop-over for migrating birds. In the autumn and winter you may see tufted duck, goldeneye, water rail and the great-crested grebe; in the summer, reed buntings and reed warblers will be flitting about in front of the hide and if you're lucky, you'll spot a hobby cruising over the lake hunting the many species of dragonflies that breed on the lake; this super fast small falcon is amazing to watch. Heading west from the bird hide, the lake trail takes you across the common land which is stile free; there are many rare orchids to be found in the meadows along with various colourful butterflies and day moth species, it's worth packing the macro lens for these.

Top: *Mynydd Troed viewed from near the bird hide. Canon 5D III, 24-70mm f/2.8 at 42mm, ISO 160, 1/80s at f/11. Polariser. June.*

Middle: *Irises and horses on the common at VP1. Canon 5D III, 24-70mm f/2.8 at 55mm, ISO 320, 1/200s at f/10. Polariser. June.*

Bottom: *Orchids and wildflowers near the bird hide. Canon 5D III, 24-70mm f/2.8 at 27mm, ISO 200, 1/400s at f/5. Polariser. June.*

*The excellently designed bird hide. Canon 5D III, 24-70mm
f/2.8 at 24mm, ISO 100, 1/60s at f/6.3. June.*

Mynydd Llangorse (515m/1690ft) stands on the western edge of the Black Mountains and is a superb vantage point to gaze out over the expanse of the Brecon Beacons National Park countryside. A variety of paths and bridleways criss-cross the mountain offering several options in a small area. This walk is all about the views with Llangorse Lake glistening in the valley below and the Pen y Fan massif summits looming in the distance to the west. This is a great hill to walk up in a short space of time with spectacular views to photograph.

What to shoot and viewpoints

To the summit: 1 mile/1.6km, 154m/506ft of ascent, 45 minutes.
Parking in the lay-by at the base of Cockit Hill, the walk takes you up a broad grassy path with a bridleway sign to Cathedine pointing the way. Although the climb up to the trig point isn't extremely steep, it is a bit of a slog. You are rewarded en route, however, with a great view of Llangorse Lake. About half way up the hill, large rocky mounds and outcrops start to appear, these are thought to have been Iron Age hill forts. Today they make a much needed shelter from the worst of the wind and rain, should it be an inclement day. They also make great foreground interests for your images.

When the ground starts to level off near the summit, the path splits, take the right path past a distinctive boulder, a small cairn and by some boggy pools. Eventually you'll reach the characteristic white trig point adorned with a red Welsh dragon. This is a great place to take a well earned rest and get the camera out.

Here you can shoot wide incorporating interesting foregrounds such as the pools, boulders or even the trig point itself. Generally, the composition is to include Llangorse Lake in the valley below and if visibility permits, Pen Y Fan in the distance. As such you'll need to check the sun angle times to make sure you're not shooting into the sun, this is a south west view so summer time sunsets should result in good side lighting. Being up high it is always good to remember to shoot with a long telephoto as well as wide-angle. Using a longer focal length will allow you to zone in on distant scenes, especially in the golden hour where the sun will cast long shadows across the farmland below. You can either follow the paths that circle the summit and come back to the parking via a different route or alternatively take various pathways down to the lake itself.

If you have the energy, from the same lay-by you can head north up Mynydd Troed (609m/1,998ft) for similar elevated views; both can be done in a day.

View to the lake from Cockit Hill. Canon 5D IV, 24-70mm f/2.8 at 28mm, ISO 200, 1/30s at f/16. Tripod. Polariser & ND Grad. Oct.

How to get here

From Merthyr Tydfil, head north east on the main A465 'Heads of the Valleys' road for around 5 miles, then take the exit towards A4281. Follow this road for about a mile or so, then take the B4560 roundabout exit towards Llangynidr. Head down here for 3 miles, then take a right turn signed Llangattock. After a further 3 miles go through Llangattock village and out the other side, coming to a T- junction. Take a left turn then a right over the bridge into Crickhowell town. Follow this road then take a left to get on the main A40 road to head west. After 6 miles you'll reach the village of Bwlch, take the right turn (B4560) signed to Llangorse. After 1.5 miles, turn right signed for Gilfach Farm. After half-a-mile take another right turn and ascend the road to a cattle grid before reaching a flat summit with two lay-bys, one either side of the road. There's parking for around four cars here, with more parking space found further along the lane. Walk up Cockit hill to reach the viewpoint – it's just over a mile walk to the trig point with good views along the way.

Parking Lat/Long: 51.947115, -3.2225018
Parking Postcode: LD3 7UL
OS Map grid ref: SO 160283
Map: OS Explorer Map OL12 – Brecon Beacons National Park (Western Area)

Top: Setting sun on hazy summer evening. Canon 5D III, 24-70mm f/2.8 at 30mm, ISO 100, 1/160s at f/18. Tripod. ND Grad. June.

Accessibility

Although the walk up this hill isn't far (a mile), it's still a fair slog and will require a good pair of walking boots and strong legs. In summer the ground is hard and compacted making the ascent easier, but when there is inclement weather the going is loose and slippery under foot in places, more so after snow. There is a small raised plateau next to the parking which has a good view down to the lake and the distant summits, ideal for those less mobile. However, the best sights of the surrounding landscape are from higher up the hill.

Best time of year/day

Sunrises and sunsets can be spectacular from this vantage point. Key times of the year are at sunrise on cold, clear autumn or winter mornings. If there is a temperature inversion when low mist hangs over the lake and the valley below, the nearby summits can appear as islands floating above the sea of clouds. In late spring into summer the sunsets are great with vivid side lighting colouring the fields and countryside along with long shadows adding to the depth. The hills are covered in heather and in August when they flower add a purple splash of colour to your foregrounds.

Above left: Looking back to Mynydd Troed. Canon 5D III, 24-70mm f/2.8 at 24mm, ISO 100, 1/6s at f/14. Tripod. Polariser. June.
Above right: Golden hour looking down on the fields. Canon 5D III, 24-70mm f/2.8 at 70mm, ISO 100, 1/10s at f/14. Tripod. June.

Looking across the Brecon Beacons in evening light. Llangorse lake below and Pen y Fan in the distance. Canon 5D III, 24-70mm f/2.8 at 24mm, ISO 100, 1/50s at f/14. Tripod. Polariser & ND Grad. June.

Meandering through the Welsh countryside the isolated Monmouthshire & Brecon Canal is a beautiful and peaceful area for canal photography amongst the wooded Usk valley. The navigable section of the canal runs for 35 miles from Brecon in the west to the Pontymoile basin in the south east. It is a haven for wildlife – bring a long lens if you have one – and is a favourite with nature-lovers, walkers and cyclists thanks to the flat and easy-going tow path that hugs the canal.

What is nowadays popularly referred to as the 'Mon & Brec' started life as two separate canals: the Brecknock & Abergavenny Canal and the Monmouthshire Canal. The 35-mile navigable section seen today is mostly the former. Though originally constructed to transport coal, lime and agricultural products the canals were used extensively by ironmasters as their main transport network, bringing raw iron ore up the canal from Newport to Llanfoist Wharf and by tramroads to the iron works and returning with trams loaded with iron, the finished product. Remains of this heritage can still be viewed along the canal today including wharfs and lime kilns.

What to shoot and viewpoints

This peaceful and almost entirely rural waterway is a must-see for nature-lovers. As the Mon & Brec is not currently accessible from any other waterway, most people cruise it on a hire-boat. There are so many places of interest along the 35 mile stretch, every mile is a picture, so I've included a variety of places to visit.

Llangynidr Locks

The main viewpoint here is the Llangynidr locks. Being a contour canal that follows the natural lie of the land, locks are in short supply on the Brecon & Abergavenny stretch but near to Llangynidr there are five to choose from, including one sequence that has three locks in short succession. Along the tow path coming from the west (bridge 136) you'll pass a picturesque area with a wooden bench situated underneath a huge oak tree, also just over the river is someone's garden home to large and vibrant rhododendrons and a beautiful weeping willow, adding a splash of colour to your shots. Walking further east, you'll pass the sign for Llangynidr locks and reach a pretty arch bridge (bridge 135). You can get good reflections here if you head to the mooring point further along and look back, with trees reflected on the far bank; spectacular in the autumn. »

Upper Llangynidr locks. Canon 5D III, 24-70mm f/2.8 at 33mm, ISO 100, 1/160s at f/10. June.

Lower Llangynidr locks. Canon 5D III, 24-70mm f/2.8 at 24mm, ISO 250, 1/400s at f/8. June.

Historic signage on canal bridge. Canon 5D III, 24-70mm f/2.8 at 45mm, ISO 160, 1/15s at f/10. June.

How to get here

From Merthyr Tydfil, head north east on the main A465 'Heads of the Valleys' road for around 5 miles, then take the exit towards A4281. Follow this road for about a mile or so, then take the B4560 roundabout exit towards Llangynidr. Head down here for 3 miles, then take a right turn signed Llangattock. After a further 3 miles go through Llangattock village and out the other side, coming to a T-junction. Take a left turn and you should see the Crickhowell bridge on your right. Head straight down this road for around 4 miles. Once in Llangynidr village, you'll cross over a bridge which goes over the canal, park in the bays to the immediate right. The locks are found to the west along the tow path.

Parking Lat/Long: 51.872603, -3.2329872
Parking Postcode: NP8 1LU
OS Map grid ref: SO 152200
Map: OS Explorer Map OL13 – Brecon Beacons National Park (Eastern Area)

Accessibility ♿

The beauty of the canal is that you can park up or be dropped off anywhere along the river and within a few steps you're onto the footpath alongside it. The tow path is flat and well maintained and is suitable for wheelchair users. Each bridge is numbered (from east to west) so if you're feeling adventurous and want to walk it all over a week, you can come back to the same point and do it in stages. There are many pubs en route so you are never far from a spot for lunch, dinner or just a well earned pint.

Best time of year/day

The canal is accessible all year round and can be good whatever the weather. It is spectacular in autumn when the vivid russet tones paint the canal side or when flush with green in spring and summer. It's a nice break from the heat in summer as there are some well wooded sections to head into the shade. Early morning or late evening provide soft, warm lighting coupled with dappled shadows from any trees or foliage. If it snows, head to the canal early to catch the freshly fallen snow without footprints, and photograph the curve of the canal and the bridges.

Flat and easy going tow path. Shaded walks in the summer.
Canon 5D III, 24-70mm f/2.8 at 59mm, ISO 250, 1/30s at f/5.6. Tripod. Polariser. June.

Reaching the cascade of three locks further on is a good point of interest, even without the camera it's great to watch the narrowboats navigate up or down through the locks as water is moved from one lock to another. If you follow the canal further east you'll reach the last two locks where the canal passes over a river and a waterfall; glimpse through the trees to see the mountains beyond. Lastly in the village is the final lock, with a great canal map carved into a bench. It's a beautiful spot, right in the heart of the national park and there's a pub here, the Coach & Horses, a great spot for a well earned lunch.

Good resting spot on the path near Llangynidr locks. Canon 5D III, 24-70mm f/2.8 at 35mm, ISO 100, 1/125s at f/10. June.

Other points of interest along the route

• **Brecon Terminus – postcode: LD3 7EW**
At the western end of the canal lies the terminus in the market town of Brecon, backed by quaint cottages. Here you can hire boats or take a day trip on the canal with one of the canal boat companies.

• **Talybont drawbridge – postcode: LD3 7UZ**
The drawbridge is a unique design in which the road swings up on one side like a lever. It allows just enough space underneath for a boat to pass. Nearby is the relic of an old aqueduct, now no longer used but handily situated next to a great pub.

• **Llanfoist Wharf – postcode: NP7 9NG**
A very picturesque location a quarter of the way up the Blorenge mountain near to Abergavenny. It dates back to the early 1800s and was built to transfer pig iron from the tramroad, which came down the side of the Blorenge mountain to the canal but today the buildings are used as holiday properties. Just to the west of here towards Govilon are some spectacular wooded sections which go vivid oranges in autumn.

Canal map engraved into a bench near Llangynidr locks. Canon 5D III, 24-70mm f/2.8 at 28mm, ISO 250, 1/400s at f/6.3. June.

Top: Near Llanfoist. Canon 5D III, 24-70mm f/2.8 at 70mm, ISO 250, 1/6s at f/5.6. Tripod. Polariser. June. **Above**: Canal slogan. Canon 5D III, 24-70mm f/2.8 at 33mm, ISO 250, 1/1000s at f/4.5. June.

Top: Llanfoist Wharf. Canon 5D III, 24-70mm f/2.8 at 35mm, ISO 250, 1/200s at f/8. June. **Above**: Talybont Drawbridge. Canon 5D III, 24-70mm f/2.8 at 24mm, ISO 320, 1/400s at f/8. June.

Cottages at the canal terminus in Brecon. Canon 5D III, 24-70mm f/2.8 at 30mm, ISO 250, 1/320s at f/8. Polariser. June.

The limestone cliffs and grassy humps of the Llangattock Escarpment are a relatively unknown location in the national park, but are surprisingly easy to reach and offer not only superb geological features but one of the best vistas in the area. This rocky ridge at the eastern end of the Brecon Beacons, dominates the skyline above Crickhowell and the view over the valley to Sugar Loaf (596m) is spectacular.

An active quarry in the 18th and 19th centuries, limestone was extracted from the ridge here and taken via tramline down to the Monmouthshire and Brecon canal in the valley below. It was then burnt in kilns and used as part of the iron-making process in the nearby iron foundries around Clydach Gorge. This was a time when the southern Welsh valleys were awash with pits and furnaces. Now the area is peaceful with just the croaks of ravens, mews of buzzards and bleat of sheep filling the air.

What to shoot and viewpoints

The best way to gain access to the cliff tops is to park at the quarry car park south of Llangattock village and walk west along the old tramline path. After a short distance along an easy going path bordered by large hawthorn trees (which are spectacular to photograph in spring when their white flowers emerge), you'll find yourself in a strange landscape of grass-covered conical spoil heaps, weathered limestone boulders and the ruins of old quarry buildings.

As you approach the first old building on your left, there's a natural pool of water on the path ahead, take a right turn and head along the wider track leading west, then after 200m or so look out for a well-worn sheep track on your left; it's easy to miss. A little narrow in places, this track takes you up and around the edge of the cliffs and along the top heading west. For what is a short ascent you really gain height fast and from here you'll have a spectacular aerial view of this majestic terrain.

To the north, you'll be tantalised by a series of wild-looking peaks and the ridges of the northern Brecon Beacons, while Crickhowell lies comfortably below in the Usk Valley. Behind you lies Abergavenny and its guardian mountain, the Sugar Loaf; this is a perfect location for sunrises all year. **»**

*Opposite top: Hawthorn trees in flower, looking to the Sugar Loaf. Canon 5D III, 24-70mm f/2.8 at 47mm, ISO 100, 1/60s at f/13. Polariser. June. **Bottom**: Table mountain and Crickhowell. Canon 5D IV, 70-200mm f/2.8 at 100mm, ISO 200, 1/20s at f/13. Tripod. Polariser & ND Grad. Oct.*

How to get here

From Merthyr Tydfil, take the A465 north east for about 10 miles, then keep an eye out for a left turn signposted Clydach North. Follow this road down into Llanelly and then out west across the mountainside, turn right at the next hairpin. Head down this single-track road and the car park is on your left after roughly a mile.

If coming from Crickhowell, head south out of the town over Crickhowell Bridge, turning left, then go right signposted Llangattock village. Follow this road for around a mile passing over the canal en-route, before taking a right turn at the woods. This is quite a narrow road which has some extreme uphill hairpin corners and cattle grids as it climbs up to the mountainside, so it is not suitable for wide or long vehicles. Once the road levels off, pass houses on the right and the car park is a few hundred metres on the right.

Parking Lat/Long: 51.831700, -3.1493211
Parking Grid Ref: NP8 1LG
OS Map grid ref: SO208154
Map: OS Explorer Map OL13 – Brecon Beacons National Park (Eastern Area)

Accessibility ♿

Most paths around the base of the cliffs are over flat ground shorn by sheep grazing. If you'd like to climb higher the going is a little trickier and in some places uneven following narrow tracks. Once on the cliff tops the paths through the heather are flat and relatively easy to walk through.

Best time of year/day

This is a superb location at sunrise when the sun rises behind the majestic Sugar Loaf. In high summer it will rise to its left and the rest of the year to the right. If the weather conditions play ball, you'll be standing on a vantage point gazing across amazing temperature inversions and misty valleys, perfect if coupled with the autumnal countryside. Late evening in summer is also good as you'll benefit from exquisite side lighting. Contrasting light is the key here to capture the depth and textures of the unique conical spoil heaps.

If you hear the clatter of metal on rocks this is because Llangattock is a very popular rock climbing spot. Going back down via the cliff top path to the original path, the gentle, level tramway winds its way west around the ridge into the Craig y Cilau National Nature Reserve at the escarpment's western edge. This area is occupied by a wonderful wealth of birdlife and wildflowers, a testament to a conscientious conservation effort. Wheatears, pied wagtails and willow warblers sing here from April to July, while frogs breed in the path side pools.

Above: *Early morning sun on the cliffs of the Craig y Cilau nature reserve. Canon 5D IV, 70-200mm f/2.8 at 200mm, ISO 320, 1/60s at f/11. Tripod. Polariser & ND Grad. Oct.* *Below*: *Sunrise at Usk valley. Canon 5D III. 16-35mm f/4 at 16mm, ISO 100, 1/2s at f/16. Tripod. ND Grad. June.*

Sheep resting in the shade and trees grow out of the quarry cliffs.
Canon 5D III, 24-70mm f/2.8 at 57mm, ISO 200, 1/125s at f/10. June.

*Early morning sun breaks through clouds causing crepuscular rays above the quarry landscape.
Canon 5D IV, 24-70mm f/2.8 at 47mm, ISO 100, 1/20s at f/16. Tripod. ND Grad. Oct.*

[12] CRICKHOWELL BRIDGE

Crickhowell is a small market town centrally located in the Brecon Beacons National Park. With many quaint shops, ancient inns and a castle ruins, there's plenty on offer for a rainy day or an easy wander around. One well known feature of Crickhowell town is its majestic thirteen-arch bridge that spans the river Usk. You'll drive over it en-route south to Llangattock Quarry or vice versa towards Llangorse Lake in the north.

This is the longest stone bridge in Wales and carries the A4077 road over the turbulent river Usk between Llangattock and Crickhowell. It has 12 or 13 arches, depending on which side you're looking at it from. Why the different number of arches on each side? A wider arch, replacing two earlier ones was added on the upstream side of the bridge at the Crickhowell end in the 1820s. All the arches aren't needed in normal conditions, but the apertures each side of the river Usk are essential when the river bursts its banks after heavy rainfall. It's a very picturesque bridge, and if viewed from the south allows views across the town towards the characteristic Sugar Loaf mountain.

What to shoot and viewpoints

You're best setting up your tripod along the south side of the river, either at the edge of the field or down by the river. Using the worn paths, head towards the tree on the left and down to the river bed. If the river is at normal levels, there should be a good amount of dry pebbles to walk along, giving lots of composition choices. Long exposures using neutral density filters could be effective here as there's a small weir that will lend itself to any water blurring. Try to find a nicely balanced composition including the river, bridge and Sugar Loaf mountain in the background. The use of wildflowers in spring provides quite an effective foreground element. As it's quite a busy road junction, you'll need to time your exposures in between the traffic lights. Distracting elements in any scene are annoying, so it's best to wait to avoid vehicles in the shot. There's also the pub on the opposite bank giving access down to the river through the beer garden.

The Usk is a very popular fishing river, so keep an eye out for any spawning salmon, sewin (Welsh sea trout) or brown trout heading up-stream during the summer. Dippers, grey wagtails and kingfishers are regularly seen on this stretch of the river.

Crickhowell Bridge and weir on the river Usk. Canon 5D III, 24-70mm f/2.8 at 24mm, ISO 100, 1/25s at f/16. Tripod. Polariser. June.

How to get here

From Merthyr Tydfil, head north east on the main A465 'Heads of the Valleys' road for around 5 miles, then take the exit towards A4281. Follow this road for about a mile, then take the B4560 roundabout exit towards Llangynidr. Head down here for 3 miles, then take a right turn signed Llangattock. After a further 3 miles go through Llangattock village and out the other side, coming to a T-junction. Take a left turn and you should see the bridge on your right. Parking is on your immediate left in the lay-by with room for about four cars just by the bridge on the south side. From here you'll need to cross the road to enter the field where the viewpoint is. You can either hop over the wall at the corner and descend the built in steps or head a further hundred yards along the field and through the gate. Access is allowed due to the local fishing rights on this stretch of river. From the gate head towards the river where you'll hook onto the well-worn paths down to the river itself.

Parking Lat/Long: 51.856257, -3.1433377
Parking Postcode: NP8 1HG
OS Map grid ref: SO213181
Map: OS Explorer Map OL13 – Brecon Beacons National Park (Eastern Area)

Accessibility

Generally easy to get to, either over the stone wall or through the field for those less agile. Nearer to the river however are uneven gullies which you'll to use to access the river so these can be loose under foot.

Best time of year/day

Being down by the river and the fact you'll always mostly be shooting in a northerly direction (to include the Sugar Loaf) early morning works best here with warm sunlight hitting the bridge side from the right, creating shadows and emphasising the stoney textures. Avoid low cloud days as the mountain will be obscured in the distance reducing the depth of the scene. The seasons will affect the shot here, not only adding a splash of green in the summer or orange in the autumn, but after heavy rainfall, the small weir will be submerged by a brown coloured raging torrent, so don't venture too close if it's like this. Some years it has been known to flood the field.

Fiery sunset and silhouetted trees at Dinefwr Park (p.308).
Canon 5D III, 24-70mm f/2.8 at 46mm, ISO 640, 1/200s at f/5, May.

CARMARTHENSHIRE

From the vast beaches of Pendine and Cefn Sidan, to the rugged hills of the Brecon Beacons, the landscape of Carmarthenshire is exceptionally varied. At its centre, rolling farmland is lined by winding rivers, ancient forests, parkland and castles. The south offers an abundance of sandy beaches and towering sea cliffs, while to the north and east, the terrain builds into the mountainous mainland regions of Wales. One of the oldest counties in Wales, Carmarthenshire, was the centre of the ancient south west Wales kingdom, formally known as Deheubarth. Even before this, the area was home to important civilisations, including the Romans, who made the region the most westerly stronghold of their empire. Today, this county, known as 'The Garden of Wales', and is a haven for visitors looking to explore its rich culture, mythical stories and legends.

Much of South Wales is predominantly English speaking, however throughout areas of mid-Wales, including Carmarthenshire, the traditional Welsh language still has a stronghold. The county resounds with words as soft as the hills and as broad as the valleys. Poet and writer Dylan Thomas settled here in the small fishing village of Laugharne, later moving into the now famous Boathouse. Close by is a clifftop garage, which Thomas transformed into his Writing Shed. Today, both buildings are museums to his life's work, containing memorabilia, photographs and notepads.

Nearby Laugharne Castle is one of the many castles dotted along this coastline but there's plenty of history to explore inland too. The Roman gold mines at Dolaucothi are worth

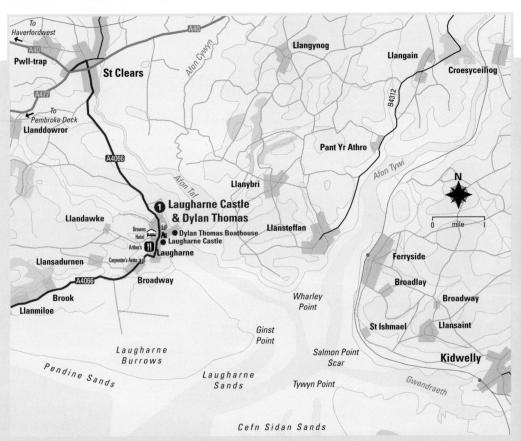

a visit as well as Paxton's Tower, a folly built high on a hill overlooking the River Towy. Along the valley, you'll discover more castles with stony ruins at Dryslwyn and Dinefwr Castle near Llandeilo, set among 800 acres of parkland.

Dinefwr Park was designed and shaped hundreds of years ago, including its picturesque deer park and fields of rare breed, White Park cattle. Dinefwr is also home to some of the oldest oak trees in Britain and if appreciation of trees and plants interests you, don't forget to stop off at the National Botanic Garden of Wales, located just to the south. Home to many exotic species of plants and flowers, it's open all year round and is a wonderful place to spend a day wandering through the themed gardens, butterfly house and the world's largest single-span glasshouse.

The north of the county is made up of dense woodland and rolling hills, a tapestry of farmland and hedgerows. To the east, the land rises as it passes the market town of Llandeilo on towards the prominent castle of Carreg Cennen, perched on a hilltop. From here, the land assumes an untamed feel – not surprisingly – as it marks the beginning of the Black Mountains and continues into the Brecon Beacons National Park.

Maps

- OS Explorer Map 177 – Carmarthen & Kidwelly, Pendine & Laugharne
- OS Explorer Map OL186 – Llandeilo & Brechfa Forest

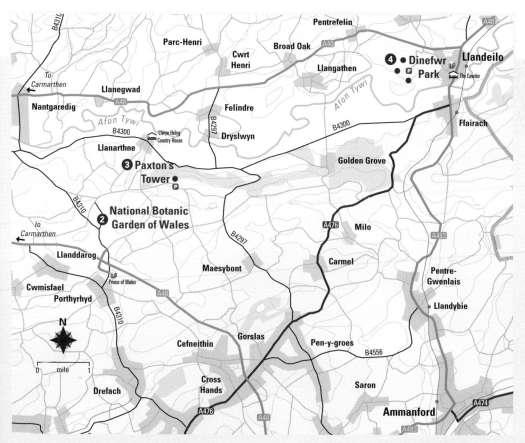

The dome-shaped glasshouse. National Botanic Garden of Wales (p.300).
Canon 5D III, 24-70mm f/2.8 at 42mm, ISO 250, 1/400s at f/7.1. ND Grad. Feb.

Wales's most famous literary figure, Dylan Thomas referred to Carmarthenshire as the 'fields of praise'. His family roots were here in Laugharne and it is Carmarthenshire that filled him with inspiration for some of his greatest works, including Under Milk Wood and Fern Hill. The Boathouse, where he lived, and the Writing Shed, where he penned his works, are now visitor attractions. They are notable features on a Dylan Thomas walk of around two miles along the Taf estuary, which also takes in views of the magnificent Laugharne castle, situated on a large rocky promontory.

What to shoot and viewpoints

Thomas and his wife lived in the Laugharne Boathouse with his family from 1949 to 1953. The Boathouse is now a museum, containing lots of memorabilia and much of the original furniture. Above the boathouse is Thomas' writing shed ("my word-splashed hut", as he described it). It is furnished with his desk and writing materials, as if Thomas himself had just nipped out. You can peer into this timeless setting through a glazed window.

Today there is a lovely two-mile route around Laugharne celebrating the author. The Dylan Thomas Birthday Walk is the setting for one of his best-loved works, 'Poem in October', in which he vividly describes a stroll around Laugharne on his 30th birthday. There are information boards full of information about Dylan's life and work at all the best viewpoints of this 'heron-priested shore'. As a bonus, if you do the walk on your own birthday (and can prove it), you can claim complimentary goodies from several local businesses. A free pint and a bag of chips anyone? »

Thomas's shed and the Boathouse, across the estuary at high tide. Canon 5D III, 70-200mm f/2.8 at 95mm, ISO 100, 1/250s at f/10. Tripod. Polariser & ND Grad. July.

Dylan Thomas's writing shed and Taf estuary. Canon 5D III, 24-70mm f/2.8 at 35mm, ISO 160, 1/1600s at f/8. Polariser. Jan.

How to get here

Carmarthen is the nearest major town so head west from here – signed the A40 road – and follow this for 9 miles. Take the left exit before the roundabout into St. Clears then take a right onto the High Street. Head down this road for 4 miles and as you enter the main square in Laugharne, turn left into the car park, where it's free to park. Here you'll find information boards and, close to the parking, the bridge. Follow the path and it will take you to the Boathouse and Writing Shed. For a different view, head south along the walk from the car park towards the water works, which allows views across the marsh towards the castle and Boathouse.

Parking Lat/Long: 51.769055, -4.4628592
Parking Postcode: SA33 4SP
OS Map grid ref: SN301106
Map: OS Explorer 177 – Carmarthen & Kidwelly, Pendine & Laugharne

Accessibility &

It's all on level ground here and in very close proximity to parking so it's a great location for those less abled. There's an incline walking up to the Writing Shed but nothing too steep. Keep an eye on the tides on full moon days and during spring tides when it comes in higher than normal, submerging the parking area. It's not uncommon to see unfortunate flooded vehicles and there are signs warning of this.

Best time of year/day

On a high tide is best; a full stream will produce reflections of the grasses and any moored boats, when shooting across the marshes. In early morning, side lighting is effective with direct illumination of the castle stonework, cobbled path and coastline buildings. Look for wading birds, when low tides reveal large mudflats with interesting sand patterns.

*Looking through the window into Dylan Thomas's
writing shed. Canon 5D III, 24-70mm f/2.8
at 44mm, ISO 400, 1/640s at f/8. Jan.*

Even if the poet, writer and broadcaster Dylan Thomas
hadn't lived in Laugharne, it is still a truly remarkable place
to visit. There's a vast amount of birdlife on the ebbing
tide here, including many wading species such as curlew,
sanderling and shelduck, not to mention interesting
migrant species stopping off to refuel. The Norman castle
is one of the highlights in this small coastal village. It dates
back to the 12th century where it was nowhere near as
imposing as it is today. The towering stone walls were built
on in the 15th and 16th centuries. Favoured compositions
of the castle include either the ford across the Coran
stream, or better still, the rocky arched bridge in the
foreground. The tide can be treacherous here, flooding this
marshy area (and the car park!) so if you catch the tide on
the way out, it can be effective with the cobblestone
pathway. Couple this with a sunrise or evening light for
lovely contrasted side lighting.

Long exposure of the footbridge and castle at Laugharne.
Canon 5D III, 16-35mm f/4 at 16mm, ISO 100, 30s at f/16. Tripod. Polariser, 6ND & ND Grad. July.

Set in the rolling hills and lush countryside of Carmarthenshire, the Garden of Wales features over 8,000 different varieties of plants across this 598-acre parkland site. It was officially opened in May 2000, and since then a stunning range of themed gardens have been developed across the site, which will appeal to a wide range of visitors.

There's the Double Walled garden, an orchard and several lakes. The recently opened Butterfly House is packed full of exotic species. Watch them fluttering past as you wind your way around the pathways through the hot and humid environment. The garden's centrepiece though is its futuristic looking Great Glasshouse, designed by world-famous architects Norman Foster and Partners. Inside its tilted glass dome is a Mediterranean landscape dominated by a six-metre-deep ravine, rock terraces and waterfalls. It's a very family-friendly site with a play area, regular kids events and a new British Bird of Prey Centre.

What to shoot and viewpoints

Situated just off the main A48 dual carriageway, the Garden, spread across historic parkland, is nestled in a wooded valley close to the village of Llanarthney. A large hall was built here in the 17th century, surrounded by formal gardens, which included a system of streams and ponds. Later, in the 18th century, William Paxton (who built nearby Paxton's Tower) purchased the estate and turned it into a fashionable leisure park. It wasn't until the late 20th century when plans were formed to create the Garden of Wales as it's known today.

You'll start your journey at the bottom of the hill at the elegant-looking Gatehouse. Purchase your admission at the small shop located here. The first part of the walk is flat and level then a broad central pathway takes you up to the top of the site and the western entrance to the Great Glasshouse. Snaking along this path is a small stream, which winds its way down to a spiral pond. From here you can either head west – out towards the Japanese Garden, straight on up the hill or east around the lakes. >>

The dome-shaped glasshouse and daffodils. Canon 5D III, 24-70mm f/2.8 at 63mm, ISO 640, 1/640s at f/7.1. ND Grad. Feb.

Many pathways and themed gardens to explore. Canon 5D IV, 24-70mm f/2.8 at 24mm, ISO 250, 1/125s at f/6.3. May.

Various exotic species can be found in the butterfly house. Canon 5D IV, 24-70mm f/2.8 at 70mm, ISO 800, 1/125s at f/4.5. May.

How to get here

A very easy place to get to with almost immediate access off the main A48 road. From Swansea, head west for 4 miles on the M4 motorway and take the second exit at Pont Abraham roundabout, signed Carmarthen/Cross Hands. On reaching Cross Hands roundabout, take the second exit (straight over) and continue towards Carmarthen. After approximately 4 miles take the B4310 exit towards Nantgaredig/Porthyrhyd, turn left at the T-junction, then take the second exit at the next roundabout. Follow this for a short distance before taking the second exit at the roundabout to enter the National Botanic Gardens of Wales. The parking entrance is on your left.

Parking Lat/Long: 51.839596, -4.1519496
Parking Grid Ref: SA32 8HN
OS Map grid ref: SN518178
Map: OS Explorer Map 186 – Llandeilo & Brechfa Forest

Accessibility ♿

The whole site has been developed with families, wheelchairs and buggies in mind so everywhere boasts flat, wide paths. There's also a shuttle buggy service should it be required. Expect to cover a few miles exploring the whole site, as it's huge. Perhaps consider splitting the visit over a day or two and make sure you bring plenty of memory cards and a picnic.

Best time of year/day

In early spring there are lots of snowdrops and daffodils dotted around the park – a welcome sight after a bleak winter – but from springtime into summer the Garden comes alive with flowering plants and activity in the ponds and streams. Autumn can be a rewarding time, with trees turning a rich orange. It's not uncommon to have snow here in winter, so check access roads prior to visiting. The glasshouse is kept at a constant temperature and the butterfly house is full of exotic life all year round.

Visit throughout the year for flowers. Canon 5D IV, 24-70mm f/2.8 at 70mm, ISO 500, 1/1000s at f/5. May.

Keep an eye out for sculptures. Canon 5D IV, 16-35mm f/4 at 16mm, ISO 320, 1/1250s at f/6.3. May.

Filled with symbolism and guided by Zen philosophy, the Japanese Garden is a lovely place to sit and contemplate. It was brought here piece by piece from the Chelsea Flower Show in 2001, where it had won a gold medal. Further out to the west is the Ice House. Cold foods were a luxury in yesteryear and many wealthy estates used these structures to store ice throughout the year. To the north of the Japanese Garden is the Double Walled garden and adjacent to this, the Butterfly House.

The whole site is linked with lots of pathways, so there's no set way to explore it. Go at your own pace and wander is my advice – there's so much to see. The Butterfly House is one of the main attractions; expect your camera and/or glasses to steam up on entry though! Keep your camera out for around ten minutes – this should be enough time for it to acclimatise. This hot and steamy glasshouse is filled with a kaleidoscope of colourful butterflies from the tropics world. There are several feeding tables along the pathways, so many of the butterflies tend to head for these, allowing fantastic close-up views. A specialist macro lens would be best here; with its very small minimum-focus distance, it can reproduce life-size objects on the camera's image sensor, making extremely detailed images. Looping round from the north west of the site you'll find the cafe and restaurant before heading east passing the Wallace and Boulders gardens towards the star of the show, the Great Glasshouse.

The Great Glasshouse has the largest single-span glasshouse roof in the world and houses the largest collection of Mediterranean plants in the Northern Hemisphere. Enter any of the dome's three entrances and the automatic doors retreat like something from a sci-fi film. The teardrop-shaped, criss-cross framework fills the sky above. It's worth visiting for the sublime architecture alone, let alone the vast array of plants on view. It houses some of the most endangered plants on the planet from California, Australia, the Canary Islands, Chile, South Africa and the Mediterranean Basin. Each of these geographical regions has its own area in the glasshouse and all enjoy a Mediterranean climate, which the glasshouse emulates. Pathways spiral around the plants on display and in the centre you'll descend to a waterfall and lake. Alternatively, take a different route around the perimeter, crossing bridges that span the paths below. There's signage everywhere guiding you and providing information on the plants and flowers.

There's so much to see at the Garden: unique sculptures line the paths, from large metal dragons to stone and wood carvings. There's a display of ancient tree boughs to the east of the dome and half way up the hill on the right an area of rocks illustrates Welsh geology spanning 300 million years. It's one of those places you could visit often and see something new with the changing seasons – a real gem in the heart of South Wales.

Above: The great roof that spans the glasshouse. Canon 5D IV, 24-70mm f/2.8 at 24mm, ISO 320, 1/800s at f/7.1. May. **Below**: Don't forget to give your camera time to acclimatise in the butterfly house. Canon 5D IV, 24-70mm f/2.8 at 70mm, ISO 1250, 1/160s at f/3.2. May.

3 PAXTON'S TOWER

'To the invincible commander, Viscount Nelson, in commemoration of deeds most brilliantly achieved at the Mouth of the Nile, before the walls of Copenhagen and on the shores of Spain; of the empire everywhere maintained by him over the sea; and of the death which in the fullness of his own glory, though untimely for his country and Europe, conquering he died; this tower was erected by William Paxton.'

The dedication to Admiral Nelson by William Paxton

Paxton's Tower was built by William Paxton sometime between 1806 and 1809 to a design by Samuel Pepys Cockerell. This Neo-Gothic folly, two storeys high, with a hexagonal castellated roof, is situated on a hilltop near Llanarthne in the Towy Valley. Paxton owned the Middleton Hall Estate, now the home of the nearby National Botanic Garden of Wales. There are as many as four theories as to why the folly was built. The most likely explanation is that it was a decorative feature – the height of fashion at the time – providing a place for Paxton to welcome guests who came to visit, dine and take in the panoramic views. The tower is thirty-six feet high and its lower part is triangular in shape with a turret at each corner. The first floor held a banqueting room and on the second floor a hexagonal prospect room – its windows now sadly bricked up – is surrounded by roof terraces. The tower was dedicated to Admiral Nelson, a friend of Paxton's, after his death at Trafalgar in October 1805.

What to shoot and viewpoints

Although in the middle of nowhere, this is an interesting and photogenic building. The site offers fabulous views of the Carmarthenshire countryside and down into the River Towy valley below. There are many compositions here, so work around the folly as you head up towards it. Using the nearby field and a medium focal length will put you at eye level with the folly, placing it in the surrounding landscape. Alternatively, attach a wide-angle lens and get up close for dynamic compositions; either shot will be compelling.

It's also a good place to test your long exposures using a high-density ND filter to capture cloud motion. Ideal weather would be a windy day with clouds scudding past to provide interest in the sky. As you move around, you'll notice you can see through two out of three doorway and window apertures, so lining up your shots through these can add interest.

Lush green countryside views in summer. Canon 5D III, 24-70mm f/2.8 at 50mm, ISO 100, 1/160s at f/13. Tripod. Polariser. Aug.

Inside the entrance archway looking out. Canon 5D III, 24-70mm f/2.8 at 24mm, ISO 100, 1/40s at f/13. Tripod. Polariser. Aug.

How to get here

Paxton's Tower is tucked away down some narrow country lanes. From Carmarthen, head east on the main A48 road for roughly 8 miles. You'll see a sign for the National Botanic Garden of Wales (B4310) – take this exit left. Head over the roundabout and continue north for a further 2 miles then turn right on a sharp junction. Head up this lane until you reach the car park on your left by a cottage.

Parking Lat/Long: 51.850851, -4.1218170
Parking Grid Ref: SA32 8HX
OS Map grid ref: SN538190
Map: OS Explorer Map 186 – Llandeilo & Brechfa Forest

Accessibility

The tower is in the care of the National Trust, but it's free of charge to visit and there's a free car park at the base of the folly. Walk out of the car park and through the kissing gate by the cottage. Sometimes livestock grazes in this field so keep dogs on leads. It's a short 150-metre walk up the hill across grass to the summit of the field, where the folly is sits in its own enclosure.

Low down, wide angle view of the tower. Canon 5D III, 16-35mm f/4 at 16mm, ISO 100, 1/160s at f/13. Tripod. Polariser. Aug.

Best time of year/day

Depending on the weather, it's possible to shoot it throughout the day in any direction, taking in the countryside views. Early morning sometimes brings low-lying mist in the Towy valley, so consider using the site as a high viewpoint for the river and Dryslwyn Castle ruins below. The folly is illuminated at night, which can add further interest to a shot, particularly on a clear starry night.

Opposite: The tower with a covering of snow. Canon 5D IV, 24-70mm f/2.8 at 63mm, ISO 100, 1/80s at f/10. Polariser. Dec.

The famous Welsh broadcaster, Wynford Vaughan-Thomas once said, *"If you take a handful of the soil at Dinefwr and squeeze it in your hand, the juice that will flow from your hands is the essence of Wales."* I would wholeheartedly agree with this evocative claim.

A stunning eight-hundred-acre estate on the outskirts of the old farming town of Llandeilo in the Carmarthenshire countryside, Dinefwr Park has a diverse range of habitats – from rich flower meadows to dense ancient woodland of historic native oaks, dating back four hundred years. From wide, open spaces of grassland where fallow deer and cattle roam, to bog woods and ponds; each provides a vital home to the numerous species that reside here. To the south, the park also features its own castle. A Sight of Special Scientific Interest (SSSI) and the only parkland National Nature Reserve (NNR) in Wales, Dinefwr Park is a microcosm of Welsh heritage and natural history. High up on a hill overlooking the river Twyi (or river Towy) valley below, provides a great vantage point over the parkland, surrounding valleys and – looking west – along the river Twyi itself, as it meanders through the countryside.

What to shoot and viewpoints

Where to start! From the main car park keep an eye out for woodland birds, especially treecreepers and flycatchers in spring. The small pond by the car park is a good spot for redstarts too. The fields you pass on the way in house rare breed White Park cattle with long curving horns throughout the year. To the north of the car park is Newton House, a grade II listed country house now restored to its former glory by Cadw and the National Trust who run the estate. Behind the house lies the medieval hundred-acre deer park, home to a herd of over a hundred fallow deer. Circling the deer park to the north are pathways through the woodland passing many old oak and beech trees, which create a spectacular tapestry of colours in autumn. These paths eventually bring you to the western end of the deer park next to a pond – a great spot for birds and dragonflies in summer. You can either go west from here to a bird hide; east along the bottom of the deer park, across boardwalks in a boggy reedbed habitat, or south east back towards the parkland. Following the paths this way will take you uphill towards the castle. There are many more paths all over the park, and the secluded church on the drive in is worth exploring, so grab a map from the visitor centre at the car park and spending a good day here. In the summer, tag onto one of the park's badger-watching evenings at its custom-built hide.

Newton House viewed from Dinefwr Castle (VP2). Canon 5D III, 24-70mm f/2.8 at 70mm, ISO 100, 1/5s at f/16. Tripod. ND Grad. May.

How to get here

From Swansea take the M4 west towards the end of the motorway at Junction 49 (Pont Abraham) then join the A48 and follow this for 4 miles until you reach Cross Hands roundabout. Take the fourth exit north signed towards Llandeilo. After 7 miles you'll come into Ffairfach, where you need to turn left at the crossroads. Follow this into Llandeilo town and take the fourth left after the buildings society. Follow this road three quarters of a mile and the Dinefwr Park entrance is on your left.

Parking Lat/Long: 51.882392 -4.0136026
Parking Postcode: SA19 6RT
OS Map Grid Ref: SN 61503 22342
Map: OS Explorer Map 186 – Llandeilo & Brechfa Forest

*Opposite left: Castle signage (VP2). Canon 5D III, 24-70mm f/2.8 at 50mm, ISO 100, 0.4s at f/16. Tripod. May. **Right**: Looking up inside the castle Keep (VP2). Canon 5D III, 16-35mm f/4 at 16mm, ISO 250, 1/640s at f/16. Tripod. Polariser. May.*

Accessibility

Most of the park is easily accessed for those with limited mobility; there are wide paths. There are some hilly sections to the south of the park – particularly the walk up to the castle and woods, which is quite steep. Once up there though it's definitely worth it for the views from the castle walls.

Best time of year/day

Dinefwr Park is open all the year round. Early morning is best for photographing birds or wildlife, while an evening visit may reveal a badger or two. It changes year on year, but mid-May is usually a safe bet when timing a visit for the bluebells; by then there's generally enough density for colour. I find outings on slightly overcast days work best, when you don't have to contend with contrasting light and there's always the golden hour to evoke some mood. Late September is best for the deer rut, though as it's quite a closely knit herd don't expect too much action.

The castle and surrounding parkland viewed from near the car park.
Canon 5D III, 24-70mm f/2.8 at 59mm, ISO 200, 1/6s at f/16. Tripod. Polariser. May.

Evening light across the Towy river valley and surrounding countryside, taken from the castle ramparts.
Canon 5D III, 24-70mm f/2.8 at 35mm, ISO 400, 1/6s at f/16. Polariser & ND Grad. May.

Castle wood bluebells and native woodland. Canon 5D III, 24-70mm f/2.8 at 55mm, ISO 1250, 1/5s at f/11. Tripod. Polariser. May.

Viewpoint 1 – Bluebells

The main burst of bluebells is situated at the foot of the castle in the aptly named, Castle Woods. For the shortest route here, follow the gravel road from the car park, passing the entrance to the deer park and boardwalks on your right. Then ascend the hill towards the castle. It's on your left through the next kissing gate. You can reach the wood from pathways leading from nearby Llandeilo Bridge, but it's easiest from the car park. The wood is comprised of two areas of ancient woodland, with veteran trees on the south and west-facing sides of the hill. Oak, ash and beech flourish here and early spring is a feast for the senses: vivid greens of new leaves, together with the purples and blues of the flowers complement one another. The perfume is unforgettable. Time your visit for early morning and the wood is filled with birdsong – magic! Photographing bluebells can be tricky; most of the time, what you see with your eyes isn't replicated by the camera. A good technique is drop to their level; this will effectively increase the density of the plants and ultimately the colour. Try using a circular polariser filter to cut down any foliage reflections and boost natural colours.

Opposite: High up in the castle keep, looking out (VP2). Canon 5D III, 24-70mm f/2.8 at 30mm, ISO 100, 1/5s at f/16. Tripod. May.

Viewpoint 2 – Dinefwr Castle

Sitting high on a hill overlooking the river Twyi valley, Dinefwr Castle is not only an interesting monument to visit but an important site in Welsh history. It is associated with the princes of Deheubarth, (an historic kingdom in south west Wales), making it a major landmark on the medieval map of Britain. Over time the castle changed hands, with the English Crown using it as a centre of royal administration in the 13th century. It was the regional capital until the early 15th century, but was later replaced by Newton House. By the 17th century it had become a picturesque, romantic attraction within Dinefwr Park. Even though the castle is in ruins, much of it remains to this day. There's good access over and around it, but walk carefully on some path sections and narrow steps. Take in the majesty of the views by accessing the high ramparts and viewing windows to the west and north.

Viewpoint 3 – Deer Park

To the north of the car park behind Dinefwr's main attraction, Newton House, lies the vast deer park. An 18th century addition, it is home to more than one hundred fallow deer, including many large bucks that come noisily to life in autumn for the deer rut. The rut usually begins in late September and lasts for three weeks. There's a pathway circling the park but you can roam freely as long as you don't spook the deer too much. Some are tamer than others, so a long lens is advisable. Surrounded by dense woodland, the park is a great place all year round. Take in wild flowers in the spring, and russet leaves and fungi in autumn.

*Opposite top: Badger emerges in early evening. Canon 5D III, 300mm f/2.8 + 1.4x Extender at 420mm, ISO 2000, 1/125s at f/4. Tripod. May. **Right**: Redstart perched on tree stump. Canon 5D III, 300mm f/2.8 + 1.4x Extender at 420mm, ISO 1600, 1/2000s at f/5.6. Tripod. July. **Middle left**: Banks of buttercups near Newton House. Canon 5D III, 300mm f/2.8 + 1.4x Extender at 420mm, ISO 800, 1/1250s at f/5.6. May. **Bottom**: Rare breed white park cattle and distant bluebell woods. Canon 5D III, 70-200mm f/2.8 at 195mm, ISO 800, 1/320s at f/5. May.*

Herd of fallow deer in the deer park by Newton House. Canon 5D III, 70-200mm f/2.8 at 70mm, ISO 800, 1/500s at f/14. May.

High tide at Three Cliffs Bay in evening light (p.344).
Canon 5D III, 24-70mm f/2.8 at 70mm, ISO 100, 1/25s at f/14. Tripod. Polariser & ND Grad. Aug.

GOWER

GOWER – INTRODUCTION

Covering around seventy square miles, the Gower Peninsula offers varied terrain from long, sandy beaches backed by vast dune systems, to salt and freshwater marshes meandering their way inland towards wooded valleys and farmland. Jutting out into the Bristol Channel, the Gower is located centrally on the South Wales coast, just a short distance from the bustling city of Swansea. It was the first area in the UK to be designated an Area of Outstanding Natural Beauty (AONB) way back in 1956, and it's easy to see why.

Much of the draw to the Gower is its stunning coastal path. Stretching from Mumbles in the east, around to the northern village of Crofty, this 38-mile section, makes up part of the Wales Coast Path, passing through all sorts of landscapes along the way. Travelling west to the end of Mumbles beach, you'll begin to exit the busy city; the buildings start to dwindle and the tree-clad limestone cliffs beckon you closer. Here's where the Gower's numerous bays – each with their own characteristics – begin.

There's the magnificent pier, lifeboat stations – old and new – and the Mumbles Lighthouse, located on an island near Bracelet Bay. This and nearby Limeslade Bay are both relatively small but offer great coastal interest and intriguing rock pools. Further along the coast, the impressive geology of Three Cliffs Bay is immediately recognisable with its triple rocky peaks jutting out onto the beach. Move westwards through more secluded coves and bays, all the time passing dramatic cliffs, and the route culminates in the Gower's showstoppers: Worm's Head and Rhossili Bay.

A dazzling three-mile crescent of flat golden sand stretches north towards Llangennith Sands and the point at Burry Holms. At the westerly tip is a rocky promontory, Worms Head; its name deriving from a Viking word for dragon. Rhossili Beach is backed by the Downs – large heathland hills and a popular launch-site for hang gliders – while surfers prefer to take on the rolling Atlantic waves that crash into the beach. From hereon round, the coastline acquires a wilder feeling, with large sand-dune systems and windswept grassland across the burrows.

Sheep & lambs on Rhossili headland (p.326). Canon 5D IV, 24-70mm f/2.8 at 50mm, ISO 100, 1/125s at f/11. Apr.

This undulating landscape rolls its way towards the unique metal lighthouse at Whiteford Point, which stands half a mile offshore, guarding the entry of the Loughor Estuary. In between is a mixture of wild moors and heathland, low-lying marshes and woodland. There's an abundance of history as well, with at least 1200 archaeological sites including caves, Iron Age forts, medieval castles and churches. There's also the stunning burial chamber of Arthur's Stone, a historical wonder that offers a great vantage point over the nearby estuary coastline.

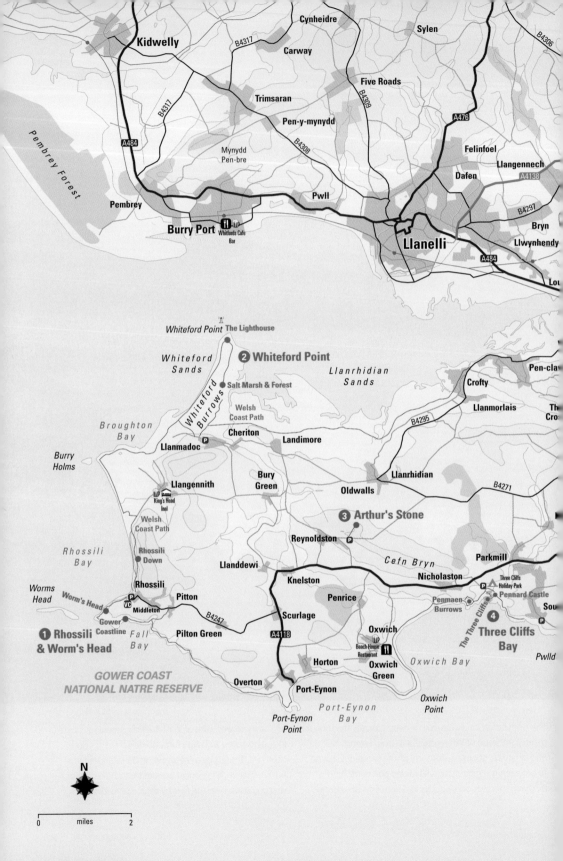

Cynheidre

Sylen

B4306

Kidwelly

B4317

Carway

Five Roads

Trimsaran

A476

Pen-y-mynydd

Felinfoel

Langennech

Mynydd
Pen-bre

B4308

Dafen

A4138

Pwll

B4297

Pembrey Forest

Bryn

Pembrey

Llanelli

Llwynhendy

A484

Burry Port

H Whitfords Cafe
Bar

A484

Lou

Whiteford Point The Lighthouse

2 Whiteford Point

Whiteford
Sands

Llanrhidian
Sands

Pen-cla

Crofty

Salt Marsh & Forest

Whiteford Burrows

Welsh
Coast Path

Llanmorlais

Th
Cro

Broughton
Bay

Cheriton

Landimore

B4295

Llanmadoc

Bury
Green

Llanrhidian

Burry
Holms

Llangennith

Oldwalls

B4271

King's Head
Innl

3 Arthur's Stone

Welsh
Coast Path

Reynoldston

Cefn Bryn

Parkmill

Rhossili
Bay

Rhossili
Down

Nicholaston

Three Cliffs
Holiday Park

Llanddewi

Worms
Head

Rhossili

Knelston

Pennard Castle

Worm's Head

Pitton

Penmaen
Burrows

Sou

VC Middleton

Penrice

**4 Three Cliffs
Bay**

**1 Rhossili
& Worm's Head**

Gower
Coastline

Fall
Bay

Pilton Green

B4247

Scurlage

A4118

Oxwich

Oxwich Bay

Pwlld

Beach House
Restaurant

H

GOWER COAST
NATIONAL NATRE RESERVE

Overton

Horton

Oxwich
Green

Oxwich
Point

Port-Eynon

Port-Eynon
Point

Port-Eynon
Bay

N

0   miles   2

5 Bracelet Bay & Mumbles Lighthouse

Map

• OS Explorer Map 164 – Gower

Long exposure on Rhossili beach, Helvetia shipwreck left of frame.
Canon 5D IV, 24-70mm f/2.8 at 50mm, ISO 50, 60s at f/16. Tripod. Polariser, 10ND & ND Grad. Apr.

It's a bit of a cliché, but the first view you'll get of Rhossili beach will take your breath away. At three miles long this is one vast beach! That alone may not pique your interest but thankfully there are plenty of inspirational locations around here.

What to shoot and viewpoints

All viewpoints are accessible via good paths from the National Trust car park so this makes for a good starting point. You'll notice a small cottage halfway along the beach. This is called the Old Rectory and could be an interesting element to include, giving your scenes some scale. At low tide an old shipwreck is visible; the Helvetia ran aground in 1887, bearing witness to the challenging sea conditions around the Gower. Backing onto the beach are the fabulous Rhossili Downs. 'Rhos' in Welsh means heath, and the downs are aptly named. Swathes of lowland heath are home to a variety of birds and insects, including the rare black bog ant. Plants are a mixture of brackens, heather and gorse, which carpet this area, coming alive in the summer months in vivid greens, purples and yellows. From the top of the Rhossili Downs stands the Beacon at 193 metres – the highest point on the Gower peninsula providing unparalleled views across the sea to West Wales, Lundy Island and the north Devon coast. Turn inland and look north up the neck of the Gower towards the Brecon Beacons. At the southern end of the Bay lies Worm's Head and at the north, Burry Holms. Both these islands are only accessible at low tide. The tide really races in here, especially on or near a full moon so keep an eye on the times and wind direction. Worm's Head (the name derives from 'wurm', a Viking word for dragon) is the most westerly tip of the Gower peninsula, jutting west out into the sea. This mystical serpent-like promontory rears up from the ocean and comprises two rocky islands linked to the mainland by a narrow causeway – consult coast watch timetables and signs for safe crossings – and to each other by a slender piece of rock known evocatively as the Devil's Bridge.

How to get here

Parking is located at the end of the B4247. To get here from the M4 motorway from the east, leave the motorway at junction 42 and follow signs towards Gower down the A483 and through Swansea. Head onto Oystermouth Road for 3 miles before turning right onto Mayals Road/B4436 for 4 miles. Turn right onto Vennaway Lane. At the end of the lane, turn left onto the A4118 and follow this for 8 miles. Finally, turn onto the B4247 and follow it for 3.5 miles until you reach the car park.

Parking Lat/Long: 51.569088, -4.2889890
Parking Postcode: SA3 1PP
OS Map Grid Ref: SS 414880
Map: OS Explorer Map 164 – Gower

Accessibility ♿

You can pretty much fall out of the car here and get a great view of Rhossili beach. Parking for all the viewpoints are at the National Trust car park where there are toilets and cafes. There's also a flat, wide, paved footpath that runs along the coast towards the Coast Watch. For those with limited mobility, look out near Worm's Head; it's a medium descent down onto the causeway and means clambering over rock pools once at sea level. Accessing Rhossili Downs begins with a steep climb out of Rhossili village, which might require a few breathers, especially when lugging camera gear. Once on the top ridge though, paths are easy going and wide, carving through the moorland.

Best time of year/day

Summer is a special time of year to be up on Rhossili Downs when the heather is spectacular. Combine this with some lovely evening side light and you're onto a winner. The tide makes every scene appear different here, so it's important to keep an eye on the times. For me, high tide is best as it floods the causeway, making Worm's Head seem like a rocky serpent breaching the flat seas. Low tide reveals many rock pools and a few bays around the head, and allows visitors to really appreciate the sheer vastness of Rhossili beach. All through the year you'll have the sun setting into the sea.

Warning sign at the tidal causeway, Worm's Head (VP3). Canon 5D III, 24-70mm f/2.8 at 35mm, ISO 640, 1/1250s at f/8. Aug.

DANGER!
FAST TIDAL CURRENTS - DANGER OF DROWNING

① Cross causeway only when dry.

② Check the times. The causeway is open approx. 2½ hrs either side of low tide.

③ If cut off by the tide, DO NOT attempt to cross causeway. Wait for the tide to recede or attract attention and wait for assistance.

④ Deaths have occurred through attempting to cross the causeway whilst flooded.

IF YOU SEE SOMEONE IN DIFFICULTY, TELEPHONE 999 AND ASK FOR THE COASTGUARD. EMERGENCY TELEPHONE SITUATED AT THE OLD COASTGUARD STATION AT TOP OF HILL.

Above: *Visitors enjoying the views to Worm's Head (VP3). Canon 5D III, 24-70mm f/2.8 at 50mm, ISO 500, 1/160s at f/10. Aug.*

Below: *Telephoto view of visitors on Rhossili beach at low tide. Canon 5D III, 24-70mm f/2.8 at 70mm, ISO 100, 1/1000s at f/5.6. Aug.*

Overview of Rhossili beach from the headland.
Canon 5D IV, 24-70mm f/2.8 at 24mm, ISO 50, 1/5s at f/16. Tripod. Polariser & ND Grad. Apr.

Sunset and heather at Rhossili Bay overlooking Worm's Head (VP1).
Canon 5D III, 24-70mm f/2.8 at 28mm, ISO 100, 4s at f/13. Tripod. Polariser, 3ND & ND Grad. Aug.

The Helvetia shipwreck and Worm's Head. Canon 5D IV, 24-70mm f/2.8 at 63mm, ISO 50, 120s at f/20. Tripod. Polariser, 10ND & ND Grad. Apr.

Viewpoint 1 – Rhossili Down

Heading north east from the car park and high up onto the Downs, is a great place to see classic Gower views. Looking down onto the beach towards Worm's Head makes for interesting compositions, leading the viewer's eye along the coastline. It's important to include recognisable elements in elevated views to maximise the scale of the scene, so include foreground features such as plants or the houses in Rhossili village. Use the natural curvature of the cliffs or Downs pathways cutting through moorland as leading lines towards the Worm.

Viewpoint 2 – Worm's Head

If you head west along the flat paths from the car park, make sure to stop off at a few of the breaks in the cliff edges en route, to photograph the interesting contours of the escarpments below. Again, use leading lines and the natural shapes of the coastline to draw the eye towards Worm's Head for an interesting background focal point.

Viewpoint 3 – Coastline

Head further around from Viewpoint 2 and you'll pass the Coast Watch hut while continuing along the coastal path towards Fall Bay. Looking back, there are interesting rock strata formations which you can use as a lead in lines, or as features in their own right.

*Opposite top: Worm's Head from the headland walk (VP2). Canon 5D III, 24-70mm f/2.8 at 24mm, ISO 200, 30s at f/11. Tripod. Polariser, 10ND & ND Grad. Aug. **Bottom**: Coastal cliffs towards the causeway at low tide. Canon 5D III, 24-70mm f/2.8 at 31mm, ISO 160, 30s at f/11. Tripod. Polariser, 10ND & ND Grad. Aug.*

The main feature in this area is the Whiteford Point Lighthouse. This lonely cast-iron structure, half a mile from the mainland, is the only wave-washed lighthouse of its kind left today on Britain's shores. It's a fair walk to reach this metallic icon on the north Gower coast, but you'll venture through all kinds of habitat en route. From wild salt marsh, through coniferous woodland on to a vast system of grassy dunes before reaching golden sands and venturing across the rocky landscape, finally reaching the Victorian lighthouse. This location is totally unique, undeniably spectacular and offers panoramic views along the surrounding Welsh coastline from Worm's Head to Pendine Sands.

What to shoot and viewpoints

This northern part of the Gower is exceptionally beautiful. It traces the Burry Estuary back inland as rolling sand dunes give way to forest and salt marsh. Getting to the lighthouse is undoubtedly one of the best walks in the area in terms of scenery and wildlife.

Viewpoint 1 – Salt Marsh & Forest
Walk out of the parking field and turn right; you'll descend down the road through the small village of Cwm Ivy, before reaching the end of the road and passing through a gate signed Whiteford Burrows. It's quite a steep descent following the path, but it's wide and level and you'll emerge onto flat ground at the bottom of the hill. Here lies a junction of the Wales Coast Path, so you can head south west here if you want to venture back in the direction of Rhossili.

Head to your right and you'll enter the forest with its coniferous scent. To your right the vast area of salt marsh begins. These salty mudflats and tidal ditches provide a unique habitat for both plant and bird life, and are home to livestock, including the famous Gower salt marsh lamb. Its meat is naturally infused with the sea lavender, samphire, sorrel and thrift that grow in this unique coastal environment. Migrating waders, geese and ducks all call this place home so it's always worth stopping for a while and scouring the landscape with your binoculars. A good spot for this is at the end of the forest. A path here heads to the right, along the top of an earthwork dyke known locally as the 'the Groose'. This offers elevated views across the salt marsh and down towards the Burry inlet – a great vantage point from which to witness the tide come and go. Further along the path the going underfoot will change to sandy gravel and then the grassy dune system will begin to your left. This is a great place to look out for stonechat, linnet on the bushes and also chough as they dig for bugs in the sandy soil. I've also heard a cuckoo calling here in spring, so keep an eye out for one in the treetops. »

The sandy pathway through the forest (VP1). Canon 5D IV, 24-70mm f/2.8 at 44mm, ISO 100, 1/30s at f/9. Polariser. May.

Whiteford burrows sand dunes and forest path (VP1). Canon 5D IV, 24-70mm f/2.8 at 65mm, ISO 100, 1/100s at f/5.6. Polariser. May.

How to get here

From Swansea city centre, head out west on the A4067/
Oystermouth road. Follow this for 2 miles, before turning right onto
Brynmill Terrace and continuing down here for half a mile. Take a
left onto Gower Road/A4118 and head down here for 2 miles
before taking the first exit at the roundabout continuing on Gower
Road/A4118. After around 1.5 miles you'll enter the common over
a cattle grid. Watch out for sheep and/or horses in the road. Take a
slight right signed the B4271 and after 6 miles you'll enter the
village of Oldwalls. At the T-junction take a left turn, signed New
Road/B4295 and follow this for just over 3 miles. When you spot
the small church, turn right signed Cwm Ivy car park. The parking is
just a short distance down here on the right in a field. It's currently
only a £1 per day, paid into the honesty box at the entrance.

Parking Lat/Long: 51.618659, -4.2551094
Parking Postcode: SA3 1DQ
OS Map Grid Ref: SS439935
Map: OS Explorer Map 164 – Gower

Above: Pathway through the edge of the salt marsh, sometimes
flooded. Canon 5D IV, 24-70mm f/2.8 at 50mm, ISO 400,
1/320s at f/9. Polariser. May.

Accessibility

This is probably one of this book's furthest locations to reach. To
get to the lighthouse from the car park is around a 3-mile walk and
although over various types of terrain, it's generally easy going. The
first part is all paved and flat, though downhill. The track through
the forest passing the salt marsh is flat too, it's only when you
venture further into the sand dunes and ultimately, the beach and
rocks, that it gets more uneven under foot.

Best time of year/day

The tide plays a bit part in the scenery here, due to the salt marsh
being tidal and many of the paths that go close to it. At certain times
in the year, on exceptionally high tides, these can be impassable.
The lighthouse can only be reached at low tide too, so time your
walk to visit this on the low water mark to allow plenty of time to
walk out, explore and return safely to the mainland before the tide
comes back in. From the approach you'll mainly be shooting in a
north-west direction, throughout the day the light will be on your
left side and sunsets will be behind the lighthouse in high summer.
Coastal flowers start to bloom in late April, while wading birds
are present all year round.

Whiteford lighthouse at low tide and flocks of gulls (VP2).
Canon 5D IV, 24-70mm f/2.8 at 70mm, ISO 100, 1/80s at f/10. Tripod. Polariser & ND Grad. May.

Further along, the path will come to a fork. Turn right to join the Wales Coast Path heading north. This route can get quite boggy and muddy with frequent puddles to jump, so I'd suggest turning left here. After a short distance, you'll be walking on soft sand into another small wood. This is such a unique environment; although venturing through a pine forest, there is sand under foot and trees growing in the dunes. It's quite remarkable. As the track winds its way further along – with a few ups and downs – it will go round to the right. Look out for a kissing gate in the middle of the burrows to your left; pick up the small track through the grass and head for this gate, passing through it, up and over the final dune, when you'll finally arrive on the beach itself.

Viewpoint 2 – Whiteford Point Lighthouse

Take it all in! This huge golden spit of beach is called Whiteford Sands and it stretches up from the western tip of the Gower peninsula at Burry Holms all the way to the north. If that wasn't enough, on most days you'll be the only one here. You can head south and climb some of the higher dunes to gain an elevated position with views across Whiteford Burrows or opt to go north up the beach towards the lighthouse. Be aware, access to the lighthouse itself is only possible around low tide; at any other time the base of the lighthouse is submerged by seawater and must be viewed from the safety of the beach. This itself could prove a successful viewpoint on windy days, as you'll witness colossal waves crashing into the lighthouse offering the opportunity for some spectacular images. Head north along the beach with the lighthouse looming ever closer and there's usually the odd piece of driftwood or gnarled rope to provide foreground interest for your wider-angled shots. At the top corner of the beach the sand will give way to a vast landscape of stones that are easy to cross but uneven, so watch you don't twist an ankle. Thankfully this stretch of stones is quite short before the ground transforms once again into a carpet of seashells. They're everywhere. Even though it's uneven, the ground here is quick to cross. Razor shells, cockles, clams and mussels carpet the sand here, crunching underfoot. It's quite an impressive sight and definitely worth a photo or two. This area is punctuated with tidal pools, which get larger the closer you get to the lighthouse, and harbour a whole host of sea and plant life.

The lighthouse is the only operational cast-iron lighthouse to actually stand in the sea on the British coast. It was built in 1865 to safeguard the increased trade in and out of Llanelli and Burry Port. The 61-ft-high structure is constructed from heavy cast-iron plates, bolted together to form seven rings. Over the years it's had many new bands and strengthening panels. Its light is solar powered and alerts passing ships of the dangerous sand banks that lie beneath the waves. Any point on the approach is a good location to photograph the lighthouse, incorporating much of the surrounding foreground. You can place the lighthouse small in the frame (on either the left or the right) for a nicely balanced image. As you venture closer, the rusty and textured metal work will become more visible, allowing you to play with available light. Side lighting can really enhance the textures on the main panels. Snap on a strong neutral-density filter and shoot some long exposures, capturing the blurring of passing clouds. This is also a handy technique to enhance reflections on windy days; perhaps the lighthouse reflected in a pool. As the wind blows the water in these pools it creates ripples, but allowing the camera to expose longer will actually smooth out the water and regain some of the reflected shapes. It won't be a perfect reflection, but helps add another dimension to your foreground. Pack a longer lens too – there's always a hive of seabird activity this far out from the mainland and it's a good location to photograph wading birds, passing gulls or seabirds that perch on the top enclosure of the lighthouse.

Opposite: *Large rock pools on the lighthouse spit. Canon 5D IV, 24-70mm f/2.8 at 28mm, ISO 100, 120s at f/16. Tripod. Polariser, 6ND & ND Grad. May.*

View of the stone and Loughor estuary behind. Canon 5D IV, 24-70mm f/2.8 at 28mm, ISO 100, 1/15s at f/13. Tripod. Polariser & ND Grad. May.

Perched high up above the Loughor Estuary in the hills of the Gower Peninsula, Arthur's Stone marks the site of two Neolithic burial tombs. Sometimes known as King Arthur's Stone, The Great Stone of Sketty or the Welsh, Maen Ceti, this huge quartz boulder weighs in at a whopping twenty-five tonnes and dates back to 2500BC.

One of the best known dolmens in Wales and an important Gower landmark, it measures an almighty four metres in length and this monolith has been the subject of myths and folklore through the ages.

What to shoot and viewpoints

Arthur's Stone stands on a north-facing slope in the large common called Cefn Bryn – known locally as the backbone of the Gower. This five-mile-long, old, red sandstone ridge protrudes from the surrounding limestone and at its highest point, reaches 188 metres above sea level. This impressive vantage point boasts superb panoramic views all around the Gower Peninsula. Gaze south across the sea towards the north Devon coastline; a glance south west reveals the offshore island of Lundy; look back inland and northwards lie the hills of Carmarthenshire and to the east, the lofty summits of the Brecon Beacons National Park. Even without the historic burial tomb, this is a great place to take in the views on a clear day.

Boggy marshland on the approach to the stone. Canon 5D IV, 24-70mm f/2.8 at 28mm, ISO 100, 1/25s at f/13. Tripod. Polariser. May.

Despite this chambered tomb's huge appearance, it was once even bigger. The large slab you see at its base today was originally part of the capstone. This piece alone is estimated to weigh ten tonnes and is said to have broken off in the late 17th century. What happened to the stone is unclear. Theories include one of a local miller, who tried to break off a piece to create a new millstone but the slab was too heavy to move. Others claim it was struck by lightning or that the Patron Saint of Wales, Saint David himself, split the stone with a mighty sword. Whatever the cause, the broken part still lies alongside the monument, demoted to the ground. The presence of this lone, gigantic stone and how it got here has puzzled people for millennia. One well-known legend tells of King Arthur finding a pebble in his shoe and throwing it across the Burry Estuary, where it landed on Cefn Bryn. This stone, touched by the hand of the King, allegedly grew and grew and was held up

by other, smaller stones in admiration. It has also been proposed that its presence illustrates a feat of engineering similar to that of Stonehenge, where Neolithic people used basic equipment to move large stones into prominent positions. Today, geologists believe it's merely a glacial erratic carried here in the last Ice Age, with settlers later excavating underneath it to create burial chambers. Whatever your thoughts on the tales and myths that surround this stone, it's a superb place to visit – not only for the colourful history but to take in the stunning coastal views.

__Opposite__: Looking across to Burry Port from the stone. Canon 5D IV, 24-70mm f/2.8 at 28mm, ISO 100, 1/13s at f/14. Tripod. Polariser & ND Grad. May.

How to get here

From Port Talbot in the east, follow the M4 motorway for 3 miles, before taking the exit at junction 42 signed Swansea/Abertawe (A483). Stay on the A483 for 5 miles as Fabian Way becomes Quay Parade (A4067). Follow this for 2 miles, before turning right onto Brynmill Terrace and continuing down here for half a mile. Take a left onto Gower Road/A4118 and head down here for 2 miles before taking the first exit at the roundabout continuing on Gower Road/A4118. After around 1.5 miles you'll enter the common over the cattle grid. Watch out for sheep and/or horses in the road. Take a slight right signed the B4271 and after 5 miles take the left turning signposted Cefn Bryn. After around 2 miles the small parking area will be on your right and you'll spot Arthur's Stone to the north.

Parking Lat/Long: 51.588831, -4.1799425
Parking Postcode: SA3 1AE
OS Map Grid Ref: SS490900
Map: OS Explorer Map 164 – Gower

Accessibility

This is a relatively easy location to get to. There's no designated parking for the stone but there is a rocky area just off the road from Cilibion to Reynoldston that's used for parking. Even though it's a largely flat walk of around half a mile north across the grassy common, suitable footwear is definitely recommended, as it's uneven in parts. About halfway along, the footpath frequently becomes muddy with water to cross as, despite its elevation and due to the surrounding heathland, it's often waterlogged and boggy here.

Best time of year/day

One option is to make the estuary a backdrop to your wider views, positioning the stone to one side. You can photograph the stone from any angle, all the way around, but there's definitely a more photogenic side when shooting from the south, using its natural edge for light and shade. Maximise the stone's appearance by timing your visit either for early morning or the end of the day, when you can take advantage of sunny side lighting. The stones are incredibly textured so will show up best when there's contrasted light. Overcast days generally work best for close ups and windy days for long exposures, with clouds streaking by. Foliage and grasses will be lush in late spring into summer, while in winter snow is possible, due to the spot's elevation.

This bay offers a much wilder experience than other serene sandy beaches in the Gower. It's a spectacular expanse of golden beach with a rocky headland on both sides. The left headland arches around towards the sea with the famed three limestone cliffs standing tall. These merge into a huge system of sand dunes heading back towards a river that snakes through pebble banks intertwined with salt marsh tributaries. The ruins of Pennard Castle perch proudly at the top. Three Cliffs Bay is a particularly photogenic part of the Gower Coast Path. Stay safe though; this is one of Wales's most beautiful beaches, but nature can be wild too – watch out for strong tides and currents at all times.

What to shoot and viewpoints

Viewpoint 1 – The Three Cliffs

Three Cliffs Bay consists of a towering headland culminating in three curving, adjoining pyramid peaks – like the spine of a Welsh dragon at rest. The cliffs, formed of limestone strata, are punctured by an archway, which leads through to the quiet and sandy Pobbles Beach. At low tide, you can walk from one beach to the other, until the sea comes in and separates the two. Once you've walked over the reasonable, flat ground from the National Trust car park via good pathways, park yourself on one of the benches dotted around the top of the headland and enjoy a moment's rest. You'll need it! For a relatively easy route onto Pobbles Beach, descend a snaking path through sand dunes. This will require some stone climbing at the bottom. However, to reach Viewpoint 1 you'll need to head back up the sand dunes on the other side – no easy task! The tricky scramble against gravity and shifting sand soon gives way to a magnificent panorama that greets you at the top. From here, head left towards the tops of the cliff promontories and use the natural curvature of the cliffs to aid composition depth and offer leading lines to your images. There are also terrific elevated views of the river inlet down below; the patterns it weaves make interesting shapes and abstracts, which morph and develop with the tide.

On the ridge at Three Cliffs Bay (VP1). Canon 5D III, 24-70mm f/2.8 at 24mm, ISO 100, 6s at f/11. Tripod. Polariser, 6ND & ND Grad. Aug.

How to get here

All viewpoints can be accessed from the campsite car park however for Viewpoint 1, a shorter and more direct route is to park in the National Trust car park in Pennard village and walk west.

VP 1 Parking Lat/Long:	51.567000, -4.0878153
VP 1 Parking Postcode:	SA3 2AS
VP 1 OS Map Grid Ref:	SS 55391 87414
VP 1 Map:	OS Explorer Map 164 – Gower

Viewpoint 1

From the M4, exit at junction 47 and take the A483/A48 to Swansea/Gorseinon. At the bottom of the dual carriageway take the second exit on the roundabout to head west on the A484. At the next roundabout take the first exit onto Victoria Road/B4296, then head straight over the next junction to Carmansel Road.

Follow this into Three Crosses, turning right and then left onto Chapel Road. Take a left at the next T-junction onto Tirmynydd Road for a mile then left again onto the B4271. After just over half a mile take a right onto the A4118 and follow this for 2 miles passing the airport, before turning left onto Vennaway Lane, which will join you on to the B4436. Follow this road through Pennard and Southgate, turning left at the roundabout into the National Trust car park. From here, walk west along the path past the houses that back onto the golf course. On reaching the first bay (Pobbles) head down the sand dune and up the other side, walking towards the end of the cliff promontory.

Above: *View down to Three Cliffs Bay from the path (VP3). Canon 5D III, 24-70mm f/2.8 at 61mm, ISO 100, 1/20s at f/13. Tripod. Polariser. Aug.*

Pennard Pill looking up towards Pennard castle.
Canon 5D III, 16-35mm f/4 at 20mm, ISO 100, 1/125s at f/13. Polariser. Aug.

Sun shines through an arrow slit on Pennard Castle (VP2). Canon 5D III, 16-35mm f/4 at 16mm, ISO 100, 1/125s at f/13. Tripod. Aug.

Viewpoint 2 – Pennard Castle

Pennard Castle's situation is dramatic and beautiful. It rests on the edge of the valley of Pennard Pill, with sheer drops to the north and west. From here extensive views towards Three Cliffs Bay below and across the valley to Penmaen Burrows entice the eyes. It was a perfect position for a castle, except for one thing: it was vulnerable to sand blow. By the end of the 14th century, sand encroachment had led to the castle's abandonment and, ultimately, to the ruin that remains today. The castle can be reached via the directions given for Viewpoint 1, as you'll already be high up and to the east of the river inlet, saving you extra walking. Another route is to walk down from the campsite, across the stepping stones and up into the dunes that lie to the east of the beach. Either way, you'll need to dig deep to climb those sand dunes, before finally reaching the relatively level headland. There's also a more level walk from inland that skirts the nearby golf course. It's an interesting route and one that provides little snippets of the coastline, thanks to views through holes and crumbling window apertures in the castle's ancient stone walls. It's quite unusual to have a castle set amongst sand dunes and marram grass, so take your time and try to capture as many different views as you can.

VP 2 & 3 Parking Lat/Long: 51.577976, -4.1163754
VP 2 & 3 Parking Postcode: SA3 2HB
VP 2 & 3 OS Map Grid Ref: SS 53447 88691
VP 2 & 3 Map: OS Explorer Map 164 – Gower

Viewpoints 2 & 3

From the M4, exit at junction 47 and take the A483/A48 to Swansea/Gorseinon. At the bottom of the dual carriageway take the second exit at the roundabout to head west on the A484. At the next roundabout take the first exit onto Victoria Road/B4296, then go straight over the next junction to Carmansel Road. Follow this into Three Crosses, turning right and then left onto Chapel Road. Take a left at the next T-junction, then after 2 miles turn right onto the B4271. After 1.5 miles take a left. After a further mile take a right onto the A4118. Look out for signs for Three Cliffs Bay campsite. There's plenty of parking here and at the time of writing it's only £3 for the day.

Accessibility

All viewpoints require some degree of climbing or a walk across uneven ground, particularly viewpoints 1 and 2, which are accessed via large sand dunes. This can be tiring and tough, especially with a backpack full of camera gear. Viewpoint 1 requires further clambering across a system of rocky ledges to reach the 'spine' of the cliffs. The back of the beach is reached down a stony track, and the main part by stepping stones that cross the tidal river. You can go around this through the lower sand dune pathways, but it still requires a short paddle to get onto the beach. Keep an eye on the tide times here as I almost got caught out: although I'd timed it just right, I still had to wade through water to locate the stepping stones beneath.

Three Cliffs Bay. Canon 5D III, 24-70mm f/2.8 at 33mm, ISO 100, 1/25s at f/13. Tripod. Polariser. Aug.

Even though the water was just a couple of feet above the stones I could definitely feel a strong push. When the tide is completely in, it becomes impossible to cross the river. If you can't climb the dunes, take great care not to get cut off. The tide sometimes comes in around the sides of the beach, leaving a sandy island in the middle ... but not for long.

Best time of year/day

Morning can prove successful for catching light down the valley to illuminate the faces of the cliffs and dune grasses. Beneath the campsite, bluebells grow on the banks – a highlight in springtime. Late evening is the best time for me however, as once the spring season progresses and the sun starts to set further to the north, you can really capture the coast bathed in enchanting light. Try using the natural curvature of the cliffs in Viewpoint 1 as a lead in to the setting sun; it's a serene scene on a summer's eve.

Viewpoint 3 – Penmaen Burrows

Penmaen Burrows are nestled between Three Cliffs Bay and Oxwich Bay. Walk down the dead end road opposite the car park then take a left through the gate and head down the gravel track. A few strides after the houses and you're out into the open with a fabulous vista across the bay. Here you can use a medium to long telephoto lens, shooting across the bracken, which lines the path down onto the beach. Fill your frame with the celebrated three cliffs, timing a visit at high tide so they're surrounded by water – it's a magical scene during the golden hour. Turn off the track down a steepish marked path and you'll find yourself in the woods at the back of the burrows. From here you'll emerge onto the beach with exquisite views out across the river inlet high up to the castle. Keep heading south and you'll find yourself in a realm of sand dunes, marram grass and coastal flowers. Attach a wide angle lens and get down low, shooting through the grasses out to sea to give your images some texture, colour and mood.

Crossing the river via the stepping stones at the back of the beach. Canon 5D III, 24-70mm f/2.8 at 35mm, ISO 100, 1/20s at f/13. Tripod. Polariser. Aug.

A stone's throw from the hustle and bustle of the city of Swansea, Bracelet Bay is a small, rocky beach, backed by dramatic limestone cliffs. Situated at the start of the Gower Peninsula, it's the first bay you'll reach when venturing west from Swansea Bay. There are lots of rock pools to explore, along with nearby Mumbles Lighthouse, standing proud on its own island. The beach offers views along the south Wales coastline and across the Bristol Channel towards Devon. It's a stunning stretch of the Gower and a real escape without being too far away from civilisation.

What to shoot and viewpoints

Viewpoint 1 – Bracelet Bay

In summer Bracelet Bay is a popular destination for holidaymakers. Parking is found at the top of the beach while to the western end a large restaurant with a terrace offers great views across the bay and beyond. The main path down to the beach from the car park is found at the eastern end. This will take you down onto a small area of sand, covered in shingle and stones. There's not much in the way of sand on this stretch of the Gower, however what it lacks in sand, it more than makes up for with rocks. The whole expanse of Bracelet Bay is a maze of intertwining rocky gullies, inlets and rock pools full of sea and plant life. The centre of the beach comprises a mix of sand patterns, formations and rocky outcrops, while to the eastern and western ends, the rocks swell into huge slabs and boulders, creating some pools more than six-feet deep. Traversing this rock-strewn landscape can be quite precarious, so take care not to twist an ankle on slippery seaweed. The colours of the rocks here are impressive: there are shades of reds, yellows, even the odd green tinge laced with quartz stripes. It's an abstract shooter's dream and should keep you entertained for some time. Popular views of the bay tend to include the lighthouse in the background with the curve of the bay leading the eye towards it. The tide plays a big part in shots here; while you'll want a low tide to explore the rocky areas on the beach, higher tides can help simplify your scenes, concealing the distraction of scattered rocks and filling your foreground with the blue colour palette of seawater. There are strong rip tides and the

waves can get pretty rough here in the winter months, which makes the bay a popular place for stormy, wave-filled images, all shot from the relative safety of the car park.

Viewpoint 2 – Mumbles Lighthouse

The Mumbles Lighthouse sits proudly at the far south-eastern point of Bracelet Bay. Like many of the lighthouses throughout Wales and the United Kingdom, it is now unmanned though would once have been occupied by more than ten people. It has guided vessels to safe passage for over 200 years, around nearby Mixon Sands and Cherry Stone Rock – two massive submerged sandbanks that have caused the destruction of countless ships over the centuries. Today it's simply a flashing light powered by solar energy and a horn sounded on foggy days to warn vessels. >>

Opposite: Sand formations and rock pools on Bracelet Bay (VP1). Canon 5D IV, 24-70mm f/2.8 at 33mm, ISO 100, 25s at f/16. Tripod. Polariser & ND Grad. Apr.

How to get here

From Swansea city head out west on Victoria Road/A4067 and follow this road for nearly 4 miles before going straight over at the roundabout and continuing for a further mile. As you enter the village of Mumbles, head over the roundabout and continue for another mile. You'll see the pier on your left and as the road veers round to the right, you can either park in the car park here or continue a few hundred yards to the main car park. Pay and display charges apply.

Parking Lat/Long: 51.566777, -3.9815167
Parking Postcode: SA3 4JT
OS Map Grid Ref: SS627871
Map: OS Explorer Map 164 – Gower

Accessibility &

The car park is very large, stretching the entire length of the bay up the sea front, so this area is flat and wheelchair/scooter friendly. The restaurant here has a terrace, so you can take in the sea views along with any refreshments. The beach, accessed via a few uneven pathways, is itself very uneven with many rocks to cross. The pier and arcade area is generally flat and offers views down across the bay and to the lighthouse.

Best time of year/day

Low tide is best to explore the tremendous number of rock pools found along the bay, while high tide coupled with windy weather is best to see waves crashing into the land. Seabirds start to nest in April and stay around until midsummer. Sunrises can be spectacular in winter months with the sun rising out of the bay behind the lighthouse, while sunsets can provide helpful side lighting to illuminate Bracelet Bay's rocks and the shapely lighthouse beacon.

Long exposure to smooth out ripples. Rock pool and lighthouse on Bracelet Bay.
Canon 5D IV, 24-70mm f/2.8 at 24mm, ISO 50, 240s at f/18. Tripod. Polariser, 10ND & ND Grad. Apr.

Favoured views of the lighthouse look from Bracelet Bay and also from the pier side of the bay. Use the rocky foreground to create a visual journey towards the island and lighthouse. Couple this with strong side lighting to highlight the white paint on the beacon itself for great effect. The going underfoot is always over boulders and rocks so watch your step. There's a fast-rising tide here though so make sure to have an exit route planned!

Viewpoint 3 – Mumbles Pier

Visible from most places in Swansea Bay, Mumbles Pier is a firm favourite with holidaymakers and day trippers. Offering the customary amusement arcades, ice cream parlours and fish and chip shops, the pier was built in 1898 and was used as a terminus for the Swansea and Mumbles Railway – the world's first passenger-carrying railway company. In the 1920s, a lifeboat station was added and today there's a second, brand-new lifeboat station at the end of the main walkway. The pier has elevated views of the surrounding coast, lighthouse and back towards Swansea itself. The summer months provide a unique offering when the pier is home to nesting kittiwakes. This breeding colony is well over twenty years old and is one of only a handful in the UK on a manmade structure. To encourage the birds, shelved platforms have been installed, mainly on the old lifeboat station, for the birds to nest on. They also gather along the rafters and framework of the pier structures. These are exceptionally noisy birds and you'll hear them before you see them. Ordinarily, kittiwakes nest on remote coastal cliffs, so it seems incongruous to observe them roosting against a city backdrop. A must see!

Top: Abstract of seaweed and rocks. Canon 5D IV, 24-70mm f/2.8 at 24mm, ISO 320, 1/125s at f/9. Tripod. Polariser. Apr.

Middle: Kittiwake nesting shelves on the old Mumbles lifeboat station. Canon 5D IV, 70-200mm f/2.8 at 140mm, ISO 800, 1/1250s at f/5.6. Apr.

Bottom: Long exposure of the new Mumbles lifeboat station. Canon 5D IV, 24-70mm f/2.8 at 30mm, ISO 50, 180s at f/18. Tripod. Polariser, 10ND & ND Grad. Apr.

Opposite: Kittiwake nests on the pier structures (VP3). Canon 5D IV, 70-200mm f/2.8 at 185mm, ISO 800, 1/640s at f/5.6. Apr.

The seaside town of New Quay.
Canon 5D IV, 70-200mm f/2.8 at 135mm, ISO 400, 1/250s at f/10. Polariser. Apr.

CEREDIGION

CEREDIGION – INTRODUCTION

Ceredigion is a county on the west coast of South Wales. Much like Pembrokeshire, it's a real hotspot for tourism and one of Wales' most popular holiday areas. Comprised of rocky coves, sea cliffs, caves, idyllic harbours and an abundance of sandy beaches, the Ceredigion coast is a lovely place to visit any time of year. Named after Prince Ceredig, Ceredigion is sheltered from the east by the Cambrian Mountains and stretches west to the shores of Cardigan Bay. As a key part of the Wales Coast Path, Ceredigion's footpath winds for sixty miles along this sweeping arc of land from Cardigan in the south to Ynys Las in the north, before taking a turn inland, down the Dyfi Valley and on to the neighbouring county of Gwynedd.

Bottlenose dolphins in Cardigan Bay.
Canon 1D IV, 70-200mm f/2.8 at 200mm,
ISO 1000, 1/3200s at f/5.6. June.

Ceredigion is known for its coast and the world-famous Cardigan Bay. The outstanding beauty of Cardigan Bay was acknowledged when it became the UK's first designated Marine Heritage Coast more than twenty-five years ago. It is a huge lee shore that faces the prevailing winds and the full force of the Atlantic in winter months. The bay itself is generally quite shallow – no more than fifty metres in places – and it's this unique habitat of reefs and sea caves that makes marine life flourish. It's no surprise then that the UK's biggest pod of bottlenose dolphins live in Cardigan Bay and these fascinating creatures are a regular sight from the shores and harbours. In New Quay, they delight visitors daily with their jumping and diving, which can be seen from the sea wall. Other marine species, such as harbour porpoise and grey seals, call these shores home too, as do a variety of nesting seabirds.

Inland treats include wooded river valleys with gushing waterfalls rich with leaping salmon; upland moors and bogs bursting with wildlife and rare flora and fauna. Medieval castles dot the landscape, while to the east, the topography changes shape, with the beginnings of the Cambrian Mountains. Then there's Aberystwyth, Ceredigion's largest town, with a large university, trendy bars, high street shops and a population of over 15,000, It's a real culture shock after experiencing the peaceful seaside villages that surround it. But venture west away from the busy streets and it's still a seaside market town at heart. With its sweeping promenade, characterful Victorian pier, working harbour and two beaches, it's the perfect place for an outing with the camera; just don't forget the fish and chips.

Maps

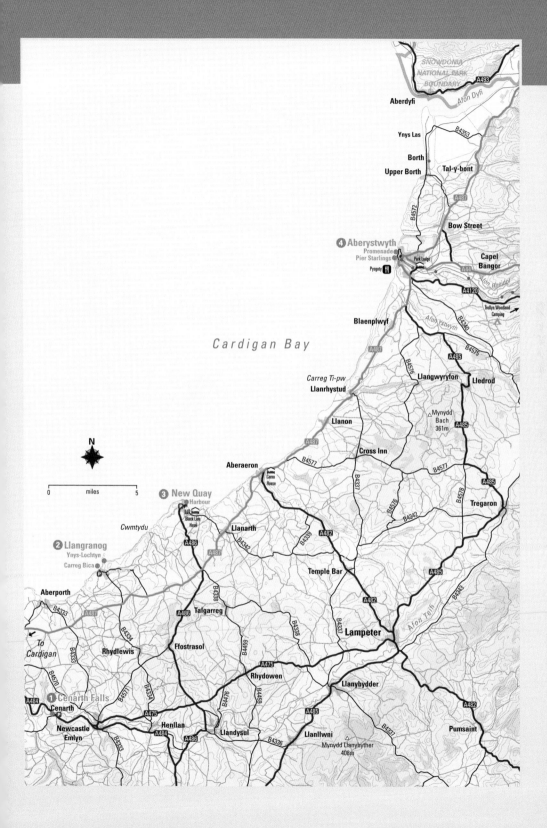

Cardigan Bay

SNOWDONIA
NATIONAL PARK
BOUNDARY

A493

Aberdyfi

Afon Dyfi

Ynys Las

B4353

Borth

Tal-y-bont

Upper Borth

A487

B4572

Bow Street

4 Aberystwyth
Promenade
Pier Starlings
Park Lodge
Pysgoty

Capel
Bangor

A4120

Afon Rheidol

Trefyn Woodland
Camping

A4340

Blaenplwyf

Afon Ystwyth

A4575

A485

A487

B4576

Llangwyryfon

Lledrod

Carreg Ti-pw

Llanrhystud

Mynydd
Bach
361m

A485

Llanon

B4577

Cross Inn

B4577

A487

B4578

Tregaron

B4337

B4576

A485

Aberaeron
Carno
House

B4342

B4339

A482

Temple Bar

A485

3 New Quay
Harbour
Black Lion
Hotel

Llanarth

A486

B4342

A487

Cwmtydu

A482

B4343

B4337

2 Llangranog
Ynys-Lochtyn
Carreg Bica

Afon Teifi

Aberporth

A486

Talgarreg

B4333

A487

B4334

*To
Cardigan*

B4570

Rhydlewis

Ffostrasol

B4459

B4338

A475

Rhydowen

Llanybydder

A482

1 Cenarth Falls
Cenarth

A484

B4571

B4334

A475

Henllan

B4476

B4459

A485

Llanllwni

Pumsaint

B4337

Newcastle
Emlyn

A484

A486

Llandysul

B4336

Mynydd Llanybyther
408m

N

0 miles 5

Ynys Lochtyn from nearby Pendinas Lochtyn (p.366).
Canon 5D IV, 24-70mm f/2.8 at 30mm, ISO 200, 1/60s at f/9. Tripod. Polariser. Oct.

Situated right on the border of the counties of Pembrokeshire, Ceredigion and Carmarthenshire, Cenarth Falls is a spectacular series of cascading waterfalls on the river Teifi near to Cardigan. The river is the heart of the village here and it's easy to see why. Over the years the running water has eroded its way through hard rock, producing a collection of tumbling waterfalls. There has been a watermill here since the 13th century and the falls are famous for leaping salmon on their journey upstream to spawn.

What to shoot and viewpoints

The dominant feature of Cenarth is the large stone bridge that spans the river and carries the main road traffic from Cardigan to Newcastle Emlyn. The bridge was built in 1787 and features large circular holes that serve to maintain strength while reducing the weight of the structure. Without these holes, there would be immense pressure on the bridge during floods. After heavy rain the falls here become submerged by a raging torrent of brown water that can flood the car park completely. It's a very dangerous place to be in such conditions, so I'd only recommend viewing from a distance. River levels can change rapidly along this wooded valley.

Just next to the main car parking area lie the falls' best features: a mixture of flowing gullies and swirling pools to photograph. Depending on the river level you can do some rock-hopping to venture closer to the centre of the falls for a different composition, but watch out for slippery surfaces. Long exposures work well here, smoothing out flowing water and a polariser filter will help to cut down surface glare and reflections. There's often a fallen log or tree that's been washed downstream, creating an interesting focal element. Inarguably though, the main background interest is provided by the old water mill, nestled within the trees. It's a timeless scene and one that's inspired photographers and painters for generations. A footpath snakes along the northern side of the river here if you wish to explore further. Just above the falls are the rapids, where you might see salmon resting before continuing their journey up river. The trees here are mainly

deciduous so most transform into rich amber colours in autumn. Many bird species call this place home with plenty of woodpeckers, nuthatch and red kite to name just a few.

Another interesting sight you may only see in Cenarth are coracles. These small, hand-crafted boats were once used all over Britain, but now only remain in a handful of places – Cenarth being one. Fisherman still use them to this day. One technique involves spanning the river with a large net held between two coracles as the boats drift down with the current, sweeping up salmon or sewin (sea trout)

Opposite: The falls and the old water mill. Canon 5D II, 17-40mm f/4 at 26mm, ISO 100, 0.8s at f/16. Tripod. Polariser & 3ND. Sep.

How to get here

From Cardigan follow the one way system around the town, before taking a left onto Priory Street. Follow the road signed Pont-Y-Cleifion for a quarter of a mile before taking the second exit at the roundabout. Head out east on the A484 main road for 7 miles until you reach the village bridge and the river will be on your right. A private car park on your immediate left is situated adjacent to the falls. There is a small charge for parking. A handful of free parking spaces lie on the south side of the river just past the bridge on the B4332.

Parking Lat/Long: 52.044995, -4.5262840
Parking Postcode: SA38 9JL
OS Map grid ref: SN268415
Map: OS Explorer Map 198 – Cardigan & New Quay

Accessibility

If limited mobility is an issue, opt for the waterfalls car park, where you can park literally next to the river and in close proximity to the falls. If you park on the south side of the river, then you'll need to cross the road bridge to access the waterfalls. It's single-file traffic over the bridge, which is used by buses and large lorries so keep your wits about you when crossing. Once down near the falls it's fairly easy going underfoot. If you want to explore closer still, the ground can be uneven although access to the viewing platform is generally flat. The pathway along the river is uneven in places, especially if flooding means you have to take the higher route.

Best time of year/day

Spring through to autumn would be my chosen window to go. Not only for tree colour but if you're shooting to include the watermill, stark trees during winter let the sky through – tricky to balance for a decent exposure. An early morning or afternoon visit would be advisable otherwise you'll be shooting into the sun. River levels change drastically throughout the year so the falls will often look different on more than one visit. Salmon jump the falls mainly in late summer and sewin between June and August.

during the open season. Coracles are made from strips of willow or ash then wrapped in canvas impregnated with tar to make them watertight. Paddling them is a real art – a figure-of-eight motion – and it takes a long time to master. In the village itself a coracle museum shows how they are made and displays examples from around the world.

Unique holes in the stone bridge allows for floods. Canon 5D IV, 24-70mm f/2.8 at 24mm, ISO 100, 1/40s at f/8. Mar.

A coracle in Cenarth village. Canon 5D IV, 24-70mm f/2.8 at 33mm, ISO 400, 1/500s at f/9. Mar.

Llangrannog is one of the county's most popular beach destinations tucked away in a valley along the coast of Ceredigion. Quaint seaside pubs and shops give way to the sea wall and a large sandy beach running into a rugged, rock-strewn coastline. Large sea stacks stand proud and rock pools are ripe for exploration in this small area on the west coast. Venture along the coastal path to see breathtaking views out across nearby islands as well as the sweep of the Cardigan Bay coastline right up to north Wales. If, like me, you went to school in South Wales, there was always an annual trip to the youth centre here, known as the 'Urdd'. So if it's a slow weather day, there are always lots of activities to enjoy, the dry ski slope being the highlight.

What to shoot and viewpoints

As with many locations across the UK, the names of our towns, cities and local landmarks are steeped in history. Sometimes myths and legends dominate; stories and folklore conjure up images of fantastical beings and Llangrannog is no exception. Both the main geological features along this coast are included in a famous tale – one where giants roam and islands are created with a mere sweep of the finger.

Legend says that the sea stack Carreg Bica (Bica's rock) on Llangrannog beach is the tooth of a giant who lived in the nearby mountains. Suffering from severe toothache, he offered a reward to anyone who could cure him. A lonely dwarf named Lochtyn suggested Bica should head to the coast, where his tooth would fall out. In return for this advice, Lochtyn's wish was to live on an island for the rest of his days. Bica set off for the coast and arrived in Llangrannog. His first footstep formed Llangrannog beach and his second, Cilborth beach. The painful tooth fell out between his feet, creating Carreg Bica and, lo and behold, the pain was gone! True to his word, Bica reached out and drew his finger across the rocky headland, shaping a tiny island for the dwarf. The island is known today as Ynys Lochtyn –Lochtyn's Island.

Viewpoint 1 – Carreg Bica

You can't miss this one but you'll need a low tide to explore around it. Llangrannog is a very small seaside town with minimal parking so it's best to take advantage of the free parking areas just outside the town and walk down the narrow hill to the seafront. The beach is straight down the slipway. To the east of the bay lies a gargantuan sea stack. It's quite the symbol of Llangrannog and a photogenic one at that. Made of Ordovician rock, it's become so weather-worn over the years that parts have fallen off and it is now balanced by little more than grace. The view from the sea reveals that it stands on a much thinner pillar than first seems from the beach. It's a great focal point on which to aim your camera and is best viewed from the shoreline. Try to incorporate tidal action in the foreground for a nice lead line towards the stack.

How to get here

From Cardigan head north east on the main A487 west coast road for around ten miles. As you enter the small village of Brynhoffnant take a left turn – signed Llangrannog/B4334 – just before the petrol station. This lane can get busy and it's quite narrow so keep an eye out for passing places. Watch out also for a couple of hairpin bends. After a caravan site, the car park is on your left. From here, walk down the road before taking a left and heading down the hill to the beach and the start of the coastal path.

Parking Lat/Long: 52.157131, -4.4626956
Parking Postcode: SA44 6RL
OS Map grid ref: SN316538
Map: OS Explorer Map 198 – Cardigan & New Quay

Accessibility

There is a private pay & display car park right on the beach, handy for those with limited mobility, to access the sandy shoreline and views of Carreg Bica. Otherwise I'd recommend parking in the free car park up the hill then walking down. Viewpoint 2 requires a good level of fitness to reach via the coastal path, especially if heading up to the hill fort, as it does get quite steep. It's good under foot as it's an access road for the observation post.

Best time of year/day

Late afternoon or sunset is the best time to visit; with the northern seaward aspect you can witness the sun setting into a watery horizon. Keep an eye on the tide, especially if venturing around Carreg Bica and the rock pools, as it can come in and separate the two beaches. Steps at the back of Cilborth Beach provide an escape route if needed. Gorse will start to flower along the pathways in early spring, while in late summer the bracken lining the coastal path turns a lovely russet orange, adding a splash of colour to any foreground.

Carreg Bica from the shoreline on Llangrannog beach.
Canon 5D III, 24-70mm f/2.8 at 35mm, ISO 100, 5s at f/18, Tripod, Polariser, 6ND & ND Grad, Oct

From the coast path near VP2 looking north in autumn. Canon 5D III, 24-70mm f/2.8 at 35mm, ISO 250, 1/100s at f/11. Polariser & ND Grad. Oct.

Viewpoint 2 – Ynys Lochtyn

From the rear right-hand corner of the beach, next to the café, you can spot the start of the coastal path. From here follow the path that ascends the steps to the top of headland with a conveniently placed bench to catch your breath. Below you lies Cilborth beach, which is a lot rockier and can be accessed at low tide via steps down to it. Continuing north eastwards the footpath skirts around fields before joining the main route at a kissing gate. Take a left here and after a few hundred yards the view across to the island reveals itself with the blue yonder of Cardigan Bay as its backdrop. Another handy bench is situated here and there are two options: either head down the carved out steps and onto the plateau at the end on the mainland – this offers great compositions over to Ynys Lochtyn and the surrounding coves and rocky bays; or continue heading east on the coastal path. If you follow it round in a spiral, you'll climb to the summit where you'll find Pendinas Lochtyn hill fort. There's now a fenced off MOD observation post here but you're free to wander the surrounding land. It commands magnificent 360-degree views sweeping from the mainland down along the coast and on towards north Pembrokeshire. In the other direction, views open up right round Cardigan Bay to Snowdonia and the Llŷn Peninsula in North Wales. These panoramic views make this the perfect spot for a picnic. It's also a great place to spot wildlife, with hovering kestrels, whirling chough and – if you're lucky – pods of dolphins in the bay below as they make their way to New Quay.

Opposite: At the end of Ynys Lochtyn. Canon 5D III, 24-70mm f/2.8 at 28mm, ISO 50, 25s at f/16. Polariser, 6ND & ND Grad. Oct.

With its picturesque houses, pubs and restaurants all clinging to a hillside above Cardigan Bay, New Quay is a very quaint seaside town on the west coast of Wales. Not to be confused with the similarly named Newquay in Cornwall, New Quay has two golden sandy beaches divided by a curved harbour wall. It's a popular fishing harbour and there are always plenty of boats moored up here, sheltering in the calmer waters of the bay.

It's one of the most-visited Welsh seaside towns in summer, when New Quay becomes a bustling, vibrant holiday resort, popular with sailing and fishing boats. There are dolphin-watching tours, watersports and superb Blue Flag beaches. Oh, and great fish and chip shops.

What to shoot and viewpoints

Most of the photographic interest at New Quay lies in and around the harbour and its sandy beaches. It's a very compact seaside town with narrow one way streets and limited parking, so can get exceptionally busy on high days and holidays. Opt for a weekday visit during these times if possible. Parking is easy with several car parks, though as a general rule of thumb, the closer you get to the beach the higher the charge. Once parked however, it's easy to cover most of the area on foot.

New Quay is a coastal photographer's dream; there are so many compositions to be had. Wide-angle lenses will be perfect to embrace the whole sweep of the harbour, including any moored boats. Pick an elevated spot to make the most of reflections and use a low tide to your advantage: wander out around beached boats to find interesting sand textures, formations and rippled pools. Up on the harbour wall itself the weather-beaten stonework is textured for close-up abstracts, along with old anchors, rope and other boating chandlery. This is a working harbour so there are plenty of lobster pots and netting lying around, along with colourful seashells at which to point your lens. When visiting New Quay, you might catch a glimpse of the wild bottlenose dolphins that call this area home. Cardigan Bay, the area around

New Quay harbour in summer. Canon 5D III, 24-70mm f/2.8 at 28mm, ISO 640, 1/125s at f/14. Polariser. June.

Llangrannog and New Quay has the largest population of dolphins in Europe. They are regularly seen, swimming in small pods and it's possible to spot them from the harbour wall as they leap into the air.

The best way to see them up close though is to head out on one of the boat trips, which take groups out from New Quay on a regular basis, I'd recommend joining the survey boats on one of their research outings as these can be up to eight-hours long. As with any wildlife, there are no guarantees of seeing dolphins on a given day, but the chances are good. Just up the hill behind New Quay beach is the Cardigan Bay Marine Wildlife site, which has lots of information on the species found in the bay and any sightings that have been recorded. Dolphins are best observed on days when the sea is calm, as they are much easier to spot. A wave from afar looks identical to a surfacing dorsal fin, so you need conditions to be on your side for any outings. May through to September are the best months. The pier at New Quay is usually a good vantage point, as is anywhere along Rock Street – the closest of the New Quay terraces to the sea. The best times for spotting dolphins from land are early morning, evening and immediately after high tide, however a boat trip usually rewards those hoping to see them. There's a wealth of other wildlife too, Atlantic grey seals are very common all along the coastline here, as well as seabirds nesting and roosting at Bird Rock and beyond towards Llangrannog.

Bottlenose dolphins in Cardigan Bay. Canon 1D IV, 70-200mm f/2.8 at 200mm, ISO 1000, 1/3200s at f/5.6. June.

Nesting seabirds along the coast, viewed from boat trip. Canon 1D IV, 70-200mm f/2.8 at 165mm, ISO 800, 1/1250s at f/5.6. June.

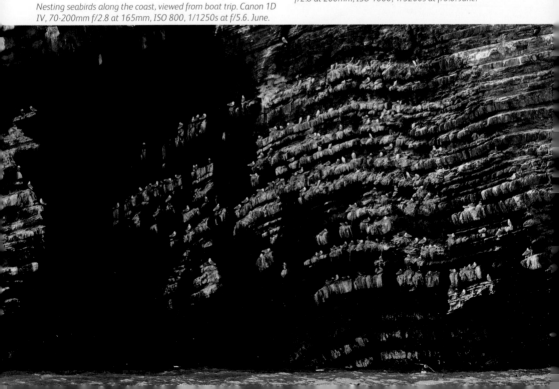

Top: *Dorsal fins of bottlenose dolphins in Cardigan Bay. Canon 1D IV, 70-200mm f/2.8 at 200mm, ISO 1000, 1/4000s at f/8. June.*

Fishing boat moored in New Quay harbour. Canon 5D III, 24-70mm f/2.8 at 28mm, ISO 640, 1/200s at f/10. Polariser. June.

How to get here

From Cardigan head north to the A487 coast road signed Aberystwyth for just over 17 miles. On approaching 'Synod Inn', take a left at the crossroads onto the A486 signed New Quay. Follow this road for 4 miles and you'll enter New Quay. You can either park here on the right at Church Road car park or continue down to Rock Street car park on the waterfront. The road will merge into Hill Street as you follow the one way system around the town for a few hundred yards. Take a left onto Glanmor Terrace/B4342 and continue around the seafront passing the slipway. The car park is on your right.

Car Parks' current charges: Rock Street – £3.30 per day; Church Road – £2.40 per day.

Parking Lat/Long: 52.215712, -4.3601641
Parking Postcode: SA45 9NY
OS Map grid ref: SN388601
Map: OS Explorer Map 198 – Cardigan & New Quay

Accessibility ♿

Most of the pathways from parking to harbour are paved and generally flat, however there's a steep descent/ascent if walking to and from the Church Road car park towards the harbour, so if this is an issue choose the parking closest to the harbour. You're free to wander around the beaches, the harbour and right to the end of the harbour wall, though there's a few stepped level changes here.

Best time of year/day

Although it doesn't feel it as you look out to sea on the west coast, New Quay has an eastern aspect, so it's nicely sheltered from choppy seas. This provides great reflections in the bay and due to the angles of sunlight, the harbour benefits from sunrises. Dolphins are most commonly seen late spring into summer on an incoming tide and seabird colonies will be most active around June.

Above: *Research boat skipper looking for dolphins. Canon 5D III, 24-70mm f/2.8 at 24mm, ISO 400, 1/60s at f/14. June.*

Nestled in between Cardigan Bay and the Cambrian Mountains on the west coast of Wales, Aberystwyth is a lively university town with bags of character and atmosphere. It has a, long, seafront promenade and a pebble beach, backed by colourful Victorian and Edwardian terraced buildings looking west out to sea. Dividing the beach and the harbour is the 242m-long historic pier, where hundreds of thousands of starlings roost in the rafters during the winter months. There are castle ruins and a funicular railway, which transports passengers high above the shops and houses and rewards them with sweeping panoramic views of the town and coast below.

What to shoot and viewpoints

Viewpoint 1 – Promenade

The jewel in Aberystwyth's coastal crown is its graceful and sweeping seafront. The prom is exceptionally picturesque whatever the weather and always busy with people enjoying the seaside. At just under two-miles long there's plenty to point your camera at here. The town's sights and landmarks include the harbour and marina in the south with its large sea wall and moored boats, and the busy main beach and Constitution Hill at the northern end. The busiest and most-photogenic section of the promenade is the aptly named Marine Terrace. Here multicoloured houses and hotels line the seafront.

The beach is made up mostly of shingle with the sand only revealed at low tide but this changing tide offers different foreground textures for your images. At the centre of the beach, a large bandstand holds a variety of events and musical performances during the summer season. There's also a long, narrow jetty that juts out at a right angle to the prom, stepping down as it reaches into the sea. For those who love minimalistic long exposure shots, this is a perfect setting thanks to the symmetrical jetty posts, which descend towards the end marker; black and white conversions work particularly well. Take care walking on the wooded surface – it can be slippery under foot. If you catch the tide right you'll be able to reach the end of the jetty, which offers a different view back towards the promenade – most effective when day transitions into night and you can photograph the town's streetlights reflected in the calm waters. Residual colour from the sky adds additional hues.

War memorial statue in castle grounds. Canon 5D III, 24-70mm f/2.8 at 53mm, ISO 250, 1/250s at f/7.1. Polariser. Jan.

__Opposite__: Shoreline waves along the promenade beach. Canon 5D III, 24-70mm f/2.8 at 28mm, ISO 250, 1/50s at f/11. Polariser. Jan.

Long exposure of promenade seafront and buildings in blue hour.
Canon 5D III, 24-70mm f/2.8 at 24mm, ISO 100, 30s at f/16, Polariser & 6ND, Jan.

Starlings flocking around the pier at sunset (VP2). Canon 5D III, 24-70mm f/2.8 at 55mm, ISO 1000, 1/1250s at f/6.3. Jan.

Viewpoint 2 – Pier Starlings

One of nature's greatest spectacles is to witness thousands of starlings flying to roost at dusk. It happens here in Aberystwyth in the autumn and winter months and they all head for the seaside pier. Even without a camera, it's a fantastic sight. You'll notice a crowd of hopeful onlookers and birdwatchers gathering, ready for the spectacle. Unless you're in the know, you'll wonder why the previously empty beach is now packed with people. As the sun starts to set, the birds begin flying in to roost. They'll arrive in separate groups and then some larger groups will filter in. With a steady flow, the numbers build and within minutes, there's a huge, dark, swirling mass of birds in the sky. If a bird of prey is present, it will dive bomb the group and scatter them, causing mass hysteria among the birds. These sychronised and mesmerising displays are called murmurations and it's a wonderful natural phenomenon to witness. Some days they'll swirl for longer in the sky than others, so it's worth visiting several times to see different displays. If you're lucky enough to have the flock pass overhead, you'll be in awe at the sound of thousands of beating wings as they whoosh past. Once the birds are finished, they circle and stream down to roost in the supports under the pier. At which point, these previously silent birds erupt in raucous chatter, illustrating just how apt the collective noun 'chattering' is for starlings. The noise can be deafening if you stand too close to the roost.

The best place to watch this natural wonder is from the beach, between the pier and the jetty. Tide times will dictate how far out you can go so check these before visiting. Anywhere along the seafront around the pier is also suitable as a viewing point, but means you'll be looking down on the roost once they've settled. Some opt to stand out on the jetty; it sticks out far enough into the sea to align it with a setting sun for stunning colour-filled skies. Try a long telephoto lens to home in on the structures and roosting birds, throwing them into silhouette by deliberately under-exposing.

The old college. Canon 5D III, 24-70mm f/2.8 at 24mm, ISO 500, 1/60s at f/9. Jan.

How to get here

Parking Lat/Long: 52.417688, -4.0842412
Parking Postcode: SY23 2BY
OS Map grid ref: SN583820
Map: OS Explorer Map 213 – Aberystwyth & Cwm Rheidol

Accessibility ♿

Aberystwyth's seafront is exceptionally mobility-friendly with flat, wide pavements, which are on the same level as the road. There is also easy, free roadside parking along Marine Terrace. There is a large slipway down to the beach just north of the bandstand. Otherwise, access to the beach is via steps at the southern end of the seafront and there are steps onto the jetty. Those less mobile can still watch the starling display from the well-maintained pavements all along the promenade.

Best time of year/day

Due to its western aspect, sunset is a great time to visit both of these viewpoints. Throughout the year, the sun's setting position will move around to the north; eventually setting right out at sea during the summer months. The starlings will start to gather and roost on the pier from late October onwards and depart around mid- to late-February or early March. The promenade can be treacherous when winter sea storms roll in teaming up with high tides. In recent years, it has been a more regular occurrence for the sea to breach defences and flood the main road and buildings, covering the road in shingle and debris.

Above: People gather to watch the starling murmuration on the beach jetty. Canon 5D III, 24-70mm f/2.8 at 24mm, ISO 1000, 1/1250s at f/3.5. Jan. *Left*: The castle ruins in late afternoon light. Canon 5D III, 24-70mm f/2.8 at 31mm, ISO 500, 1/60s at f/9. Polariser. Jan.

Slow shutter speed of starlings silhouetted at roost on the pier.
Canon 5D III, 500mm f/4 at 500mm, ISO 100, 1/30s at f/8. Tripod. Jan.

East Usk lighthouse in evening light, Newport Wetlands (p.408).
Canon 5D III, 70-200mm f/2.8 at 200mm, ISO 800, 1/1250s at f/5. Nov.

SOUTH EAST WALES

South East Wales offers a mixture of rugged sea cliffs, meandering rivers, castles and cities. Home to the country's capital, Cardiff, it is Wales's most populated region; over twelve per cent of Wales's population live in Cardiff alone. Even so, you don't need to go far from the hustle and bustle of the city to enjoy a wild escape. Within an hour's drive, you can be among the Brecon Beacons or striding along the cliff tops of the Gower coastline in splendid isolation.

Along its base, the main artery of the M4 motorway winds its way half the length of South Wales, connecting Wales to England via the Second Severn Crossing road bridge. The coastline in this region is varied and although much of it has been industrialised, there are some real gems to explore here. Just a forty-five minute drive west from Cardiff you can take in the views along the spectacular Glamorgan Heritage Coast.

This fourteen-mile stretch of fossil-rich coastline offers plunging cliffs, secluded coves and breathtaking views across the Bristol Channel – all of it accessible on foot via the Wales Coast Path. Dunraven Bay near Southerndown is one of the more popular beaches, while the lighthouse, shapely sea cliffs and boulder-strewn beach at Nash Point are definitely worth a visit too.

Many castles dot this part of Wales and you may spot one as you drive along the motorway near Cardiff. Castell Coch, nestled on a hillside and surrounded by rich woodland, wouldn't look out of place in a fairytale. Cardiff too has its own castle and is a great location for a city break with plenty of bars, shops and parks. To the south, Cardiff Bay is extremely popular and the juxtaposition of traditional old buildings and modern architecture is a sight to behold, complemented by views across the water. There's a small wetland area here for bird watching and other places for wildlife encounters such as Forest Farm in Cardiff and the RSPB site of Newport Wetlands just up the coast to the east.

Escape the city northwards and you'll find yourself in the eastern part of the Brecon Beacons, with the Black Mountains providing a backdrop to the small market

town of Abergavenny. A short hop east into Monmouthshire and you're approaching the English borderlands of the Wye Valley. Spectacular limestone gorges and dense woodlands greet you as the river winds its way down to the beautiful Forest of Dean.

Illuminated words on the Millennium Centre, Cardiff Bay (p.402). Canon 5D IV, 24-70mm f/2.8 at 24mm, ISO 100, 3.2s at f/9. Tripod. Polariser & ND Grad. Dec.

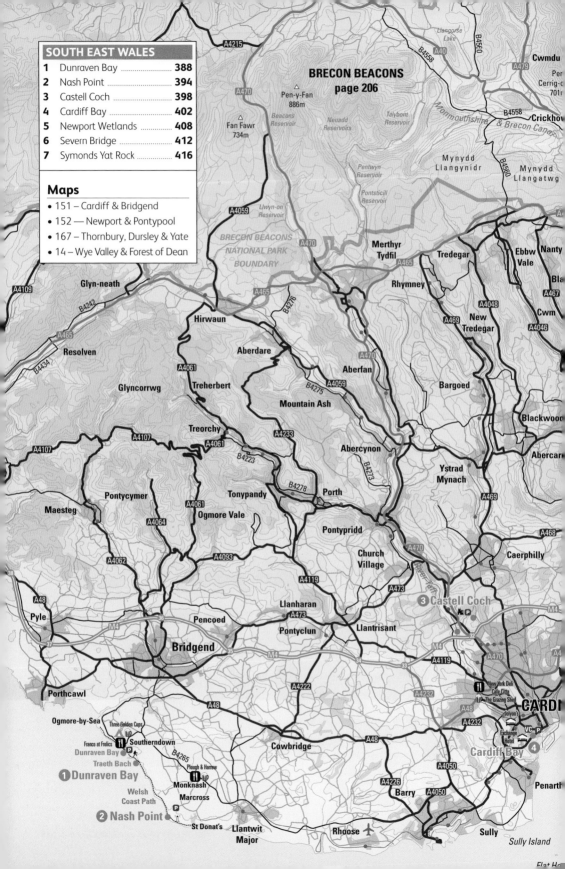

Sun shines through autumn woodland, Forest of Dean (p.416).
Canon 5D IV, 24-70mm f/2.8 at 28mm, ISO 100, 1/30s at f/16. Tripod. Nov.

Just to the west of the iconic Nash Point headland, Dunraven Bay is a fabulous location along the Glamorgan Heritage Coast. Southerndown, the nearby village, is arguably the most scenic of the numerous coastal villages in the Vale of Glamorgan and is certainly the most popular with locals. Although the beach is officially called Dunraven Bay, the locals call it Southerndown Beach. The beach itself is backed by large round boulders, which have been shaped by the powerful waves. When the tide is out there's a great expanse of sand and many rock pools to explore. It's a good place to look for fossils too.

There's a second beach, just over the headland to the south that rarely has anyone on it, partly due to the steep steps down the cliffs. This second beach is one of the largest in Glamorgan but be careful as tide conditions can cut you off from the steps. To the east of the bay you can hop onto the Glamorgan Coastal Path and explore the ruins and gardens of Dunraven Castle, climbing up right onto the cliff edge for spectacular views of coastline and wave-cut platforms hundreds of metres below.

What to shoot and viewpoints

Viewpoint 1 – Dunraven Bay

This is a very picturesque bay offering a variety of views. On exiting the car park you're met by an area of large smooth boulders that back onto the beach. These make great foreground focal points to your shots, not only providing scale and interest for those wider views but also abstracts and close ups too – especially on cloudy days when they'll expose nicely with subtle shading. Visits to the bay at high tide are rewarding: these boulders look superb as they get covered with water, reflecting colour from the sky, so test out some longer exposures here as the tide rushes back and forth creating white trails. With the tide further out, more of the sandy beach is exposed. This large, flat smooth bay is inundated with rock pools, sand ripples and formations. To the west of the bay a large slipway heads down to the sea. This allows you to position yourself in the centre of and slightly above the incoming tide, so you can shoot from the heart of the action without getting wet. Venturing in either direction means a climb up the coastal path onto the headland. To the west the path climbs rapidly, allowing views down into the bay and also across to the north Devon coastline, a short distance away over the Bristol Channel . To the east lies the interestingly named Witches Point, a towering headland that juts out into the bay. This cliff face will most likely form many of your backgrounds. The very end of the Witches Point headland is accessible, if you follow the coastal path east from the bay then the worn tracks to the very end. Here a different view of the bay looks west. It's a great viewpoint when large waves are forecast as they smash against the rocky outcrop.

How to get here

From the M4 motorway, exit at junction 37 and take the A4229. At the next main roundabout follow signs for A48 south. Follow the A48 for around 5 miles before turning right onto New Inn Road. Head down here for 1.5 miles then turn right onto the B4265 towards Southerndown. After 2 miles turn onto the B4524 and continue for a further mile or so. This will bring you out onto the coast road passing the cliff-top car park. The main car park sits at the bottom of the hill.

Parking Lat/Long: 51.446165, -3.6053617
Parking Postcode: CF32 0RT
OS Map grid ref: SS 885731
Map: OS Explorer Map 151 – Cardiff & Bridgend

Accessibility ♿

There's a charge in the daytime (approximately £3) at the Dunraven Bay car park, but visit out of hours and it's generally free. The car park is almost on the beach here so it's an easy location to reach if you're short on time or don't fancy a long walk. There are also paved pathways along the seafront that go down onto the beach via the slipway. Elsewhere, access to the beach is across boulders or rocks. The coastal path is generally easy going over flat ground with a gentle incline in both directions.

Best time of year/day

The bay makes a great sunset location thanks to its south west aspect, benefiting from side lighting during the golden hour which illuminates the cliffs, colours the clouds or (in winter) sets directly out to sea. Ultimately it will be the tides that dictate your images here. From both viewpoints and Dunraven Bay you'll lose almost all of the sand on a high tide. The wave-cut platform too will be submerged so shoot this at mid or low tide for the best views of this geological spectacle.

Fossil rich sandstone cliffs reflected in rock pool (VP1).
Canon 5D III, 24-70mm f/2.8 at 35mm, ISO 100, 1/60s at f/16. Tripod. Polariser. Mar.

Long exposure along the Glamorgan Heritage coastline. Sunlit cliffs and a passing hail shower. Canon 5D III, 24-70mm f/2.8 at 70mm, ISO 50, 13s at f/18. Tripod. Polariser, 6ND & ND Grad. Mar.

View along the heritage coast (VP2). Canon 5D III, 24-70mm f/2.8 at 67mm, ISO 50, 25s at f/16. Tripod. Polariser & 6ND. Mar.

Viewpoint 2 – Traeth Bach

This viewpoint requires a bit more walking but it's worth it for the spectacular views of the coast. From the car park, head east past the entrance and up the road. You can either follow this road all the way along, passing the castle ruins en route to the end of the lane, which loops around, or take the scenic route: turn off the road after the small pond and climb up onto the headland. Either way there's an incline, leading you to the viewpoint and the start of the coastal path. From here you'll look down along the towering cliff faces, which slope off into the distance. These are best photographed with side lighting (from the south) to emphasise the depth and texture of the unique, layered rocks. Late afternoon into the golden hour will infuse them with colour in the right conditions. Along Traeth Bach beach there's a huge wave-cut platform, which protrudes out of the sand. Look for winding patterns and rock shapes where the limestone has been broken into blocks by the sea. This platform is mostly exposed at low tide though a mid tide can also reveal interesting patterns. This is a great place to test your neutral density filters and create some long exposures of the tidal surf.

Waves rush around rocks at Dunraven Bay (VP1). Canon 5D III, 16-35mm f/4 at 19mm, ISO 100, 0.8s at f/16. Tripod. Polariser, 3ND & ND Grad. Mar.

An extremely photogenic yet compact stretch of coastline and a place synonymous with photographers, the bay of Nash Point on the Glamorgan Heritage Coast is a superb spot to place your tripod.

A rocky wave-cut platform, peppered with pools and gullies covers the bay. It is backed by increasingly large pebbles and boulders leading up to the Sphynx-like rocky headland of Nash Point, which stands proud above in a display of raw geology and nature.

What to shoot and viewpoints

The main focus along this wonderful stretch of Welsh coastline is the rocky bay below this stunning headland. It's a great place to test out neutral density filters and long exposures, capturing the tides rushing in and around the pools. Walk down through the boulder field that backs the beach, and it will soon morph into wave-cut slabs, where pitted, craggy-edged pools have been carved out by fearsome Atlantic waves. This landscape has been shaped over millennia into basins and crevices teeming with life. This area of the bay is the best place to plant your tripod, shooting wide and filling your frame with the photogenic foreground rock formations. Nash Point will most likely form your background focal element, giving any composition considerable scale. Remember to photograph the orange cliff faces unique to this area of coastline and to Wales. Use the golden hour to bathe cliffs in light, boosting the already colourful rock faces. Or, on cloudy days, slot in a heavy neutral density filter, extending your exposure time to minutes and lending mood to the sky and sea. Either way, you should come away with some evocative images from this little bay courtesy of its unique geology.

How to get here

Heading east along the M4, exit the motorway at Pencoed (Junction 35) and take the A473. Follow this for two miles. At the roundabout join onto the A48 and follow this for a further mile, taking the first exit at the roundabout onto Ewenny Road/B4265. This road snakes through countryside and villages for around 4 miles, after which a right-turn filter take you down a road called Heol Las. Follow this for 2.5 miles through Monknash and into a village called Marcross. Here, take a right turn towards the lighthouse. Head about a mile down this lane and you'll find the small parking area at the top of the bay. Parking charges may apply depending on the time of day.

Parking Lat/Long: 51.403944, -3.5592404
Parking Postcode: CF61 1ZH
OS Map grid ref: SS916683
Map: OS Explorer Map 151 – Cardiff & Bridgend

Accessibility

Park at the car park located above the bay and head down the road (passing a little hut) to access the beach. A steeper but quicker route lies straight down the bank using the well-worn paths, while a gentler way is to walk back along the road a short distance before turning left. There's no really easy way to enter the bay as it's backed by large boulders that you'll need to clamber over. These gradually reduce in size, transitioning into a gentler wave-cut platform, pocketed by rock pools. You can also head up either side of the bay – high up onto the cliff tops. It's relatively easy going and flat on both sides, offering great coastal views.

Best time of year/day

Undoubtedly these vividly coloured cliffs come alive in the golden hour. The position of the setting sun changes throughout the year, so the best time to capture this glorious scene is during late autumn, winter and early spring. Outside these times –in late spring or summer for instance – the sun is obscured by the coastline. This orange side lighting gives the blocky patchwork of cliff face tremendous contrast, emphasising depth and texture. Time your visit with an incoming tide (around mid state) and you'll be able to capture water rushing into and around the pools and crevices. White water dances and swirls, advances and retreats, all while your camera is exposing. Superb!

Opposite: *Evening sunset illuminates Nash Point cliffs as the tide rushes in. Canon 5D III, 16-35mm f/4 at 16mm, ISO 125, 0.8s at f/14. Tripod. Polariser & ND Grad. Mar.*

Waves rush in at Nash Point, while evening sunset light colours the cliffs orange.
Canon 5D III, 16-35mm f/4 at 20mm, ISO 50, 0.4s at f/14. Tripod. Polariser & ND Grad. Mar.

Castell Coch sits on the side of a wooded hill overlooking the valley that carries the river Taff (afon Taf) down towards Wales's capital, Cardiff. Translating to 'Red Castle', it takes its name from the red sandstone used to construct it. Most visitors' first view of this fairytale castle is a quick glimpse through trees, as they whizz by on the M4 motorway.

Despite its Disney-like appearance, the castle was actually built in the 13th century by a Welsh lord. It's located just outside of the village of Tongwynlais and has undergone a full reconstruction in recent times. The castle is eye catching and so is the surrounding countryside. Castle Coch and Forest Fawr woods are ancient forests containing many old species of trees, including native beech, that turn vivid colours in the spring and autumn. This area also forms part of the Taff Trail – a great route from which to take in the scenery.

What to shoot and viewpoints

One option is to head straight for the castle. For a small admission fee, you can venture inside, explore rooms and climb the towers. However, due to the castle's splendid exterior, I think it's best admired from afar. Using the unique setting, photographing it nestled in its woodland home. This produces the best photos in my opinion. The following viewpoints will show the castle at its best, together with the surrounding woodland.

Autumn colour surrounds the castle viewed from the river footbridge (VP1). Canon 5D III, 70-200mm f/2.8 at 140mm, ISO 100, 1/25s at f/11. Tripod. Polariser & ND Grad. Nov.

Opposite: *Afternoon light shines through the summer trees near the castle. Canon 5D IV, 16-35mm f/4 at 16mm, ISO 100, 1/160s at f/16. Tripod. July.*

Viewpoint 1 – Taff River

The easier of the two viewpoints to reach, this will take you onto a small bridge that crosses the Taff. The walkway is quite narrow and it's a popular footpath so don't be surprised if you have to keep moving your tripod aside for passersby. Regardless, this is a great view, elevated over the rushing waters below as they lead the eye up and towards the castle, snug in its woodland setting. Generally I'd recommend a longer telephoto lens for this image – something in the region of 100–150mm focal length should render the castle large enough in the frame for stonework detail, yet wide enough to give the building scale and context. Long exposures work well here, helping smooth out water movement and eradicating reflections. I'd always opt for a circular polariser; it helps cut down any surface glare and boosts the colour of natural foliage. One gripe with this viewpoint is the power lines that cross the river. You'll need to compose your image carefully or – in extreme cases – get handy with the cloning brush tool. Explore the field to the west of this viewpoint as it offers a different perspective of the castle.

How to get here

Viewpoint 1

From the east, exit the M4 motorway at junction 32 and head round the roundabout taking the sixth exit, A4054 signed Tongwynlais. Follow this road for half a mile before turning left onto Iron Bridge Road. This takes you under the main A470 road before bearing right. It's a dead end with limited turning space so I'd recommend parking in this area where there's plenty of space to pull over out of the way. Walk the rest of the way down the road heading west and after a short distance the road ends just beyond the electric substation. The footbridge path is immediately on your right.

VP 1 Parking Lat/Long:	51.528547, -3.2499830
VP 1 Parking Postcode:	CF15 7NJ
VP 1 OS Map Grid Ref:	ST133818
VP 1 Map:	OS Explorer Map 151 – Cardiff & Bridgend

Viewpoint 2

Exit the M4 motorway at Junction 32 and take the sixth exit at the roundabout – A4054 signed Tongwynlais. Follow this road into the town for half a mile, before turning right onto Mill Road. Continue on this road passing the golf course entrance on your left, before turning right into Catherine Drive. Park anywhere here. The footpath is found at the entrance junction to Maes Y Draenog.

VP 2 Parking Lat/Long:	51.536287 -3.2481169
VP 2 Parking Postcode:	CF15 7JL
VP 2 OS Map Grid Ref:	ST135826
VP 2 Map:	OS Explorer Map 151 – Cardiff & Bridgend

Accessibility

Viewpoint 1 is a great location for those with limited mobility as it's relatively flat and easy going. The second viewpoint requires a slightly higher level of fitness as parts of the lane are uneven and could be slippery in inclement weather.

Best time of year/day

Autumn is the best season to experience this location. On a bright day the trees and foliage that surround the castle are truly stunning. Time your visit so the sun provides side lighting and you'll reap the rewards; it gives great contrast, shading the cylindrical turrets. Combine side lighting with a circular polariser to boost the natural colours of the trees and sky.

Viewpoint 2 – Elevated

It's bit of a walk to this one and perhaps not in a location you'd expect, however it offers great views. In Tongwynlais, behind Catherine Drive towards the reservoir there's a pathway that heads up the hill. Park anywhere in the housing estate. You'll find the start of the path at the

Wales' fairytale castle – Castell Coch from VP2. Canon 5D IV, 70-200mm f/2.8 at 100mm, ISO 50, 1/8s at f/11. Tripod. Polariser & ND Grad. Nov.

entrance junction to Maes Y Draenog. Follow this small wooded lane up the hill, around the gate and on for about another hundred yards. You'll come to an opening by a field. Look over to your right and you'll see the castle standing tall. The increased elevation means you're now almost eye-level with the castle and above many of the lower treetops. From here you can peer down into the valley and glimpse parts of the golf course. Again, a telephoto lens (around 100mm) here is advised, allowing you to zoom in and position the castle among the wooded landscape.

Cardiff Bay is an attractive waterfront area built around a 200-hectare freshwater lake known as the Bay. This compact area provides the perfect focal point for a day out with the camera. Visitors can explore the rich heritage and range of activities around Cardiff's vibrant waterfront. With landmark buildings, tourist attractions, eateries, boat trips and cultural attractions, there's enough to keep you occupied all day and into the night.

What to shoot and viewpoints

There's no denying the water plays a big part in potential images here. Cut off from any tidal changes, on a calm day the Bay can be like glass, resulting in mirrored reflections of the surrounding buildings. If a light breeze or boat creates ripples, using a neutral density filter to extend your shutter speeds into multiple seconds can work wonders in terms of smoothing out the water. And when photographing the buildings in nearby Mermaid Quay, using the same technique can be just as effective with passersby. As this is a popular place, it's likely there will be people wandering through your shots, so shooting with long exposures means you can photograph populated scenes without people in them. As long as the people keep walking, they won't be rendered on the final image. If they pause however – even for a short time during a long exposure – they will appear like ghosts, which itself can make an interesting image if that's what you're after. The architecture is striking here and there's a surprisingly large number of bird species around the Bay. Cormorants, grebes and diving birds such as coots and moorhens are abundant so it's worth packing a larger lens.

Pierhead Building

One of the Bay's most familiar landmarks and built in 1897 as the headquarters of the Bute Dock Company, the now Grade I listed Pierhead Building has remained a constant feature in Cardiff Bay. Its clock is unofficially known as the Big Ben of Wales. Restored in 2010 it hosts exhibitions on the history of the Bay and is a venue for public debate. For photography, the stark contrast of the Pierhead with the surrounding buildings is draw

enough. French Gothic in design, deep red in colour, with terracotta panels, it's a real show stopper, adding a bold splash of colour to the waterfront.

Y Senedd

Opened in 2006, the Senedd was designed by renowned British architect Richard Rogers. It's the Welsh Assembly Government's debating chamber and the word Senedd means senate or parliament in Welsh. The building has a glass façade and is dominated by a steel roof with a wooden ceiling. Many of the materials used to construct it were locally sourced. It is one of the most environmentally friendly parliament buildings in the world. Up close the architecture is stunning; wood panelling curves from the roof down to the interior and into the heart of the building.

Wales Millennium Centre

Opened in 2004, the Wales Millennium Centre is a key cultural landmark in the Bay hosting a wide range of performances from opera and ballet to comedy and musicals. The striking main building is created from

How to get here

From the M4 (in either direction) exit at junction 33 signed Cardiff Bay. Follow the A4232 for around nine miles. After heading over the River Taff, and before the tunnel, take the exit signposted Techniquest. Take the first exit at the roundabout, then the next right. Follow this road towards the hotel and the car park will be on your right.

Parking Lat/Long: 51.461237, -3.1679604
Parking Postcode: CF10 5SG
OS Map grid ref: ST 189742
Map: OS Explorer Map 151 – Cardiff & Bridgend

Accessibility &

Parking at Havannah Street car park (the cheapest around) all the Bay's attractions are easily accessed by well-maintained pavements or decking walkways. Ramps are built into the walkways, making level changes easy so it's a perfect place for those less mobile to explore this picturesque marina.

Best time of year/day

For the best reflections of lights and photos of the inscribed words, the blue hour is preferable and will add some colour to the sky. To photograph architecture, visit during the golden hour, when side lighting is soft, or on a cloudy day for global illumination, textures and an absence of harsh shadows. Avoid the Bay on very windy days – these ruin reflections in the water. Weekends and holidays can be exceptionally busy.

Long exposure of the Pierhead building reflected in the bay. Canon 5D III, 24-70mm f/2.8 at 50mm, ISO 125, 30s at f/11. Tripod. Polariser, 6ND & ND Grad. Dec.

Five image stitch of Cardiff Bay in the blue hour, taken near St David's Hotel. Canon 5D III, 24-70mm f/2.8 at 70mm, ISO 100, 30s at f/16. Tripod. Polariser & 6ND. Dec.

multicoloured rows of slate divided up by stained glass. The centre's large dome covers the Donald Gordon Theatre and is clad in steel treated with copper oxide, giving it a bronze colour. As day turns into night, the building comes alive: inscribed on the front of the dome above the main entrance are two lines by poet Gwyneth Lewis, one in Welsh, one in English. The Welsh – 'Creu Gwir fel Gwydr o Ffwrnais Awen' – translates to 'Creating truth like glass from inspiration's furnace'. Lewis said, "I wanted the words to reflect the architecture of the building. Its copper dome reminded me of the furnaces from Wales's industrial heritage". The English words, 'In these Stones Horizons Sing', were inspired by the strata of the slate walls, which reminded Lewis of the horizons beyond Penarth Head in South Wales. She felt the stones would "literally be singing" once the building opened.

Merchant Seafarers' War Memorial

Some lost-at-sea memorials are touched by genius. The images they convey – like all great art – are timeless and universal. Approach this sculpture from one side and you'll see the hull of a ship, torn from the rest of the vessel, resting on a beach or the ocean floor. Walk around the other side and you'll see the face of a person, lost forever

to the sea. The Cardiff Bay Arts Trust commissioned Brian Fell (whose father was a merchant seaman) to create the memorial in 1994. The galvanized steel hull rests on a circular mosaic by artists Louise Shenstone and Adrian Butler. Inscribed around the edge of the mosaic are the words: "IN MEMORY OF THE MERCHANT SEAFARERS FROM THE PORTS OF BARRY PENARTH CARDIFF WHO DIED IN TIMES OF WAR". It's a thought-provoking memorial and a photogenic one. Position your camera close to the hull and use a wide angle lens to make it dominate the foreground. With some careful alignment you can create a pleasing composition with the Pierhead Building in the background.

Panorama

As day turns to night the bay's buildings are imbued with a vast array of colours and illuminations. I find this is best viewed from nearby St. David's Hotel. From here you'll be close to the water level so the reflections will be vivid. A still night will produce fantastic reflections. Use the footpath that circles the hotel to find your favourite viewpoint. I chose the corner just before the pathway begins heading back towards the wetlands reserve. You'll need to catch this in the blue hour just after sunset to capture some colour

in the sky, but before it's completely dark. Otherwise the sky will take on an orange tone caused by light pollution. Exposure blending works well here too as some streetlights will over expose during a long exposure (of 30 seconds for example) so it's worth keeping the camera in the same position and shooting some shorter exposure frames to blend later on just in case. Another option to try here: keep the tripod nice and level and you can photograph the whole bay. Merge all these images into a panorama.

There are so many buildings and activities around the bay, here are just a few:

Roald Dahl Plass – The former Oval Basin dock is now a 10,000-capacity outdoor entertainment arena located immediately adjacent to Mermaid Quay.

Norweigan Church – Formerly the church of the Norwegian sailors, the building was moved to its present location in 1992, and is now a thriving cultural and arts centre.

Techniquest – The UK's longest established science and discovery centre is just two minutes from Mermaid Quay and offers visitors a hands-on approach to science.

Doctor Who Experience – Adventure though time and space; step through a crack in time to help the Doctor escape his foes; fly the TARDIS and come face-to-face with Daleks, Cybermen and Sontarans. This experience is packed with amazing special effects, original props, costumes and artefacts.

Cardiff Bay Barrage – Boasting stunning sea views, the Barrage is the perfect place for a scenic stroll or bike ride.

Flat Holm Island – Not strictly in Cardiff, but five miles off the coast, the tranquil island of Flat Holm is a different world with a wealth of history and wildlife. Enjoy a boat trip, guided tour and a drink at The Gull and Leek, Wales's most southerly pub.

Cardiff Bay Wetland Reserve – Easily accessible via a gravel walkway and boardwalk, the eight-hectare reserve supports a diverse range of plants and animals, including invertebrates, fish and other wildlife. A viewing area extends out over the water, providing the perfect location for bird watching.

Above: Cardiff's Wales Millennium Centre arts complex lit in early evening. Canon 5D III, 24-70mm f/2.8 at 24mm, ISO 100, 3.2s at f/11. Tripod. 6ND. Dec.

Below: Merchant Seafarers' War Memorial and Pierhead building. Canon 5D III, 24-70mm f/2.8 at 25mm, ISO 320, 30s at f/10. Tripod. Polariser, 6ND & ND Grad. Dec.

Above: Welsh Assembly building – Y Senedd. Canon 5D III, 24-70mm f/2.8 at 24mm, ISO 320, 30s at f/10. Tripod. Polariser & 6ND. Dec.

Below: Pierhead building and Y Senedd lit at night. Canon 5D III, 70-200mm f/2.8 at 130mm, ISO 50, 13s at f/14. Tripod. Polariser & 6ND. Dec.

Newport Wetlands is a real gem on the south-east Wales coast. Opened in 2000 by the RSPB, it covers over a thousand acres. It consists predominately of reed-bed and freshwater lagoons, making it one of the best birding sites in Wales. A visit here is worthwhile at any time of year and it's not just about the birds. There are numerous pathways to explore, a lighthouse on the sea wall and, nearby, the Gwent Levels, home to number of interesting plants. The entire site is largely flat and offers good walking opportunities. It's a wildlife escape on the edge of the city.

What to shoot and viewpoints

After a short walk from the car park you'll reach the visitor centre. There's a host of information on what to find across the site, maps, a shop and a cafe. Newport Wetlands is made up of four marked trails: head south from the visitor centre and you'll find yourself on the Orchid trail. This pathway loops around in a clockwise direction, eventually taking you back to the car park. The habitat here is perfect for these delicate plants in late spring and early summer, so keep your eyes peeled for different species.

On reaching the junction of trails south of the visitor centre, there are a few options: head straight on and you'll pass through rich reed beds and watery lagoons bursting with birds. Blinds and screens with holes act as makeshift bird hides, allowing you to go relatively unnoticed. This north-to-south track will eventually bring you to the sea wall. Here you'll find the smaller than average East Usk lighthouse, dating from 1893 and standing guard at the eastern entrance to the River Usk in the Severn Estuary. From here you can either go west on the Sculpture trail or east on the Woodland and Estuary trail. The Sculpture trail circles around the inner part of the reed-bed area and there are many sculptures en route. The eastern pathway – the Woodland and Estuary trail – is a 1.5-mile route through reed beds, woodland and past open water and the estuary to the south. At the eastern-most point of this path a bird hide overlooks a large pool. It's perfect for spotting migrant ducks and waterfowl. If you fancy stretching your legs, the Wetlands Experience trail takes in the whole area. At nearly three miles long, it combines three trails with an extra region to the reserve's west. The pathway along the south is part of the Wales Coast Path – a superb area for seeing wading birds on the mudflats. Most of the paths here are easy going and flat, allowing access for pushchairs and wheelchairs. >>

Birdwatcher using the blinds to scan for birds on the pools. Canon 5D III, 70-200mm f/2.8 at 70mm, ISO 800, 1/1600s at f/5.6. Nov.

How to get here

From the M4 leave at either junction 24 or 28, joining onto the A48. Follow the A48 until you come to the Newport Retail Park roundabout. Exit onto the A4810 Queensway Meadows. At the first roundabout take the third exit onto Meadows Road and follow the brown tourist signs to the reserve. There's a large car park and the visitor centre is a short walk away.

Parking Lat/Long: 51.546128, -2.9609643
Parking Postcode: NP18 2YH
OS Map grid ref: ST334834
Map: OS Explorer Map 152 – Newport & Pontypool

Accessibility ♿

This is an RSPB reserve and consequently, great thought has gone into making the whole site accessible and people friendly. Most, if not all pathways are hard-standing compacted gravel which are wheelchair and pushchair friendly. Some areas include floating walkways so caution should be taken on these buoyant structures.

Best time of year/day

Autumn and into winter is the best time of year for bird watching at Newport Wetlands, when migratory wildfowl and wading birds begin to arrive ready for their winter stay. Starlings display at dusk in their thousands from October until December, while in spring and summer, orchids and dragonflies bring a splash of exotic colour to the area. Morning and late-evening light is best for warm glowing reed beds. Winter storms can whip up some fantastic waves. View these from beneath the lighthouse on the sea wall.

East Usk lighthouse with passing flock of starlings above the reed beds. Canon 5D III, 70-200mm f/2.8 at 200mm, ISO 3200, 1/100s at f/5. Nov.

Mudflats and the Bristol Channel from the sea wall. Canon 5D III, 70-200mm f/2.8 at 100mm, ISO 800, 1/320s at f/14. Nov.

As with most birding and wildlife sites, the seasons not only change the look of the landscape but what you're likely to see. Spring marks the start of the breeding season, a very active and exciting time of year as birds set about finding their mates and building nests. Breeding birds at the reserve include lapwings, oystercatchers and even the bearded tit. As April shifts into May, swallows and swifts begin arriving from Africa. This is a great time of year to listen out for the distinctive call of the cuckoo too, most likely heard in the wooded parts. Many plants, including orchids, will begin to burst into colourful flower. In the height of summer and if you're lucky, grass snakes can sometimes be seen soaking up the sun or swimming among the reed beds. A huge number of insects also call Newport home in the summer. Around sixteen species of dragonflies, twenty-three species of butterfly and two hundred species of moth are found at Newport Wetlands. The reserve is also home to badgers, moles, wood mice and otters, however the latter are notoriously shy of humans and so can be hard to spot. Their droppings (called spraint) are the most common clue to their presence.

Autumn is when the migratory wildfowl and wading birds begin to arrive ready for their winter stay. Curlews, redshanks, dunlins, sanderlings and oystercatchers feed on the estuary at low tide, using their long, pointy beaks to sift through the mud for worms and grubs. The reed beds turn from a vibrant lush green to yellowy brown and groups of goldfinches can be seen flitting around the reserve, extracting seeds from the teasel heads found along Perry Lane. The real highlight of the year is the starling roost and it's not to be missed. From October onwards, large groups of starlings gather at dusk in great numbers. At its peak, around 50,000 birds swoop and soar overhead, chattering noisily. After a breathtaking display of murmurations, the birds drop dramatically into the reed beds, where they settle for the night. Throughout winter, although the days are short, the birds are active throughout the day. Parts of the reserve provide a winter home for nationally important numbers of black-tailed godwits, shovelers and dunlins. You might even see a bittern; one has been spotted here most winters since 2001. Bitterns are similar to heron only smaller and stockier but they're rare and very secretive, moving silently through the reeds to look for fish.

Top: Starlings flock together above the wetlands. Canon 5D III, 70-200mm f/2.8 at 200mm, ISO 800, 1/640s at f/6.3. Nov.
Above: Newport Wetlands RSPB centre. Canon 5D III, 70-200mm f/2.8 at 70mm, ISO 800, 1/250s at f/5. Nov.

Above: Winter wildfowl on the pools at sunset. Canon 5D III, 70-200mm f/2.8 at 140mm, ISO 3200, 1/160s at f/6.3. Nov.
Below: Starlings flying in to roost in reed beds. Canon 5D III, 70-200mm f/2.8 at 200mm, ISO 1600, 1/200s at f/6.3. Nov.

[6] SEVERN BRIDGE

The gateway to Wales makes a superb photographic subject in its own right. The Second Severn Crossing was opened in 1996 and spans a considerable three miles across the Severn Estuary. Much of the estuary consists of mudflats at low tide, but as the tide comes in, the bridge's large pillar supports can be submerged by as much as fourteen metres of water.

The estuary has the second highest tidal range in the world and presented engineers with a conundrum. The construction of the bridge was a real feat of engineering, with foundation work scheduled only at low tide. It was completed in the narrow windows allowed by the tide. Today it carries over 60,000 vehicles a day over the turbulent waters below, forming a vital link between South Wales and England.

What to shoot and viewpoints

There are a few places in the vicinity from which to photograph the Second Severn Crossing. There's an old slipway on the Welsh side, where the ferry used to disembark in days gone by. This has lovely cobbled stonework that works well with soft lighting and retreating waves. It can be

Long exposure at high tide of the Second Severn Crossing. Canon 5D III, 24-70mm f/2.8 at 45mm, ISO 100, 30s at f/13. Tripod. Polariser, 6ND & ND Grad. Sep.

South side of the bridge. Canon 5D III, 24-70mm f/2.8 at 53mm, ISO 200, 20s at f/16. Tripod. Polariser, 6ND & ND Grad. Sep.

How to get here

Parking is on the dead end road at the start of the Severn Way footpath on the English side of the bridge. After crossing the bridge (heading east on the M4), come off at junction 20 onto the M5. Follow the motorway south west for 3 miles, before turning off at junction 17, Head around the roundabout and take the third exit for A4018. Continue down this road for 3 miles before turning right at the mini roundabout onto Redwick Road/B4055. You'll find the parking area at the end. Walk north west for a few hundred yards before turning left and joining the Severn Way footpath. It's about half a mile from this point to beneath the bridge.

Parking Lat/Long: 51.573731, -2.6595987
Parking Postcode: BS35 4LZ
OS Map grid ref: ST543863
Map: OS Explorer Map 167 – Thornbury, Dursley & Yate

Accessibility ♿

The footpath is a great place to walk. It's wide and flat with ramps when the levels change, allowing access for those with all levels of mobility. The walk from the parking is relatively short – well under a mile – and there are no gates or stiles so the viewpoint is accessible day or night.

Best time of year/day

Due to the mainly seaward aspect, a visit during high tide is advisable as the water will cover most of the mudflats and offer less distracting foregrounds. A visit at any time of year should be rewarding but especially so either side of the summer months, when the sun will appear to set between the bridge towers. Choose cloudy, windy days for long exposures to create streaky skies above the bridge.

Formations in the mudflats looking towards the bridge. Canon 5D III, 24-70mm f/2.8 at 35mm, ISO 200, 30s at f/16. Tripod. Polariser, 6ND & ND Grad. Sep.

great at sunrise too, as it faces east. My preferred location though is on the English side of the bridge, which offers more in the way of composition opportunities. From the eastern end of the crossing, you'll see the sweep of the bridge more clearly as it snakes off into Wales. On clear days, the summits of the eastern and central Brecon Beacons rear their impressive heads above the distant shoreline. Sunsets can be spectacular here too as the bridge's streetlights glow in the twilight. Couple this with an orange sky as a backdrop and the bridge will appear in glorious silhouette.

Always try and time your visit near high tide. The mudflats here are a fantastic habitat for wading birds and also make a great foreground. The branching patterns and shapes work well as close-up abstracts. The sea wall is made up of massive boulders along the whole of the Severn Way footpath, which skirts the banks of the estuary. The boulders too – many coated with vivid yellow lichen – provide an interesting foreground. Long exposures would be my method of choice here. With a colourful sunset and the use of neutral density filters, they'll help to smooth out the waves and blur any cloud movement. When shooting from this location either side of the summer months, the setting sun should position itself in between the two bridge towers so remember to pack a telephoto lens. Something in the range of 175mm should give you a bold frame-filling composition.

***Opposite**: Vivid yellow lichen on the sea wall boulders. Canon 5D III, 24-70mm f/2.8 at 26mm, ISO 250, 30s at f/16. Tripod. Polariser, 6ND & ND Grad. Sep.*

[7] SYMONDS YAT ROCK

Situated at the top of the Upper Wye Gorge and just over the Welsh border, Symonds Yat Rock is a limestone outcrop towering more than 120 metres above the river below. This world-renowned viewpoint is famed for its natural river scenery and wooded expanses. As well as being a favourite spot for walkers, Yat Rock is a popular place for bird watchers, with resident peregrine falcons nesting in the surrounding cliffs throughout the spring and summer months.

What to shoot and viewpoints

Symonds Yat is not actually in Wales, however it's a short hop over the border and well worth a visit for the views alone. The main viewpoint here reveals the sweeping horseshoe bend of the River Wye in the gorge below. Lined with trees, it's a fantastic place to witness the changing seasons. Species found here include sweet chestnut, oak, beech, silver birch – the list goes on – and they all turn fabulous golden-russet tones in autumn. To the south and east from Yat Rock lies one of the most ancient forests in Britain: the forty-two square miles of mixed woodland, the Forest of Dean. The village of Symonds Yat marks the point where it meets the Wye Valley, making this a popular area to explore. The forest and many of the car parks in the Forest of Dean are looked after by the Forestry Commission

and as such are well maintained. The main pathway from the car park takes you north past The Log Cabin cafe and over a footbridge that crosses the road. Take a left here and head up to the viewpoint.

As you gaze out at magnificent views, you'll notice a large hump of exposed rock. The clifftop was acknowledged as a great vantage point by its Iron Age inhabitants, who built a fort here 2500 years. Most of the settlement remains are now surrounded by the car park (created for the forest park) with all the walking trails marked out. Yat Rock is also a place people go to watch the peregrine falcons that nest on the cliff faces to the viewpoint's right. In the daytime, from April through to August, there are usually helpful volunteers from the RSPB here, helping visitors find the birds and giving advice on sightings and the area in general.

It's not just nature's fastest bird that visitors come to see; a wealth of birds and mammals call the Forest of Dean home. Famed for its different types of deer, the forest was a Royal Hunting ground in Norman times. Since then, more species have populated the forest, including muntjac, roe, red deer and the most common: fallow deer. You might also see wild boar here if you're lucky. The boars are normally secretive and largely nocturnal but you may encounter them in the daytime. They're fascinating animals and lend any scene a timeless feel.

How to get here

From Ross-on-Wye head south on Hill Street towards Corpus Christie Lane, then turn right onto Gloucester Road/B4260 for a quarter of a mile. Turn left, signed B4234 and after 3.5 miles, take a right onto the B4229 – you'll cross over the River Wye. Follow this road for a further mile then take a left signed Yat Rock. After a short distance the road will cross the river again via a narrow bridge; be prepared to give way here. Follow this lane as it climbs the hill – it's narrow with passing places. As you reach the summit, the road goes under the footbridge and you'll find the car park on your right. The charge for cars and minibuses is currently: £3.50 Mar–Oct, £3.00 Nov–Feb. At the time of writing, a year pass to the Forest of Dean costs £25.

Parking Lat/Long: 51.840836, -2.6347178
Parking Postcode: HR9 6JL
OS Map grid ref: SO563159
Map: OS Explorer Leisure Map OL14 – Wye Valley & Forest of Dean

Accessibility

Most of the pathways from Yat Rock car park are flat and easy going. Access to the viewpoint is well maintained – great for those with limited mobility. Venture deeper into the forest and the going underfoot can be uneven and muddy in places, though the main tracks are easy going.

Best time of year/day

As expected in a wooded environment, spring will produce the most vivid greens while autumn is also spectacular. I regard it as one of the best places in Britain to witness the changing of the colours, due to the sheer variety of species in this ancient forest. The peregrine falcons start nesting in late March or April, so there's a good chance of seeing busy parents feeding their young from May onwards. Wild Boar and deer are best seen early in the morning and just before dusk but you'll need to venture away from the car parks and deep into the woods.

Striking autumn beech trees in Forest of Dean. Canon 5D III, 17-40mm f/4 at 28mm, ISO 800, 6s at f/16. Tripod. Polariser. Oct.

Wild boar rooting through forest floor, Forest of Dean. Canon 5D III, 300mm f/2.8 at 300mm, ISO 800, 1/100s at f/3.2. Oct.

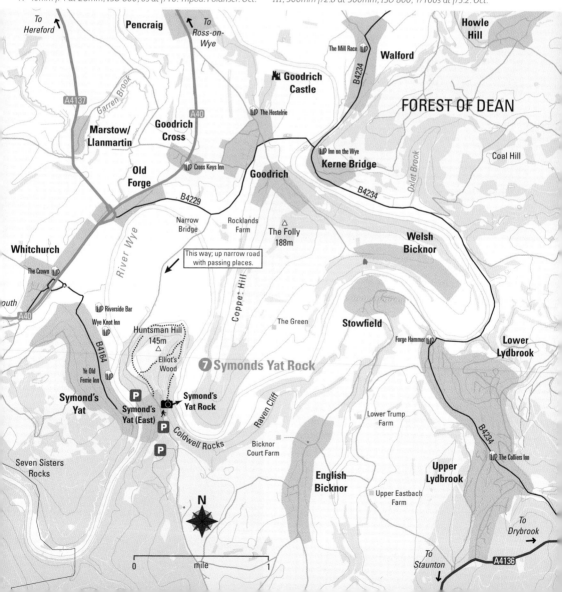

Four image stitch of the rock viewpoint in summer. Canon 5D III, 24-70mm f/2.8 at 24mm, ISO 100, 1/25s at f/14. Tripod. Polariser. June.

Nearby Location: Ross-on-Wye

There's no mistaking the market town of Ross-on-Wye, thanks to its historic church. The spire at St. Mary's has shaped the skyline here for over 700 years. Perched dramatically above the River Wye, Ross is the southern gateway to Herefordshire, the Wye Valley and the Forest of Dean. As with many town or city skylines, it's best viewed from afar and this viewpoint above the river Wye is a classic. Unconventionally, the viewpoint isn't as serene as it might be; it is in fact on the bridge of the very busy A40 dual carriageway. Park in the small lay-by on the southbound carriageway and it's a short walk of about a hundred yards along the path to the bridge. Be vigilant about passing traffic and stay behind the footpath barrier at all times.

The middle of the bridge provides the best photographic angles, enhancing the diagonal appearance of the river and directing the eye towards the town. Early morning or an afternoon visit work best, with the sun providing side light across the scene. Combine this with blue skies, billowing white clouds and a polarising filter for great effect. Midsummer is my preferred time to visit, when the fields and trees glow luscious green and add a timeless mood to images.

Autumn colours in the Forest of Dean. Canon 5D III, 300mm f/2.8 at 300mm, ISO 1000, 1/640s at f/5. Oct.

Autumn works well, when the trees in the Forest of Dean turn rich reds and oranges. The keener eyed reader will notice a few power lines missing from the images here; I rarely remove anything from my photos, choosing instead to recompose if something mars a shot, but limited angles here mean they're hard to avoid. Keep an eye on rainfall levels if visiting this spot. Heavy downpours cause flooding and the river looks murky brown – not ideal for pictures.

How to get here

From the Symonds Yat Rock parking head north back down the hill for 2 miles, then turn left onto the B4229. Follow this for nearly a mile, turning right onto the A4137 crossing the A40. Take an immediate left – it will bring you round to join onto the A40 northbound. After 5 miles head straight over the roundabout and continue for another 1.5 miles. At the next roundabout, take the fifth exit, doubling back on yourself. Head down here for a mile then, *before* the bridge, park in the lay-by on your left.

Parking Lat/Long: 51.919564, -2.5927647
Parking Postcode: HR9 7DG
OS Map Grid Ref: SO593247
Map: OS Explorer Leisure Map OL14 – Wye Valley
                                        & Forest of Dean

Fungi are abundant in the Forest of Dean in autumn. Canon 5D III, 17-40mm f/4 at 40mm, ISO 160, 4s at f/5.6. Tripod. Polariser. Oct.

Ross on Wye town and river scene from road bridge.
Canon 5D IV, 24-70mm f/2.8 at 57mm, ISO 400, 1/160s at f/11. Tripod. Polariser. July.

The Craig Goch dam at sunset in Elan Valley (p.428).
Canon 5D IV, 24-70mm f/2.8 at 35mm, ISO 100, 30s at f/10. Tripod. Polariser, 6ND & ND Grad. July.

POWYS

Powys is Wales's largest county, covering a whopping 2,000 square miles stretching from Pontneddfechan in the south right up to Oswestry in the north. It's made up of the historic counties of Montgomeryshire and Radnorshire, most of Brecknockshire (Breconshire), and a small part of Denbighshire and covers about half the width of Wales. The rivers Severn, Wye and Usk all flow through Powys. Bordering England on its eastern flank, the county encompasses most of the Brecon Beacons National Park. Consequently, in this book the Brecon Beacons locations have been grouped together in a section devoted to the National Park.

The upper part of Penygarreg Reservoir in Elan Valley (p.428). Canon 5D IV, 24-70mm f/2.8 at 33mm, ISO 100, 1s at f/13. Tripod. Polariser. July.

Mid Wales contains several old spa towns, three of which have 'Wells' in their name. During the 18th century, there was a craze for spas; these water sources supposedly had healing powers and the pure water of Welsh rivers and springs was held in high regard by Victorian royalty. A new railway linked up many of these towns, bringing in the masses and putting Llanwrtyd Wells, Llandrindod Wells and Builth Wells on the map. Today, these rural towns are generally much quieter than in their Victorian heyday but in mid-July Builth Wells showground is busy with the prestigious Royal Welsh Agricultural Show.

In the heart of mid Wales lies Rhayader, a small market town on the river Wye, known as the gateway to the Elan Valley. This stunning nine-mile-long string of reservoirs, surrounded by woods and heathland, was built in the 19th century and supplies drinking water to the city of Birmingham, some seventy-five miles east. Powys is made up of rolling hills, river valleys, farmland and undulating mountains; perfect terrain for upland bird species and wherever you roam here, you're sure to see a red kite or two soaring overhead. It's one of the grandest sights in Wales, particularly as these beautiful birds were recently pushed to near extinction. Thanks to heroic conservation efforts, they're now a common sight across Powys and beyond as they spread to other Welsh counties.

Red kite soars against blue sky at Gigrin Red Kite Centre (p.434). Canon 1DX, 300mm f/2.8 + 1.4x Extender at 420mm, ISO 1250, 1/5000s at f/5.6. Feb.

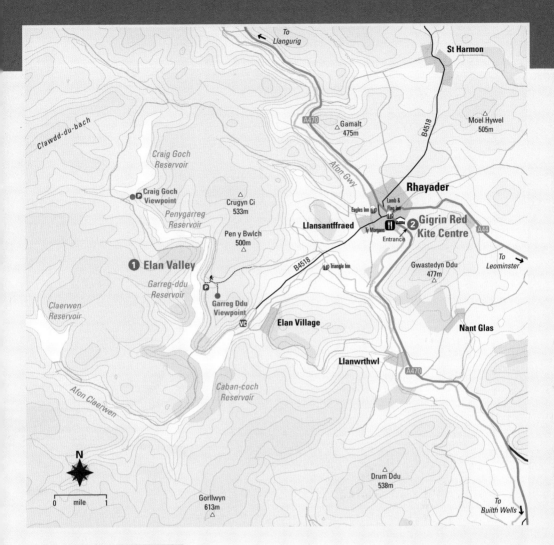

Map

- OS Explorer Map 200 –
  Llandrindod Wells & Elan Valley

Red Kite flying through snowfall at Gigrin Red Kite Centre (p.434).
Canon 5D IV, 500mm f/4 at 500mm, ISO 2000, 1/2500s at f/4. Tripod. Dec.

Making up part of the rugged Cambrian Mountain range in mid-Wales, the Elan Valley is a beautiful and unspoiled area made even more compelling by its many dams and reservoirs. Just a short drive away from the nearby town of Rhayader, Elan is a peaceful retreat and a true wilderness. Covering a vast seventy square miles it starts low down along the banks of a river – the Afon Elan.

The road winds its way up through wooded river valleys, allowing visitors who pass the reservoirs and huge dams to marvel at the engineering enterprise of the Victorians. The land reaches for the sky on both sides of the road, with rocky crags towering above. The road levels off before reaching the wild, barren, treeless landscape of the upland hills. Elan is a real haven for wildlife too, one of the most important sites in Wales for rare birds and insects. It's also a superb place to witness the changing of the seasons and a stunning Dark Sky area.

What to shoot and viewpoints

Elan is first and foremost synonymous with the many the dams and reservoirs that run through its valley. They're here to supply drinking water to the Midlands. The amazing system of pipelines, tunnels and bridges was constructed by the Victorians to carry huge amounts of water seventy-three miles from the valley to Birmingham. This system is called the Elan Valley Aqueduct, and although it has to cross many hills, valleys and rivers, it transports the water all the way by gravity alone. The water travels gently downhill at about two miles an hour, and takes one and a half days to get to Birmingham. Wales is famed for its rain and this area is no exception, collecting vast amounts throughout the year. In autumn and winter, the reservoirs fill up in spectacular fashion, with white water overflowing the shoots and dam walls. From late spring into summer, water levels drop rapidly and the valley returns to a peaceful place, with the soothing sound of running rivers, bleating sheep and mewing buzzards and red kites.

Viewpoint 1 – Craig Goch

Craig Goch, the highest of the series of dams in the Elan Valley, is often referred to as the top dam. It's 317m above sea level and the treeline stops here, creating a wild, sparse upland environment where red kites soar overhead. Craig Goch is the most popular dam among visitors and is regarded by many as the most photogenic. It has an elegantly curved retaining wall that carries a narrow roadway across the top and a domed valve tower is situated two thirds of the way along. Below the roadway lies a series of arches which, when water levels allow, fill with white water overflowing from the reservoir. This creates an immense and thunderous waterfall that plunges down the dam face into Penygarreg Reservoir below.

Parking is located at either end of the dam roadway and there are many walking routes up the hillsides to explore from here. Take in views of the dam and the surrounding countryside at the viewpoint just to the south west of the dam. Park in the lay-by at the western end and you'll find a gate across the road. Head through it and follow the pathway as it travels southwards, slowly ascending a series of steps before it turns right in a south-west direction. Anywhere along here offers fabulous elevated views of the dam and reservoir above. Due to the increase in altitude you can look down on the dam walls and tower, making them stand out against the water, adding depth to your shots. Late afternoon and evening are good times to visit, offering moody side lighting or vibrant sunsets to colour the skies above.

Viewpoint 2 – Garreg Ddu

Access to this viewpoint requires a reasonable level of fitness. It overlooks the Garreg Ddu Reservoir in the lower Elan Valley from a rocky outcrop – a superb vantage point and one worth making effort to reach. Park in one of the lay-bys near to SN913656, take the main footpath on the right and climb the hill. It's a really steep ascent for a good ten minutes up a rocky path and would, I imagine, be tough going after heavy rain, when it would act like a gully for rainwater. You'll rise 300 feet in just a quarter of a mile then the pathway levels off around a corner. The main path

Opposite: Craig Goch dam (VP1) in late winter with falls flowing. Canon 5D III, 24-70mm f/2.8 at 65mm, ISO 100, 1/25s at f/14. Tripod. Polariser. Feb.

*Drew standing at VP2 above Garreg Ddu reservoir.
Canon 5D IV, 16-35mm f/4 at 20mm, ISO 500,
1/50s at f/16. Tripod. Polariser. July.*

*The Craig Goch dam at sunset (VP1). Canon 5D IV, 24-70mm
f/2.8 at 35mm, ISO 100, 25s at f/13. Tripod.
Polariser, 6ND & ND Grad. July.*

is quite obvious to follow, but the route from here is all via sheep tracks through the heather. Double back on yourself and head south, following the sheep track as it firstly takes you up (passing a slate area) then winds down the hill. It's up once again then down towards a large boggy area with a small stream running through it. There's sporadic cotton grass here in summer, which is an attractive addition to the hillside. Head to where the bog is at its narrowest to hop over – this is roughly at SN916655. It's a short walk uphill again towards the rocky area, where you can have a well-earned rest and gaze out over the landscape below. Magnificent! It's only around half a mile from the car, but feels longer due to the undulating terrain. Standing on the rocks there's a sheer drop below you. Look down to see the road snaking around the reservoir towards Llannerchi Wood; look left for Y Foel summit. There are many elevated panoramic views like this in the area but none, in my opinion, with such a superb view of the surrounding countryside. This stretch, along the eastern hills by Garreg Ddu, is one of the best areas in summer for flowering heather, which will add a colourful splash to any foreground.

How to get here

Viewpoint 1

From Newtown take the A489 south for 5 miles until you reach Caersws, then continue over the roundabout onto the A470 and follow this for 8 miles. Head over the roundabout, taking the second exit and follow for a further 5 miles towards Llanidloes. Again, go straight over at the roundabout and continue on the A470 for another 9 miles. Once in Rhayader, take a right at the crossroads following the B4518 a short distance before taking a right signed 'Mountain Road'. After 3 miles, take a left signed 'Elan Valley' and descend through the valley for a further 3 miles until you reach the Craig Goch dam. The start of the viewpoint walk will be on your right through the small gate.

VP 1 Parking Lat/Long:	52.304536, -3.6253743
VP 1 Parking Postcode:	LD6 5HS
VP 1 OS Map Grid Ref:	SN892686
VP 1 Map:	OS Explorer Map 200 – Llandrindod Wells & Elan Valley

Viewpoint 2

Follow initial directions to Viewpoint 1 but after turning right at Rhayader, continue on the B4518 for 6 miles as the road winds up through the valley. At the grid reference you'll see a large lay-by on the left-hand side of the road. Park here; the pathway begins a short distance up the road and on the right.

VP 2 Parking Lat/Long:	52.278366, -3.5937551
VP 2 Parking Postcode:	LD6 5HE
VP 2 OS Map Grid Ref:	SN913656
VP 2 Map:	OS Explorer Map 200 – Llandrindod Wells & Elan Valley

Accessibility

You can park right next to the dam for Viewpoint 1, and drive across it to access the other side. Those with limited mobility can make the most of the countryside views and the architecture of the dam itself. The viewpoint is up an uneven path, with many steps but is only a short walk from the parking area on the western end of the dam. Viewpoint 2 requires a good level of fitness; a steep ascent followed by many ups and downs – including a stream crossing – means you'll need to be fairly agile. At some points en route it can feel as though you're walking across wilderness though it's generally easy going. Thankfully all the reservoirs and dams in the Elan Valley are accessible by car and short walks, making the area accessible for everyone.

Best time of year/day

The seasons play a big role in the appearance of your shots here. Autumn is spectacular in the Elan Valley, especially in the lower wooded areas, where trees turn every shade of yellow and orange. Autumn usually signifies more rainfall too, so this is when the reservoirs start to overflow once again. Winter is best for flowing waterfalls (to the extreme at times!) and snow is not uncommon in higher parts of the valley. In summertime heather and flowers bloom and birdlife is abundant. Red kites and buzzards are a common sight all year round as are upland bird species. Summer produces some lovely golden-hour light as shade falls in the valley basin. It's also an excellent place to gaze up at the stars as it has been granted Dark Sky Park status.

Craig Goch dam (VP1) in between sleet showers with falls flowing. Canon 5D III, 24-70mm f/2.8 at 53mm, ISO 100, 1/320s at f/14. Tripod. Polariser. Feb.

Stunning dark skies in Elan Valley. Canon 5D IV, 50mm f/1.4 at 50mm, ISO 6400, 10s at f/1.4. Tripod. July.

Shapely trees line the valleys. Canon 5D IV, 70-200mm f/2.8 at 200mm, ISO 400, 0.6s at f/8. Tripod. Polarise. July.

Spoiled for choice

As you drive along and ascend the valley, it seems there's a photo to be had around every corner. The whole area is exceptionally photogenic and there are plenty of lay-bys and areas to make a stop at en route. There's an interesting wooded island in the middle of Penygarreg Reservoir to photograph from the roadside on your way to Craig Goch, and there are waterfalls at the top of Garreg Ddu by the bridge crossing. All of these are in easy reach of the road and can be accessed via pathways. There are many walking routes and a total of six dams across the valley – any one of them would make an interesting viewpoint. There's so much to see, allow a couple of days to visit and get a feel for the topography of the area.

At VP2 high above Garreg Ddu reservoir.
Canon 5D IV, 16-35mm f/4 at 18mm, ISO 100, 1/6s at f/18. Tripod. Polariser. July.

Everyone should experience Gigrin Red Kite Centre at least once. Get ready to be wowed by the aerial acrobatics performed by one of the finest raptors in Britain: the red kite. These majestic birds soaring overhead provide one of the grandest sights Welsh skies have to offer. Not too long ago these beautiful creatures were pushed to the edge of extinction, with only a handful of pairs surviving. But thanks to heroic conservation efforts, they're now a common sight in Mid Wales. Furthermore, they're spreading beyond Wales across the rest of the country. The kites are fed every day here and they fly in from far and wide. During the colder months, when natural food is scarce, there can be up to 600 birds in the sky at once – an impressive sight to behold.

What to shoot and viewpoints

Gigrin is just off the main road at the eastern end of Rhayader. Approach the farm along the small lane and you'll be greeted by the resident peacocks strutting their stuff. Once parked, you might see the odd kite lazily gliding overhead but it's nothing compared to what's in store. At Gigrin you'll view the feeding session from purpose-built hides. There are a number to choose from; the three lower ones are known as the general admission hides and are all wheelchair friendly. Another one is designated for wheelchair users who want to get a better view of the kites. This hide has adjacent parking and – thanks to its partial roof – unobstructed views.

Over the years Gigrin has accommodated photographers and film-makers alike by creating larger hides close to the action allowing land-locked, in-flight shots. There's the Gateway hide, set to the left of the feeding area and boasting a large opening, which allows photography from ground level to the sky for action shots. The Field hide is

Opposite: A red kite's wings and plumage illuminate as it turns into the autumn sunlight. Canon 1DX, 500mm f/4 at 500mm, ISO 1600, 1/5000s at f/6.3. Tripod. Oct.

set right among the action and two larger ones – the Tower hides – are raised up above the ground on stilts, with exposed fronts and partial roofs. These are my pick whenever I visit. One downside is you are more exposed to the elements, however they give you much more freedom to follow the birds with your lens. This elevated position also offers the chance to photograph birds in flight against the landscape, which changes colour with the seasons. The Tower hides are exposed and these are wild birds, so keep noise to a minimum. Clothing should be dull or dark in colour. This is Wales, so the weather can be changeable. It's wise to wear warm layers under a water and windproof coat. Settle into the hides at least an hour before feeding time at 15.00 (14.00 GMT). This is when the fun starts! >>

How to get here

From Aberystwyth head out east on the A44 and after 2 miles, head over the roundabout signed Llangurig. Follow this road for 21 miles as it winds through mid Wales towards Llangurig. After passing through the town, take the second exit onto the A470 signed Rhayader. Follow this for a further 10 miles, going straight over the cross roads in the centre of Rhayader. Shortly after leaving the town, the entrance to Gigrin Red Kite Centre will be on your left. Follow this lane for a short distance uphill to the car park.

Parking Lat/Long: 52.298681 -3.4975402
Parking Postcode: LD6 5BL
OS Map grid ref: SN979677
Map: OS Explorer Map 200 – Llandrindod Wells & Elan Valley

Accessibility &

All the hides are accessed via well-maintained, reasonable, level pathways. Other than the Tower hides, all are wheelchair friendly with ramps provided. There's also a wheelchair-accessible photographic hide with adjacent parking. The hides are just a short walk from the car park and other pathways and walking routes criss-cross the land providing extended views across the landscape.

Best time of year/day

Feeding takes place at 14.00 GMT and 15.00 during BST. You'll want to get here at least an hour before to get settled in the hide and set up your camera ready for the action. Autumn (just before the clocks change) is probably my favourite time to visit, as the light can be magical during the golden hour. Gigrin is nearly a thousand feet above sea level so it's not uncommon to get snow here.

Red kite flips into a dive in the autumn sunlight backed by clouds.
Canon 1DX, 500mm f/4 at 500mm, ISO 1600, 1/4000s at f/6.3. Tripod. Oct.

Red Kite flying through heavy snowfall. Canon 5D IV, 500mm f/4 at 500mm, ISO 1000, 1/2500s at f/4. Tripod. Dec.

You'll hear the rumble of a tractor as it gets closer and the crows and ravens are first to arrive in the trees. The tractor stops in two places, spreading meat scraps on the grass outside the hides. The sky will subsequently fill with hundreds of circling kites. Red kites have a wingspan of almost five feet so up close they look huge. They come quite near the hide so try to get some good close ups. The kites dive down to grab food, testing your tracking skills. While buzzards will feed on the ground along with ravens and crows, a kite will clutch meat in its talons and make for clear airspace, where it feels secure enough to feed. You'll notice many birds feed on the wing, their heads turning down to meet forward-lifted legs. After the early feeding frenzy tails off, another wave of kites appears in

smaller groups, which makes picking out individuals much easier. The kites are far more leisurely in their approach to feeding and frequently float around in front of the hides for some time before seizing their morsel of choice. You'll definitely come away with some soaring kite images (against blue skies if you're lucky) but the shots I aim for are those split-second moments when the kite twists instantly into a dive. It will take many attempts, changing auto focus and tracking settings, but with enough patience and perseverance, you'll bag a shot to be proud of. My advice is to choose one bird (without wing tags preferably) and just follow it around. It may do a dozen or more circles but sooner or later it will dive and you'll be ready. Buzzards and ravens will also be airborne so practice your bird-in-flight techniques on these slower birds. Eventually kite numbers will start to decrease but you'll still get groups hanging around or perching in the nearby trees. If possible, stay to the end; the light will improve as the afternoon wears on – particularly in autumn, when stunning golden light combines with moody skies. These are the conditions I always hope for, making the birds' orange and red plumage truly 'pop' in the viewfinder.

A Red Kite and Buzzard in flight with rainbow backdrop. Canon 5D III, 300mm f/2.8 + 1.4x Extender at 420mm, ISO 1250, 1/8000s at f/6.3. Jan.

*Red kites gather at feeding time in vivid light and a rainbow arcs across the sky.
Canon 5D III, 24-70mm f/2.8 at 51mm, ISO 640, 1/1250s at f/10. Polariser. Jan.*

The Red Arrows performing the 'Gypo Break' manoeuvre.
Canon 1DX, 100-400mm f/5.6 at 360mm, ISO 1000, 1/2500s at f/9. July.

SHOWS
AND
EVENTS

SHOWS AND EVENTS

South Wales hosts a diverse programme of outdoor shows and events that offer great opportunities for photography. There are air shows, rural and agricultural shows, literary festivals and the world bog snorkelling championships

There are full listings of events at *visitwales.com* and *showmewales.co.uk*, but here are some highlights:

JANUARY
New Year's Day Swims
The fun (and very cold) Barry Island New Year's Day Dip and the Saundersfoot New Year's Day swim take place each 1 January. Fancy dress is optional.

Hen Galan – Welsh New Year
If you're in the Gwaun Valley in Pembrokeshire the New Year starts on the 13th.

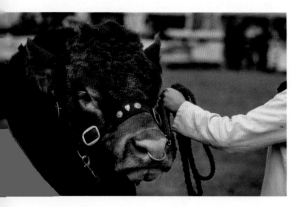

FEBRUARY
Six Nations
Rugby Internationals, Principality Stadium in Cardiff

MARCH
St. David's Day – 1st March

Crickhowell Walking Festival
9 Days of Guided Walks and Events in and around Crickhowell and the Black Mountains. And now a weekend of walks in the autumn.

APRIL
Barley Saturday
The last Saturday in April. Judging of various horse competitions, then the crowds gather to watch the horses parade around the Cardigan streets at approximately 2pm.

RHS Flower Show – Cardiff
Fabulous floral displays and perfect plants. With more than 50 exhibitors celebrating spring.

MAY
The Hay Festival
World famous literature event in the town of Hay on Wye. *hayfestival.com*

JUNE
Wales Airshow
Breathtaking aerobatic displays over Swansea Bay. *walesnationalairshow.com*

JULY
Royal Welsh Show
The biggest and best attended agricultural event of its kind. The annual show is the shop window for Welsh farming and food production. It's a real celebration of all things rural. Held at Llanelwedd, Builth Wells. *rwas.wales/royal-welsh-show*

Bridgend County Show at Bridgend College
An agricultural and horticultural show at the Pencoed Campus. *bridgendcountyshow.org.uk*

Gower Festival
A music festival featuring internationally acclaimed musicians performing in churches. *gowerfestival.org*

AUGUST
Pembrokeshire County Show
Biggest county show in Wales. Featuring all things agricultural plus crafts, exhibitions and entertainment. *pembsshow.org*

World Bog Snorkelling Championships

An event that Lonely Planet described as one of the top 50 "must do" things from around the world. Held at the at Waen Rhydd bog near Llanwrtyd Wells. There is also a Bog Triathlon the day before.

National Eisteddfod

The National Eisteddfod is a celebration of the culture and language in Wales. It is held in a different Welsh venue each year. *eisteddfod.wales*

Summer Spectacular

Tenby harbour most Sundays. Fun, music, food and drink ending in a firework display.

Green Man Festival

An alternative folk festival at the Glanusk Estate in the Brecon Beacons. *greenman.net*

Brecon Jazz

A jazz festival set in the beautiful Brecon Beacons, featuring over twenty concerts from cosy gigs to big bands, from an emerging artists to late-night jam sessions. *breconjazz.org*

Cardiff Harbour Festival and Extreme Sailing Series

Elite-level international sailing teams compete in Cardiff bay. *visitcardiff.com*

SEPTEMBER

Tenby Arts Festival

A week-long festival of the arts and music. *tenbyartsfest.co.uk*

Narberth Food Festival

Thousands of visitors descend on the market town of Narberth for its annual food festival. The festival is relatively small with more than 50 independent stall-holders showcasing their best dishes, produce and drinks to the crowds of visitors.

Ironman Wales

Tenby & South Pembrokeshire. Athletes must complete a two-mile swim, a gruelling 112-mile bike route and a 26-mile marathon in one day to be crowned an Ironman.

OCTOBER

Dylan Thomas Festival

Based in Swansea, talks, performances, exhibitions, readings and music with a Dylan Thomas theme.

NOVEMBER

Pembroke Castle Christmas Market

A Christmas market featuring hundreds of stalls of food, drinks and gifts, all based in this fantastic castle setting.

Christmas Fayre at Dinefwr

Set in Llandeilo, this is a great Christmas fayre to visit and browse the many stall holders to get in the festive spirit.

DECEMBER

Cardiff's Winter Wonderland

Kick start your Christmas celebrations at Cardiff's Winter Wonderland and Ice Rink.

Some quick tips for photographing at events

- Check the event programme to see what is happening when and get there early to scout the best viewpoints.
- Keep in mind where the sun will be, it's better to have your subject nicely lit rather than struggling to photograph into the sun.
- Use longer focal lengths to get in close to the action or subject. A wide to mid zoom lens is best for events allowing you to zoo into the action as well as taking more contextual images.
- Isolate the subject by using a wide aperture (f/2.8) to get a narrow depth of field.
- If the action is fast paced use the Auto or 'P' Program setting – better to get the shot than miss it whilst fiddling with settings.
- Set the scene, look for compositions or subjects that identify the event.
- Photography in public places is allowed under UK law. Always ask permission if you want to take close ups of a person. There may be restrictions for photography if you are on private land or at a private event. For commercial use you will need a model release from the person you have photographed, or a property release if on private land.

DREW BUCKLEY

Biography

Drew Buckley is one of the most well-respected and accomplished photographers in the UK. Based in Pembrokeshire, 32-year old Drew's talents cover landscape, wildlife and astro photography, photo-journalism and all aspects of commercial photography.

Inspired by his brothers he picked up a camera at young age and got a 35mm film Canon SLR back in the late 90s. After a career as a 3D artist working on PlayStation and Xbox games he became a full-time professional photographer in 2010.

Previous book titles include *Puffins* and *Wilder Wales*, published by Graffeg. His work has been featured in *BBC Countryfile*, *BBC Wildlife*, *Outdoor Photography*, *Digital SLR*, *Photo Plus*, *The Great Outdoors* and *Country Walking*; and national newspapers such as *The Times* and the *Guardian*. Drew regularly takes on photography commissions. His clients include Pembrokeshire Coast National Park, National Trust, RSPB, Wildlife Trust, NHS Wales and many South Wales businesses and organisations. He's currently working on a time-lapse project for the BBC in his home county of Pembrokeshire.

Drew runs photography workshops in Pembrokeshire for all abilities of photographer, and is an official Wildlife Trust commercial operator permitted to run day and overnight courses on Skomer Island. He runs processing classes in Lightroom, and is a website designer. His commercial work also includes food, product and property photography.

In 2017 Drew received his fourth *Highly Commended* award at the British Wildlife Photography Awards and since 2012 has won awards at the GDT European Wildlife Photographer of the Year, 2018 & 2015 *International Garden Photographer of the Year*, *Landscape Photographer of the Year* at the National Photography Awards, *Outdoor Photographer of the Year* and *Bird Photographer of the Year*.

Find out more about Drew, purchase prints of his work, or book a photography workshop at:
drewbuckleyphotography.com

*Pre-dawn pastel skies from Pen y Fan (p.256). Looking at Cribyn and west to Sugar Loaf.
Canon 5D IV, 24-70mm f/2.8 at 47mm, ISO 100, 1/50s at f/14. Tripod. ND Grad. Sep.*

If you are a keen photographer or want to take the best photos when out and about or on holiday, fotoVUE guidebooks show you where and how to take photographs in the world's most beautiful places.

Website – *www.fotovue.com*

Visit our website for articles on how to improve your photography, view inspirational photographs and learn more about our guidebooks.

- Find out about our books
- Additional viewpoints
- Photography tutorials
- News and special offers
- Inspiration – full of amazing photographs
- Articles and features by leading photographers

Register for the fotoVUE newsletter to get regular updates and offers on our guidebooks.

Existing books

fotoVUE photographer-authors use their local knowledge and expertise to show you the best locations to photograph and the best times to visit.

- *Photographing The Lake District* – by Stuart Holmes
- *Photographing North Wales* – by Simon Kitchin
- *Photographing Wildlife in the UK* – by Andrew Marshall
- *Photographing Cornwall and Devon* – by Adam Burton
- *Photographing Dorset* – Mark Bauer

- *Photographing The Dolomites* – James Rushforth
- *Photographing The Peak District* – Chris Gilbert & Mick Ryan
- *Photographing Scotland* – Dougie Cunningham
- *Photographing South Wales* – Drew Buckley

Forthcoming titles

- *Photographing The Snowdonia Mountains* – Nick Livesey
- *Photographing London* – George Johnson
- *Photographing Northumberland* – Anita Nicholson
- *Photographing East Anglia* – Justin Minns
- *Photographing The Cotswolds* – Sarah Howard
- *Photographing West Ireland* – Carsten Krieger
- *Photographing The Yorkshire Dales* – Lizzie Shepherd & Oliver Wright
- *Photographing Iceland* – James Rushforth, Geraldine Westrupp and Martin Sammtleben
- *Photographing Kent* – Alex Hare
- *Photographing Dublin and Wicklow* – Adrian Hendroff
- *Photographing The Night Sky* – Alyn Wallace

Check the website for the latest on release dates.

Upload your own photographs and viewpoints at:

www.fotovue.com

Opposite: Bamburgh Castle, Northumberland. Canon 7D, Sigma 10–20mm at 10mm, 200s at f/16, ISO 100. © Anita Nicholson from the forthcoming fotoVUE title *PHOTOGRAPHING NORTHUMBERLAND by ANITA NICHOLSON*

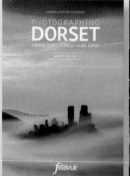
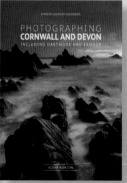

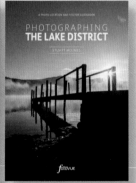

#fotovue

Hashtag your images **#fotovue** on Instagram to be in
with a chance of winning a fotoVUE
guidebook each month.

*The winter of 2017/18 high up on the Pennine moors above Hebden Bridge, West Yorkshire.
Sony A7RII, Sony 24-105 f/4 G @ 24mm, ISO 100, 1/500s at f/9.5, © Mick Ryan*